DRIVING TITO

Through the Balkan Backroads with a Celebrity

EMMA CARMICHAEL

Travelling Through… Press is an independent publishing
house whose address can be found at
www.travellingthrough.co.uk

Every effort has been made to obtain the necessary permissions with reference
to copyright material, both illustrative and quoted. We apologise for any
omissions in this respect and will be pleased to make the appropriate
acknowledgements in any future edition.

First published in London, 2019

A CIP catalogue record for this book is available from the British Library

Paperback ISBN 978-1-9161423-0-5

Typeset: Palatino
Cover Design by: © Drawn by Hand
Map Illustration by: © Drawn by Hand
Printed and bound in Great Britain

For my mother, sister and brother,
with love,
For my father,
who is with me in spirit,
For Steve,
who pulled me over the finishing line,
And, for Tito,
my Zastava 750 (Fića),
without whom there would be no tale to tell.

© Photographed by Emma Carmichael

Contents

Author's Note

Please be aware that everyone the author meets on her journey has been given a fictitious name to protect their identity.

Also, while travelling through Macedonia, the country's official name was the 'former Yugoslav Republic of Macedonia' (FYROM) but recently the country has been renamed the Republic of North Macedonia. For ease, my chapter headings are merely entitled 'Macedonia', with no offence intended to either the Macedonians or the Greeks, nor, for that matter, to anyone else.

Indicative Map of Our Travels through the Balkans

 X = Car Breakdown

The journey was taken in an anti-clockwise direction starting and finishing in **Skopje**. Major car breakdowns are marked with an 'X' and occurred in **Provatonas**, Greece; **Samokov**, Bulgaria; and **Prilep**, North Macedonia.

Love at First Sight

SKOPJE

S *ummer, 2004*

In the bustling capital city of Skopje, parked incongruously by the side of the road and half the height of any other vehicle in the street, sat a Zastava. Were it not for its bright purple body it would have been lost in the jungle of silver, black and white 4-wheel drive monsters surrounding it. As it was, its small, neat form and boldly colourful exterior aroused my curiosity. I bent down to peer through the tiny windscreen. Everything about the car seemed uncomplicated and strangely endearing, from its simple dashboard, chequered upholstery, and slim steering wheel to its delicate ruler-length windscreen wipers, and playful eyes for headlights. I was instantly captivated.

"Ah, this is Fića!" said my Macedonian colleague proudly, "Our car from Yugoslav times."

A wave of nostalgia seemed to pass over him as he looked with genuine pleasure at this miniature vehicle. He opened his mouth as if to say more but changed his mind. Instead he just smiled and kept his thoughts to himself.

As soon as I could get near a computer with an internet connection, I eagerly got onto Google for more information and discovered the car was originally modelled on the 1950s *"cinquecento"* Italian Fiat 500. The Balkan model, the Zastava 750, was designed and launched in the 1960s and, being relatively affordable for many, the car became an overnight sensation. For the first time, Yugoslavs took to the road together. Although compact in size, the car still had the capacity to transport a family of four whilst piling their luggage onto a neatly designed roof rack. The Zastava was considered to be practical and functional and easily stole the hearts of the nation.

The car became affectionately known as the "Fića" (pronounced Fee-cha), a name derived from the word "Fiat", and its popularity in both style and colour choice spanned a number of decades. Today, the Zastava continues to be revered but undeniably represents a classic car from another age. For most, the Zastava has largely become a rusting relic from the former Yugoslavia.

However, this chance meeting with a functioning – although admittedly parked – Zastava model in Skopje had had an instant effect on me. It had been love at first sight, and with increasing work commitments in the Balkans between 2004 and 2009 came an opportunity to spot more of these vehicles on and off the road in varying degrees of road-worthiness. But with each sighting of a Zastava 750 came an increasing desire to drive one.

Five years on, the moment suddenly presented itself and I threw caution to the wind and took action. Much to everyone's disbelief, I had decided to jack in my well-paid, stressful and highly-politicised work; instead, I would drive full-circle around, through and across the Balkans in a Zastava 750. The Yugoslavs had been doing something similar for several decades. So… how hard could it be? This was the 21st century.

An Idea Blossoms

J*une, 2009*

I had always imagined the Balkans to be a dark, imposing and mysterious landmass inhabited by equally tall, dark and mysterious people, speaking a strange unfathomable language. A vague sweeping movement of the hand had generally accompanied most people's description of the former Yugoslavia when, with the prospect of a job in cultural heritage protection back in 2004, I had first asked people what they knew of the region. 'The Balkans. That place. Over there. Somewhere.' The Balkans. A word frequently associated with blood, death, wars, oppression, suppression and cheap '80s Yugoslav beach holidays.

My school history classes – and, for that matter, geography lessons – had rarely taken me beyond the heroes of Scotland or the importance of the weather and cloud formations. The Balkans were thus a void in my already sadly dismal knowledge of world history generally. However, Google was a fount of information and although I learned how Yugoslavia had split into the seven new countries of Bosnia and Herzegovina, Croatia, the 'former Yugoslav Republic of Macedonia' (officially renamed the Republic of

North Macedonia this year), Montenegro, Serbia, Slovenia and most recently, (if – still – somewhat controversially) Kosovo, it came as a surprise to find there is no singular definition of the Balkans.

The Balkan people were at odds in terms of those whom they considered Balkan and those not. This has meant multiple definitions have arisen, so I plumped for the one I rather liked, encompassing more than just the former Yugoslavian territories. This, the geographical definition, refers to all lands south of the Sava and Danube rivers enclosed by the Adriatic, Aegean, Ionian, Mediterranean and Marmara seas. This meant excluding parts of Croatia, Serbia, Slovenia and the majority of Romania but including Albania, Bulgaria, mainland Greece including the Peloponnese, and northern Turkey in my understanding of the Balkans. Secretly, I considered Slovenia to be far too European to be included in the first place – this assumption being based rather tenuously on a fleeting visit to Ljubljana, where the visible influence of tourism had clashed with my romantic notion of how I believed the place should be: a land cloaked in mystery.

My suppositions were challenged while working in Kosovo, my first taste of the former Yugoslav world, and the Balkans. Surrounded by Montenegro, Macedonia, Albania and Serbia, Kosovo is a politically fragile place, accommodating an alarming international working presence (myself included) in relation to its local population, and although declaring its independence from Serbia in February 2008, Kosovo continues to be locked in an extraordinarily delicate and complex situation – and a subject for another book, another day.

Working in the international field of post-conflict development had been eye-opening, life-changing, character building and all the other clichés one imagines it would be, but it had also consumed me, and my life. I knew that it would do so, yet I had continued to ignore the signs until one day, after more than four years in this work-intense environment, I realised I had to get out, and get out fast before I locked myself into a world in which I really did not belong and, more importantly, struggled to understand. Simultaneously, the idea of travelling across the Balkans in a Zastava was taking hold with alarming clarity.

It is true to say that to travel is in my blood. I have no fear of it and at times the yearning for adventure – to be out there, somewhere, anywhere – could consume my thoughts for days until I hit upon an idea. It was usually a spontaneous yet instinctive decision and, although neither a hardcore traveller nor a particularly brave one, the prospect of going travelling always excited me. Taking a journey, after working in Kosovo, around my now expanded knowledge although certainly not my understanding of the Balkan region, seemed the most natural thing to do.

I had found my escape route, a chance to simplify my life once more, and the opportunity to reclaim a sense of freedom. The way to experience more of everyday Balkan life would have to be through my own initiative. An independent approach was needed. It meant I would need to resign, move on, and turn away from the web of restrictions of the international working environment. Only then would I get a closer look at the landscape, the architecture, the people and their culture.

Although I had no useful knowledge of the languages spoken in this part of the world, my mother tongue was English, I had a smattering of French and a scant knowledge of German, which I hoped would be enough.

My mode of transport? I would find my very own Fića – hopefully while I was working through my notice period – and then drive away in a flourish of Yugoslav vintage glory (or something to that effect).

———

F ive years previously (2004) I had been in Skopje and had fallen in love with the Zastava car. Therefore, I decided that this should be the place where I would look first to find my very own Fića. I set about the task with unstoppable enthusiasm but almost immediately I hit upon an unforeseen problem. To buy a car in Macedonia, one had to live there or, better still, be a Macedonian. I met neither criterion. In a moment of panic, followed by some swift thinking, I quickly deduced that my work colleague, Liljana, fulfilled both; the question would be whether she could be persuaded to help.

A robust woman with a personality to match, Liljana had a presence to be reckoned with. Like most Balkan women I had met, she was extremely expressive and unreservedly blunt. She was a hugely jovial person whom I liked immensely and I believed if anyone would be willing enough to help me, it would be her. When I broached the subject, however, the response was not quite the one I was anticipating.

"But why?" she protested, nonchalantly smoking a cigarette, listening to my idea with growing amusement. "They are so old! And they do not go up hills very well. You will not get very far in a Fića!"

I argued it would be the perfect way to blend in and live a Yugoslav experience retrospectively, in a vehicle that was accepted and liked by all! A Zastava was the perfect camouflage in which to travel without drawing undue attention to myself. People would be less suspicious of a Fića coming through their village. She lifted her arms in mock resignation at my rather weak counter-argument and sighed.

"Ok, ok! I agree! Buy your Fića and I shall be the owner." She then chuckled with genuine delight at the thought. "Me, the owner of a Fića!"

Finding One's Zastava

S *ummer, 2009*

In all honesty I knew absolutely nothing about Zastava cars except that the engine was in the boot and the petrol tank was under the bonnet. A quick glance at Zastava's own website informed me I had two possibilities: the original 1950s Zastava 600, which as yet I had not seen anywhere on the roads, with doors rather coolly opening 'northwards'; or the slightly later and more popular 1960s model, the Zastava 750, which seemed to have a more robust frame. Originally, this car could reach a top speed of 110km/h, a fact which impressed me greatly but brought much derision from my Kosovo colleagues. Apparently that had been in their heyday. Today it was unlikely I would find a car at all, let alone one which could do more than 70km/h, and that on the flat with a tailwind.

It appeared my colleagues were right. I found Zastava sightings to be a very rare occurrence, and most were to be found abandoned in fields, missing many of their parts. Undeterred by the diminishing prospect of availability, slow speed and continued mockery from my office team, I persisted with my search.

The first potentially roadworthy car came unexpectedly from Kosovo's capital, Pristina – a town more notable for its 4-wheel drive and European models, rather than the home-produced Balkan brands such as the Zastava or Yugo. Now all I needed was a willing accomplice to inspect it with me.

Without any persuasion, I won the enthusiastic support of Tomi, my translator from the office. He was a Serb from northwest Bosnia and Herzegovina who had experienced war as a young boy. His family had been permanently displaced to live in the newly created Serb-dominated region of Republika Srpska within Bosnia and Herzegovina but in 1999 his mother had moved the family to Kosovo in search of work when it too was just recovering from a separate armed conflict with Serbia. A United Nations presence had been installed across the region but, with continued rising tensions between Kosovo Serbs and Kosovo Albanians, a second wave of ethnic unrest was not successfully contained in 2004, the result of which ironically brought me to the region to assist with a politically- driven cultural heritage programme of rehabilitation, and my first encounter with Tomi.

As a young man in his early twenties, Tomi lived in a world of instability, ethnic division and an uncertain future. There were very few opportunities or choices on offer in Kosovo – politics influenced daily life – but Tomi's situation could arguably be considered better than most. He had a job within the safety net of an international institution employing both Albanians and Serbs, while at least 70 per cent of the young in Kosovo remained unemployed.

Like Tomi, many of the young living across the ex-Yugoslav region were children during the war and have been indelibly affected by it in one way or another. Whether Kosovo Albanian, Muslim, Serb, Orthodox, Croat, Catholic, Bosniak, Roma, Turk or one of a number of minority groups, many have become trapped in a reality of personal or politically motivated ethnic division and an opportunity for escapism in any form is generally welcomed. Tomi was no different from anyone else and, to my delight, he wholeheartedly embraced the challenge to find a roadworthy Zastava for me. Together we set off to test-drive one incongruously parked on the forecourt of a Pristina garage with the sign "*Shitje*" planted firmly on the windscreen. The fact that it was the only car for sale in the garage was a detail we both decided to overlook.

———

The white Zastava sprang into life and my heart started to race. I set off gingerly, venturing into second gear with a lurch and a nervous excited laugh.

"Emma, have you ever driven one of these cars before?"

"Of course not!" I replied.

Tomi turned a pale shade of grey. The car was so small, his kneecaps were up beside his ears, and his head was jammed against the roof. Stifling a laugh at his discomfort, we kangaroo-hopped around the forecourt and back to the car's starting position.

"You're not scared, are you?" I asked in surprise.

Tomi grinned defiantly. "No! But if you are going out on the road, let me out!"

It was getting dark and, although I felt a step closer to realising my quest for freedom and journeying through the Balkans in a Zastava, I was not yet ready to face a road full of maniac drivers (as they all seemed to be in Pristina) when I had not yet managed to get into fourth gear.

The car felt good to me but I was not sure if it would be up to the challenge of a long journey. I needed a second opinion. Tomi phoned Edon, a family friend, who agreed to come and inspect it while we stayed out of sight in a nearby café. Edon was a handsome man in his early fifties. He was moderately tall, solidly built, like many Kosovo Albanians, and he had a thick head of straight steely grey hair and reassuring dark brown eyes. His native tongue was Albanian and he spoke Serbian also. When he had something important to say he would transmit this to Tomi in Serbian, since Tomi's Albanian was not up to the task of translating his comments into English for me, but for the rest he just listened placidly. Next to talkative Tomi with his shock of unruly brown hair, cheeky smile and six-foot gangly frame, Edon was a dignified and gently smiling contrast. They were a good combination and happily volunteered themselves to be my "Fića-finding management team". I readily accepted, marvelling at their knowledge, enthusiasm, language skills and, most endearing of all, their desire to help.

Edon had inspected the Zastava on the garage forecourt by masquerading as an independent prospective buyer and was amused to learn from the garage attendant that "an international lady was also showing interest in the car and, incredibly, had managed to start the engine on the first try!" – a feat he had apparently believed impossible. Surely a positive sign, I thought, as Tomi, Edon and I sat drinking strong macchiato coffees.

As a former Zastava taxi driver, Edon knew Zastavas inside out. He regarded me thoughtfully, took a deep breath and said as diplomatically as he could, "I'm afraid that Zastava will not get you very far." Then he added, more frankly, "You know it's going to be impossible to drive a Zastava around the Balkans. There are too many design flaws with these cars. They break down frequently, they are no good on hills as the engine overheats too easily, and you have to keep the engine door open at all times, and stop regularly to allow it to cool down. It is even more important to have a car with a good chassis and no rust. Even so, to take a Zastava on this kind of a journey across all Balkans will be a miracle."

Tomi translated Edon's words to me with gathering disappointment in his voice.

I stared pensively into my empty coffee cup appreciating Edon's honesty but my gut feeling was telling me I could do this.

"Well, I shall have to buy lots of spare parts, drive no more than a few hours during the coolest part of the day, take the hills very slowly and keep the engine door open, and find a car with minimal rust problems. I am sure it is possible." Tomi laughed as he translated my determined response back to Edon.

"Well, if you do all these things as you say, perhaps it will be possible but I am sure it will not."

Edon's air of pessimism was tinged with just a glimmer of hope and it was to this that I clung optimistically as I continued my search for the 'right' Zastava.

————

A 40-degree wall of summer heat rose from the dust and hung in the air of Pristina's city centre. It was mid-July. Just two days earlier I had cleared my desk, said my farewells to colleagues and, with great relief, declared myself on sabbatical. Liljana had given me precise instructions on how to find the weekend Skopje car market and I was on my way. Now in Skopje, a surprising number of drivers were out enjoying the Sunday sunshine in their Zastavas of every colour imaginable – green, white, red, yellow, orange. It filled me with hope, but on reaching the market my expectations were dashed. There were none there for sale and any thoughts I had of finding my Fića were slipping away.

However, it seemed I must remain open to all possibilities. I broadcasted my quest to find a Zastava to everyone I knew in Pristina, although nothing quite prepared me for the response. A Pandora's box of old cars suddenly appeared for private sale. They were the most amazing collection of antiquities I had ever seen. Some lay silently in sheds, nestled in with the cows, pigs and hens; some had been upgraded; some were being driven despite their rusted shells and life-threatening state; one had been turned into a retro-fitted boy's toy with garish wild orange flames painted down its sides and fake white leather seats. Everyone was proud of their Zastavas, whatever the condition, and with each car came a personal story. These cars, whether owned by Kosovo Albanian or Kosovo Serb, seemed to unlock a place in their hearts. Their tales were not of conflict, destruction, deprivation or politics, but about life in Kosovo and the Balkans before the recent wars, and as the owners told their stories, they could not help themselves from smiling. My Macedonian colleague had reacted similarly in Skopje when I first encountered the purple Fića five years ago, and with each smile and story, I was catching a glimpse of everyday Balkan life and it fuelled my curiosity to learn more.

However, I was still no closer to finding a Zastava sturdy enough to get me anywhere but the end of the road, and summer was marching on. Resolutely, I turned my attention back to Macedonia and the car sales websites. With the help of my Fića-finding management team, three or four hopefuls were identified and, with high expectations, we headed back to Skopje on a summer's day of peak searing heat.

We picked up a wilting Liljana, who had valiantly given up her Saturday morning to join our Zastava search as the potential owner and, just as importantly, act as our translator. Although many Macedonian words are similar to Serbian, the nuances of conversation can be lost, particularly when striking a deal. Representing four nationalities and four languages, we had all eventualities covered but we must have appeared an unusual car-buying posse. Our first seller had a yellow Zastava 750 for sale. It had been recently painted but even I could see it concealed a multitude of rust problems and the owner was earnest in his appeal that his Zastava be driven "about town" and no further!

Our second potential seller was in a quiet residential area. With a roar, a white Zastava appeared while the four of us stood expectantly in the shade of the only tree in the street. The owner looked at us in astonishment but, regaining his composure, he regaled us with the attributes of his Fiča. This one looked more promising. Tomi fortified himself for another passenger experience with me behind the wheel.

We circled the neighbourhood while he navigated, shouting nervously, "Brake!" whenever we reached a crossroads.

"I AM braking," I shouted back, but it became clear that this car would not get me very far either and with high hopes dashed once more, Liljana phoned our third appointment. Apparently, this one was now sunning himself 200km away by Lake Ohrid in southwest Macedonia. Our fourth and final appointment for the day was not answering his phone.

Finding a suitable Zastava was becoming almost as impossible as Edon's predictions for the journey itself. Liljana's solution was distraction and since nobody had a better idea, we took her back home and then Tomi, Edon and I headed for the Treska Valley National Park, 10km southwest of Skopje, for some calm reflection. Not really in the mood for appreciating beautiful scenery, I slid out of Tomi's car and stood gloomily in the car park watching the Treska River as it crashed down the mountainside. Above, the cliffs soared upwards, sleek and graceful, creating welcoming natural canopies of cool shade. I took in my surroundings with uncharacteristic indifference when all of a sudden I became transfixed by what was parked opposite.

"Look!"

Tomi and Edon followed the direction of my excited gaze. A gleaming white Zastava had been parked away from all other vehicles in front of two bright blue Portaloos. It was a

marvellous if somewhat unexpected sight. Had the driver
been in a hurry to answer a call of nature? We wandered over
and Edon gently rocked the car from side to side and bounced
it up and down to test its suspension. He looked at its
undercarriage and we peered in through the windows. This
was the one. I was sure of it. The only problem: it was
someone's private car. No one had reappeared from the
Portaloos and despite Edon's robust manhandling of the
Zastava, it did not result in the appearance of an enraged
owner. We loitered for a while just the same but no one
arrived. Eventually, the smell of barbecued corn on the cob
lured us towards one of the ardent flame-fanning cart sellers.
There was nothing to do but eat something and take a walk in
the National Park like everyone else.

———

As we returned to the car park some hours later, a rather
short, stockily-built man, substantially tanned by the
sun and dressed casually in shorts, a vest and shoes that
looked far too big for his feet, was locking up the Fića. The
owner? I held my breath. We walked towards him and Edon
engaged him in idle conversation. The language switched
perceptibly from Serbian to Albanian. He was a Macedonian
Albanian. He continued to hold Edon's attention and before I
knew it, Edon was on the ground looking under the car while
the man rocked his Zastava backwards and forwards. I
swallowed my laughter and grinned at Tomi while he
strained to understand the Albanian and translate what he
could to me. Edon chatted in his unhurried, relaxed way,
smiling and nodding encouragement as the man opened the
boot to expose the engine. I did not dare to believe this was
happening. Then came the invitation to go for a drive.
Needing no further encouragement, Tomi dived into the back
and I jumped in to the front passenger seat.

He drove at breakneck speed down the narrow single lane of the National Park. We hurtled past children, stray dogs and cows but, despite my fear, I felt exhilarated and I am sure the owner could tell. He pulled over and offered me the wheel. Tomi groaned nervously from the back. I shot him a reassuring look and flew round the car and into the driver's seat. This was it. This was the car. Everything about it felt right. But could the man be persuaded to sell?

As if reading my thoughts, Tomi whispered in my ear, "You know, everything is for sale in the Balkans; just you watch." Sure enough, as we parked and rejoined Edon, a more intense exchange began. Tomi winked at me as a look of disbelief flashed across the Macedonian man's face. He had just learnt about my travel intentions. Grasping the full weight of the situation in which he had unwittingly found himself, he drew himself up to his full 5ft5" height, re-tucked his khaki-coloured vest into the elasticated waistband of his grey knee-length shorts and crossed his arms tightly around his chest in anticipation of doing a serious business deal. The discussions were extensive; even Tomi's knowledge of Albanian could not keep up with the speed of the negotiations, so we watched and waited.

After a time, Edon indicated we should leave. We all smiled and shook hands good-naturedly but it seemed there was no sale. I climbed into Tomi's car, trying desperately to conceal my disappointment, and closed the door. Edon turned to me with a confident smile.

"Do not worry," Tomi translated, "this is the Balkan way of doing business. You'll see."

Edon was right. Within a day of returning to Pristina, the Zastava owner had phoned from Macedonia. The sale was on. In a whirlwind of phone calls, price haggling and Turkish coffees, a deal was struck and suddenly the car was mine for the princely sum of 1,100 Euros. Most certainly more than I had anticipated paying but, as a foreigner in the Balkan world, I believed I had got the best price I could hope to achieve, with my Fića-finding management team clinching the sale on my behalf. In any case, I was hugely grateful to this man for selling me his car. Days earlier it had surely been the furthest thing from his mind while he had been picnicking with his family in the Treska National Park.

Battling Balkan Bureaucracy

J *uly, 2009*

Although Liljana never admitted regretting her decision to help, the process of registering the car became more of a challenge than I could possibly have imagined. Copious quantities of coffee were consumed and, in Liljana's case, intensive chain-smoking episodes were necessary to overcome the stress of it all.

It was just eight o'clock and a week later. I could already feel the sun's strength on my skin as Edon, Tomi's mother Adrijana and I crossed the Kosovo/Macedonian border on foot. The sale was to be finalised. Contracts would be signed between Liljana and the seller, and I would part with 1,100 Euros in return for a Zastava. Tomi had disappeared for his summer holidays to the Croatian coast. I did not blame him for wanting to exchange the inland summer heat for a cooling sea breeze. Like Edon, Adrijana spoke no English but was eager to be a part of the Zastava-buying saga. A woman with entrepreneurial ambitions, Adrijana had recently established a flower shop in the optimistic hope of making a sustainable living in Kosovo. Today, she was representing Tomi, although

I suspect more out of curiosity and the chance of an unusual day trip to Skopje.

The owner of the Zastava waited patiently as our passports were scrutinised and stamped, beaming at us in anticipation of the forthcoming sale. He shook our hands as we stepped onto Macedonian soil and, while waiting for Adrijana to join us, he openly boasted to Edon of cross-border smuggling stories. He paid no attention to me or the sign that stood behind us which read 'DECLARE SMUGGLING AND CORRUPTION AT CUSTOMS' in large bold lettering, and I could only wonder from his arm movements what the car had been involved in. Cigars, I thought distractedly, hoping I was not going to be tailed by police all around the Balkans as a result of his shady antics, yet strangely the thought intrigued me.

The temperature rose steadily towards 40 degrees as we all squashed into the Zastava and drove to meet Liljana, in whose name the car was to be registered, she being Macedonian. There was an air of excitement amongst us all as we clambered out of the Zastava, peeling ourselves away from one another in the heat. The pleasantries were brief. Liljana was suffering. She hated Skopje's summer heat and was anxious to get to the Registrar's office. She glanced casually at the car documentation the owner had proudly presented to her and then, all at once, gave a cry of dismay. We all stared at her in equal amounts of consternation as she raised her hands in disbelief.

"You are not the owner! We cannot sign anything without him. The owner must be here!"

The man we had all thought to be the owner looked at us sheepishly. It was his elderly father, and not he, who was the official owner of the car.

"And where is he?" demanded Liljana impatiently.

"Walking in the forest," came the response.

Pandemonium broke out. Everyone started shouting at

everyone else in every available language except English and I looked on, not knowing whether to laugh or cry as my Zastava-to-be left the scene with a squeal of tyres, the man's son behind the wheel, having been dispatched to find his poor unsuspecting grandfather who was undoubtedly having a relaxing morning in the cool of the forest.

We piled into a nearby hotel and I bought endless rounds of coffee for everyone while we waited. Liljana's nerves peaked and troughed as the caffeine and cigarettes took effect. After several hours, the grandfather was located as he emerged from the forest and headed, as was his custom at noon, towards the mosque. Not today. Instead, he was intercepted by his grandson and whisked off to Skopje in haste.

————

The slight, serene-faced grandfather was an elderly Macedonian Albanian. He wore a crocheted black skullcap and was neatly attired in a freshly ironed shirt and grey trousers. He smiled gently at us, completely unaware of the importance of his presence, although, curiously, he had three packets of cigarettes stuffed into his shirt pocket. He was clearly expecting things to take some time.

With all the necessary representatives now assembled, Edon accompanied the grandfather, father and son in the Zastava, while Adrijana and I accompanied Liljana in her car. She led the way at speed to the Registrar's office, keen to get the car registration process over and done with; already enough time had been wasted. Straining to keep up with us, the Zastava jumped the traffic lights. There was a screech of brakes and blare of car horns. Liljana pulled over, muttering loudly under her breath as we turned to watch an altercation between the Zastava and a police car. I cast Liljana a guilty look, beginning to regret involving her in such a circus of events. Luckily, all was resolved quickly. The four men sat grinning like schoolboys as we continued towards the Registrar's office but the grins soon disappeared when it was discovered that the Registrar's office was now closed for the day. We were too late. Before Liljana had time to protest, the Zastava team, fearing the deal could be off, took charge of the situation. We followed them across the outskirts of Skopje, rising up past a rundown area of earth brick houses, where I momentarily glimpsed the onslaught of a boisterous water fight between Roma children, before we dropped down into the historic part of Skopje. Here, at least, an Advocate's office was open which would allow us to proceed with the first step of the bureaucratic registration process. All seven of us piled inside the box-sized bureau out of the heat and sat in a row, waiting patiently as the Advocate unhurriedly prepared a large sandwich of blank papers divided by sheets of carbon copy and rolled them gently into his old typewriter. A computer monitor sat prominently on his cluttered desk but seemed to have no useful function whatsoever.

After stabbing determinedly at the typewriter keys, he unscrolled the plethora of sheets from his typewriter with a final flourish and peered at us over his half-rimmed spectacles with a smile. Papers and signatures flew backwards and forwards between Liljana and the grandfather while I looked on helplessly, unable to contribute except by paying for the Advocate's services. We piled back into the cars and the Zastava team drove us on to the only Registrar's office in Skopje that was open. The receptionist stared vacantly at us as we all trouped into her dimly lit clinical surroundings. The Advocate's document was scrutinised by a gloomy-looking Registrar, officially stamped, registered and signed. There was a collective sigh from us all. The grandfather was pushed forward by his son and, with a grateful handshake, I parted with my Euros and he with the key to what was now my Zastava, courtesy of Liljana, acting owner.

———

Over the following week, Liljana registered the car at the police station and for 50 Euros I received a Green Card which allowed the car entry across every imaginable border, near and far, except, ironically, to its nearest neighbour, Kosovo. Surprisingly, a further one-off fee of 50 Euros would be required for that privilege. At last, almost everything was in place. I just needed a certificate from a lawyer's office authorising me to drive the car, it being officially registered in Liljana's name. Then I would be on my way.

———

"No, it is not possible. You cannot drive the car outside Macedonia. It is against Macedonian law."

I looked at the lawyer in disbelief. "What? I cannot leave the country?" I replied, dumbfounded. Was this really the law or just his interpretation? I had come to the end of my tether with all the ludicrous running around and paper chasing. How did Liljana manage to work in such a frustratingly bureaucratic environment? How did anything ever get done in Macedonia? Liljana sighed in defeat, resigned to my tragic fate. I sat totally speechless, inwardly fuming at the farcical situation I seemed to have created for myself, all because of a ridiculous notion to drive through the Balkans in a Zastava – now restricted to travelling in ever-decreasing circles around Macedonia for the next three months.

In desperation, I sought advice from the British Embassy but, apart from patiently listening to my woes and administering some sympathy, there was nothing they could do to help. Fortunately, it was at this moment I was introduced by a friend to John who lived in Skopje and, for several years, had worked on a number of international assignments across the Balkan region. Luckily for me, he was between projects, and was all too ready to put his mind to my predicament.

On first appearances, John was not your archetypal British male. For one thing, he appeared to prefer life in Macedonia to that in Britain, preferred *rakija* (the local home-brewed spirit) to beer and, most surprisingly, was not a man affected by the 40-degree summer heat, and while we all subsided into mushy heaps, he continued to look cool and composed. Despite these unusual traits, he had the British knack of getting right to the heart of my dilemma in a very matter-of-fact and refreshingly logical way.

"All you need is a privately signed Agreement between you and Liljana as the official owner which states that Liljana authorises you to drive the car outside of Macedonia. Simple! Macedonian law is Macedonian law, but once you leave Macedonia, it is no longer Macedonian law, *it is international law.*"

He delivered the last four words with great emphasis, followed by a triumphant grin. Undeniably, it made perfect sense. However, I was not sure whether Liljana could be persuaded to sign such a document. Secondly, would the border crossing authorities accept it?

"In any case," John continued, "no one will care once you have left Macedonia. Why should they stop you? You are doing nothing illegal. You are not stealing a car, merely borrowing it to take a trip around the Balkans. And you are driving a Zastava, for goodness' sake! No one even wants them anymore!"

I was not sure whether to be deeply offended or vastly encouraged by this.

"You will have no problems, I promise you," he said,

looking at me reassuringly. Then, as an afterthought, he added, "Well, if you do, it will be at the Macedonian border and we can come and rescue you!"

His eyes twinkled with amusement at the thought. It appeared I had nothing to lose.

Although Liljana was not so sure and feared ending up in prison, she nobly signed the Authorisation Agreement I had created. Gratefully, I hugged her. "We will see you in three months," I said, referring to the car and myself. She looked rather doubtful at this pronouncement but, whatever she was thinking, she hid it well and just smiled.

———

J ohn was filled with enthusiasm for my impending adventure and was more than happy to accompany me on my maiden voyage from Liljana's apartment to a temporary parking place outside his home. I tested all the knobs and buttons on the dashboard and flicked the levers on the steering column and, under John's instruction, practised the double de-clutch technique, which was a bit like dancing on the pedals with a bit of gear changing, and then we set off down the main road. He navigated us round the block into a residential street and at the corner pointed towards a gap in the shrubbery, an unexpected shortcut between streets which involved scaling a steep, muddy bank.

I stopped. "You are joking?" I said.

John laughed mischievously. "No. Go on, you can do it; the car is built for this, honestly."

I looked at him doubtfully but found first gear, took a deep breath and pushed down hard on the accelerator. The car sped up the slope. With a whoop and a sense of exhilaration I had successfully overcome my first "off roading" challenge. Little did I suspect how tame a test this had been compared to what was to come. For now, I felt prepared for anything the Balkan roads may bring.

─────

I took a last trip back to Pristina to pack up my belongings, say farewell to a few friends and get a haircut. Veton was a confident young Kosovo Albanian filled with good humour. He had travelled greatly in the region and overseas, and had learned his hairdressing trade in London. As he snipped away at my hair, he rattled off all sorts of travel advice, the most significant being how to act at Balkan border crossings.

"Never be in a hurry, Emma, and never hand over all your documents at the same time. This is the Balkans. Take your time. One document, then another," and with that he had flourished a mirror behind my head so I could admire his handiwork.

─────

Under the bonnet lay a mass of nuts, bolts, wires, bulbs, carburettors and indeed every spare part I could possibly imagine. John patiently explained what each item might do. I knew nothing about mechanics and although breaking down was probably going to be part of the journey, I was too excited to give it much thought at that moment.

"That's when you will meet interesting people," a friend had assured me.

I climbed into the driver's seat. "Brilliant!" I exclaimed in admiration as John completed the finishing touches to his masterpiece, an ingenious coat hanger locking device for the passenger door. He had dexterously hooked it through a hole in the door handle and then looped it over and through the hinged door pull. It was a locking mechanism like no other, and now both doors could be secured, although I chose to ignore the fact that John's mailbox key opened the driver's door with relative ease. It was too late to worry about break-ins. I was at the moment of departure!

John picked up a couple of bricks from a discarded pile outside his apartment and with a wink put them under the bonnet. "These might come in handy. Now, go!"

Nervously, I put the car into first gear and set off across the grassed verge. As I ventured onto the road, he shouted after me.

"Don't forget to turn off the headlights or your battery will go flat!" I nodded and waved as my Fića and I turned right and John's slim frame disappeared from view.

The journey had begun.

MACEDONIA

OFF ON THE OPEN ROAD

- Skopje/Gostivar (60km) -

I could not wipe the smile off my face. It was Thursday, 6th August 2009. Finally I had my Zastava and was leaving Skopje. It felt strangely liberating to be driving a car you could actually feel responding to every braking action, or turn of the steering wheel. It was almost as if the vehicle were alive. With each gear change came a new sound as the engine responded with a slow acceleration. I wound down the window and opened the adjoining quarter light. A warm flow of air circulated around me while another stream blew in across my feet from an unidentified hole in the floor, keeping them pleasantly cool. As we drove along at a steady 60 km/h, I noticed people turning their heads to look and smiling to themselves, a reaction I found rather comforting as if somehow we were being accepted.

It was the smallest car I had ever driven and I named him El Petito (a word of mixed European languages which actually means nothing, but to me, means the little one). Very soon I shortened it to Petito and finally shortened it even further to Tito. Perhaps sub-consciously it had been going this way from the start but the name suited him; he was, in any case, a car from the Yugoslav period and the era of President Tito.

I hoped to cross the Balkan peninsula with this four-wheeled thirty-one-year-old classic car. A Zastava 750S. Manufactured in 1978 by the Kragujevac Zastava factory in central Serbia. He was white in colour with chrome fixtures, clunky brakes, a manual choke and badly sprung seats. He had had a number of alterations made by the previous owner, including the introduction of a Yugo part which was designed to overcome one of the Fića's major flaws, the constant breaking of 'knuckle discs'. Although I was not too sure what this meant, Edon had convinced me Tito would get me further than any other car we had seen. The only part of him I did not like was the horn. The original had been deactivated and replaced with a dubious looking white plastic light switch which dangled rather pathetically from a cable on the steering column. When pressed, it made a squealing sound similar to a police siren. It was embarrassingly loud and totally out of character for a classic Zastava and I hoped I would never have to use it. Liljana's mechanic had changed Tito's battery and carried out a number of adjustments, which had cost me a lot more than I had anticipated but, in the end, if all went well, Tito would be my errant travelling companion for the next few months.

My idea was to travel anti-clockwise across the Balkan peninsula through eastern Greece, northern Turkey, Bulgaria, Romania, Serbia, Bosnia and Herzegovina, Croatia, Montenegro, Albania, the Peloponnese region of Greece and back through Macedonia to Skopje before the car registration documents expired in late October, giving me approximately two-and-a-half months. I had plenty of time ahead of me, or so it seemed. Today, the intention was to reach the town of Gostivar before dark and, not being too sure how long it would take to travel the sixty or so kilometres, I decided to "keep things simple" and to try not to get too distracted on the way.

Enormous road signs pointed us in the direction of a wide, two-lane dual carriageway sweeping gently upwards to the hills. We would bypass Tetovo, despite it being a town of historic interest and a very tempting first diversion. It was mid-afternoon and already I was beginning to realise that Tito's capacity to "nip by for a look" was limited. I wriggled around trying to find a comfortable position between the protruding seat springs and breathed deeply, hardly believing the journey had begun.

As the mountains and Tetovo neared, a red light started to flash slowly but insistently on the dashboard, drawing my attention away from my smug reverie and back to reality. *What on earth?* The fuel dial was pointing almost to twelve o'clock. Surely that meant the tank was full? Perhaps there was a malfunction with the needle? I pressed on, hoping this was just one of the car's idiosyncrasies. I had been so anxious to set off on my travels, I had only been given the simplest of instructions by John on how to fill the petrol tank, check the oil, cool the engine when it overheated and to jack up the car in the event of a flat tyre. The rest, I decided, I would have to work out as I went along, although secretly I hoped it would not be too difficult to find a mechanic.

We started to climb and I could feel Tito labouring. Although the lack of speed did not faze me, the flashing red light did. I slid him down into third gear as we began to plough our way slowly up the hill. Gripping the steering wheel tightly, I fixed my gaze on the road. We reached the top and Tito seemed to exhale with relief as we free-wheeled for 100 metres or so downhill. The red light stopped flashing. Perhaps the dial was just a little over-sensitive to the movement of petrol in the tank. However, as we began to climb, the red light started to flash again. It was a deceptively steep slope. I changed back into third and then down into second. The accelerator pedal was flat to the floor and my body tensed as Tito slowly crawled his way up at 30km/h. A road sign indicated petrol ahead but how far away was anyone's guess. We continued to climb. The petrol sign appeared again with an arrow indicating right. I took the turn and we glided down the slip road to a junction. There I hesitated. The sign appeared to be directing us down a deserted minor road. What if we broke down in the middle of nowhere?

As I sat there contemplating my situation, my courage failed. Instinct told me to get back onto the main road again as the enormity of the journey I was undertaking suddenly hit me and I wondered for the first time whether I actually had the nerve to do it. The plan was to take the minor routes across the Balkans and here I was too intimidated to go down my first country road. A mixture of fear and firm resolve convinced me I was making the right decision and I headed up the opposite slip road and back onto the empty two-laned highway. The red petrol light flashed unrelentingly but we made it to the top of the next incline. Here the road flattened out to reveal the petrol station in front of us but on a parallel road. I breathed a sigh of relief and pulled onto the hard shoulder, searching for the hazard light switch. There was none to be found. *Why would there be?* I reminded myself, *this is a Classic car!* I left the headlights on instead and turned off the engine.

The main road was still devoid of traffic, while in contrast the petrol station forecourt was crowded with people drinking coffee and smoking. I jumped over the roadside barrier and walked nervously towards them. The talking stopped. Eyes followed my progress, looked beyond to Tito and then back to me. Admittedly, I must have appeared an unusual sight but I had no option but to advance; I needed petrol. I had forgotten to bring a jerry can as Veton, my hairdresser in Pristina, had advised, so I walked over empty-handed and addressed the only man wearing oily dungarees in the hope he was the garage attendant.

With a lot of pointing in the direction of Tito and at the petrol pump, he piped up knowingly, "*Benzene?*" and disappeared into his workshop, coming out a moment later with an empty one-litre water bottle. He filled it with petrol and I offered him the one Euro which had clocked up on the petrol pump. He took it and set off across the road with the intent of helping me in my dilemma. The all-male café clientele looked on with a mixture of surprise and curiosity. I shrugged my shoulders to indicate *"Well, these things happen,"* and followed the garage attendant back over the roadside barrier. He spoke to me in Macedonian and then Albanian. I raised my hands apologetically. Although I could recognise the difference between the two languages, I could understand very little of either of them. Undeterred, he smiled at Tito and continued to talk rapidly. I caught the words, *"Dobro, dobro,"* *"Fića"* and *"Zastava"* and a sudden interjection of German, *"Sehr gut."*

He lifted up seven fingers and said the word *"Benzene"*, which I took to mean the next petrol station was 7km away and with that he gave Tito's bonnet a friendly pat and waved us off.

My confidence bolstered by the positive outcome to this first, slightly alarming episode, Tito and I headed towards the motorway toll. A short queue of cars was waiting. Expensive looking 4-wheel drives, a few Mercedes and us. A group of skinny young children wearing an assortment of clothes either too big or too small for them was running between the cars, asking for money, proposing a windscreen clean and selling strawberries. The children milled in amongst us with their dark eyes, dark hair, and dark skin already weather-beaten by the sun – they were almost certainly Roma children. I watched with growing interest as these canny-minded individuals passed in front and behind Tito, targeting the rich, sleek car owners and ignoring me and my supposedly poor man's Zastava almost as though we did not exist. Not one child gave us a second look. We reached the toll and I handed over a one-hundred Macedonian dinar note with a polite good day: "*Dobar den.*" The man took the note and then solemnly handed it back, lifting the barrier as he did so. Bewildered, I drove on, wondering whether he also considered me too poor to pay.

As expected, a petrol station lay ahead. I stopped Tito beside the pump. The garage attendant stared at me in amazement. I pulled the release handle under the dashboard and the bonnet hook unclicked. The tank was indeed empty. As the fuel gushed in, the petrol gauge swept clockwise to the six o'clock position, revealing as it did so a zero at the top of the dial. I peered more closely. It was marked '*Gorivo*' which I took to mean fuel. The needle now rested at a 4/4 mark. Was the car a gas guzzler? Or had the needle stuck? Or had I really set off from Skopje rashly assuming Liljana's mechanic had filled the tank when a momentary glance at the dial would have told me otherwise? Whatever the answer, in future I would be taking nothing for granted and would top up regularly.

———

We passed Tetovo and the town of Negotino, which my guidebook rather disregarded as a town with a "communist concrete" character, and pushed on west to Gostivar. Every vehicle travelling on the road seemed to overtake us but as they did so we were acknowledged with a smile, a nod or just a stare. Another toll fee was solemnly handed back to me, but this time in a different configuration of dinar notes, and the barrier raised once more. I laughed with growing incomprehension. Why was I exempt from paying? I was using the road like everyone else. I quickly dismissed the theory they thought I was a local and took the slip road to Gostivar just as daylight was fading.

The illuminated sign *BALKAN HOTEL* with its one-star symbol guided me to my first night's rest. I parked and gratefully got out of the driver's seat, only to jump back in with a horrified gasp, slam hard on the brakes and put the car into reverse as Tito rolled gently forward. It seemed John's parting gift of two bricks was going to come in very handy!

"Is your car?" asked the hotel manager as he came out to help me with my luggage.

"Yes."

He began to laugh. "Where you come from?"

"Skopje," I replied.

"Is long way in little car."

"Oh, but this is just the beginning!" I said, "I still have a long way to go. I am driving around the Balkans."

"With Fića?" he asked incredulously. "Is many mountains and…." His words trailed off as he realised I was completely serious, and was about to be his hotel guest.

"Actually it seems I have a problem with the handbrake. Do you know a mechanic?"

Changing his tone to one of helpful assurance, he replied, "No problem, we have mechanic. Tomorrow morning, I talk with him."

The muezzin's call to prayer rang out from a nearby mosque across the still evening air as I found my room and gladly collapsed onto the bed. With sixty kilometres covered and only one incident to report, I felt rather pleased with myself on surviving my first day of the journey.

- Gostivar/Bitola (110km) -

I awoke and momentarily wondered where I was as the bright colour scheme of my hotel bedroom came into focus. Day two had begun. I ate a rather uninspiring hotel breakfast of cheese and white bread accompanied by a strong coffee. A circling fly seemed more interested than I in having its share of the food on offer.

The tables began to fill with men of all ages drinking coffee and smoking strong-smelling cigarettes, maintaining an eye on everything going on around them while at the same time carrying on an intense conversation with one another. This was something I would soon come to recognise as a well-honed Balkan trait. For now, however, my experience was confined to being the one under observation as the hotel owner ushered me outside to meet the mechanic, who just happened to have a garage directly opposite. He studied Tito's handbrake, shook his head and drove the car across to the garage for further investigation. I went back to the café to finish my coffee and await the outcome with growing trepidation.

The mechanic reappeared and, with the help of one of the café's younger coffee-drinking clientele who spoke carefully constructed English phrases, explained that the handbrake would be too complicated to fix, but assured me that, in an emergency, it could still be manually applied. A more pressing concern were the brakes. They needed to be replaced, a recommendation I could not ignore. Tito was raised up on jacks and sparks started to fly out from the garage. It was too agonising to watch and I headed for the town centre on foot, hoping the mechanic would handle my Yugoslav relic with care.

Despite the intense heat of the morning sun, Gostivar was buzzing with life. Everyone was purposefully going about their business. A car parked outside a florist shop had been adorned with ribbons and bows from bonnet to boot in preparation for a wedding. It looked like a decorated cake on wheels. How the chauffeur would manage, I did not dare imagine. In the main, wide "communist style" square, aptly named Maršal Tito, a man sat in the shade of a pink flowering tree leaning against a large drum. He was wearing modern clothes but on his head sat a traditional white squarish-shaped hat. I waited a while to see if he would start playing but clearly for him it was just too hot. He moved in closer to the tree trunk, leant against it and closed his eyes.

The one obvious historic site in town, a stone clock tower from the 16th century, was sandwiched uncomfortably between a new modern glass building and a minaret. Down some narrower streets, old earth brick traditional houses reflected the town's previous architectural style. Now in such a deteriorated state, they would soon collapse or be demolished to make way for more modern buildings, eroding Gostivar's past still further.

With a raging thirst, I dived into a café and ordered a *Schweppes*. A bottle of *Bitter Lemon* appeared. The clientele, as before, were all men. They regarded me critically. A foreign woman travelling by herself was unlikely to be a common sight in those parts and, self-consciously, I stuck my head in my guidebook.

———

I t was almost one o'clock as the muezzin began his lilting call to prayer. I headed back towards the garage, passing a shopfront filled with every imaginable car part and accessory. The shop turned out to be a veritable gold mine and a chance to buy engine oil, a jerry can, an emergency roadside kit and a fire extinguisher, all of which my guidebook had reliably informed me were necessary to meet the legal European driving regulations for Greece, our next destination. The young shopkeeper negotiated his way around the compact space stacked precariously high with stock. "I have to go to the mosque now but let's find what you need." I paid up and apologised for making him late for prayer. "No, no problem," he said with a reassuring wink. "Have a good journey."

The hotel manager ushered me out to Tito. The brakes were fixed, and the handbrake would manually hold when I needed to negotiate hill starts, which I imagined would soon become quite frequent, considering the height and length of the mountain chain (Balkans in Turkish) that dominates the southeast European peninsula. I stowed my new purchases under the bonnet, reminding myself as I did so that I still needed to find a fire extinguisher from somewhere. I paid my hotel bill and mechanic's fee, which amounted to an incredibly inexpensive 40 Euros in total, packed up the car, topped up the petrol tank, and off we went.

———

Heading south, our ultimate destination on this second day of the trip was the former embassy and merchant-trading town of Bitola. However, first there was a 1700m high mountain road to negotiate. Tito seemed fine in third gear and we took the bends nice and easy but it was not long before Edon's advice was ringing in my ears. "Go slow; keep the engine door open otherwise he will overheat." The problem was that the engine door was hinged to open upwards, blocking my view out of the back window, and I had not found anything with which to partially wedge it open. I eyed the heat gauge nervously as the needle began to rise. We were doing 40km/h and my foot on the accelerator pedal was flat to the floor. My body tensed as I willed the car up the mountain road. We slowed to 30km/h while a string of cars overtook us, peering curiously at me as they passed. With a decisive sweep, the heat gauge abruptly hit red. In panic I careered across the road, driving Tito into the only piece of shade I could see.

Hot water squirted through the ventilation fins as I struggled with the key and eventually threw the engine door open. Boiling water spurted out like a fountain from a hole in the grimy water container on the left, while on the right, the oil bubbled out rather alarmingly through a joint in the mechanism. A truly dramatic spectacle; I stared helplessly at it and waited. Eventually everything cooled down. Tentatively, we set off once more but within ten minutes the needle had swung back into the red and once again I had to stop and rush to fling the engine door upwards. So began our slow climb to the top of the mountain pass. Cars zoomed by, drivers smiled and after the third stop, I began to take the drama in my stride and enjoy the mountain scenery. I felt an endearing sense of pride in my little car as eventually, wheezing and spluttering, Tito made it to the top. It was a triumph made all the more exhilarating by the long downhill ride from 1700 metres into the town of Kičevo while the heat gauge needle swung back to 'cool'.

––––––

I t was after three o'clock and the traffic was bumper to bumper up the main street, the two lanes separated by a wide grassy strip. Down one side, old trees provided plenty of shade for pedestrians and café dwellers alike. I tucked Tito into a pocket-sized parking space and, fearing to go too far from him or my worldly possessions stowed on the backseat, I took refuge in a nearby café filled with young and old drinking coffee and eating ice cream. It was Friday afternoon and everyone was out enjoying the start of the weekend. I ordered a Shopska salad, the most popular salad in the Balkans. It consists of chopped tomato, cucumber, sometimes onion, and maybe peppers and olives, all in an olive oil and often vinegar dressing, topped with a mountain of grated brine cheese similar to feta. One is never sure which ingredients will turn up on your plate but it is refreshing and tasty whatever the combination.

A group of Roma children boldly entered the café begging

for money. They eyed the Kičevo children playing with the new toys their parents had just bought them. One little boy fired a large plastic gun in all directions accompanied by the usual boy-gun-shooting sounds. The Roma children watched distractedly with a mixture of curiosity and envy before turning back to the job in hand until they were shooed out by a waiter.

Car horns sounded incessantly from Mercedes, BMWs, Porsche Cayennes and expensive looking 4-wheel drive vehicles adorned with ribbons and sashes as they made their way slowly up the main street, children and adults hanging out of every available window and sunroof. A wedding party was on the move. Traditionally, in the past, guns were fired in the air at weddings and I have been told this practice still goes on but certainly no guns were present today except for the toy gun in the café. Perhaps it was the visible presence of policemen directing the traffic that deterred their use.

The café's hi-fi system was pounding out the Balkan sounds of turbo-folk, a style of music fusing traditional folk song with modern upbeat dance rhythms. I was still in the early stages of trying to appreciate it but not today. It was time to get on the road.

———

I paid up and headed off initially in the direction of Ohrid, soon turning left towards Bitola. The road twisted and turned along on the flat and then started to rise. Clouds gathered out of nowhere and three or four large drops of rain hit the windscreen, followed by a sudden downpour. Raindrops the size of bullets hammered down on the roof. Deafened by the sound, I wound up the window as fast as I could, keeping the quarter light open to prevent the windscreen from steaming up. Tito's ruler-sized wipers squeaked left and right leaving smeary marks across the

windscreen, as I strained to see between the streaks. I tested
the brakes tentatively. They still seemed to work but I slowed
down and we motored along at 40km/h enjoying a sense of
intrepid survival in the rain. A rivulet of water trickled in
through a point at the base of the windscreen and landed
with a splash on my foot, but that was our only leak. As
quickly as the rainstorm arrived, it disappeared. The sun re-
emerged and I unwound the window once more, glad to have
survived another "first" on the road.

The road carried us past traditional houses of stone,
timber frames and earth brick with large balconies and
verandas, jettied second floors, and roofs covered in old
terracotta tiles. There were barns with sapling wood woven
walls and, on the hillsides, rows of beehive boxes painted
light blue, yellow, red and gold added an unexpected splash
of colour to the green landscape. The temptation to explore
these villages was immense but with no interpreter I
hesitated, conscious that being a foreign woman alone in a
Fića was perhaps a little more startling than I had imagined. I
settled for admiring the scene from a distance with the hope
of returning another day with someone able to help with
communication. The road flattened out past fields of crops
and on into the town of Bitola, with its impressive 19th
century stone mansion houses dominating the streetscape on
either side of the fast-flowing River Dragor.

Uncertain where I was going, and with no navigator on
hand to help, I was soon hopelessly lost in the narrow lanes of
the old town. We emerged into a square where three old men
waved at us. I smiled back and navigated my way out, only to
find myself re- emerging into the square for a second time.
The old men laughed and I waved in embarrassment. When I
navigated back into the square for a third time, there was
genuine concern written on the three old men's faces and they
rose to their feet to assist.

A test of varying languages proved ineffectual. They stuck

to Macedonian and I to my guidebook page of "phrases". It did not really help much but they recognised the words "De Niro's Hotel". One of them was appointed to accompany me in the car and he, with a beaming smile, eagerly approached the passenger door as I unwound John's coat hanger locking device from the handle and let him in. The old man happily sat with my half-empty bottles of water at his feet, while my collection of maps, books, straw hat and handbag was piled onto his lap. He patted the dashboard gleefully. "Zastava, *dobro, dobro*. Fića."

"*Da, da, dobro, dobro*," I laughed, nodding in agreement. He directed me through the cobbled lanes in a mixture of German and Macedonian until eventually we arrived at De Niro's and I parked in the shade of an ancient tree. Fighting off all my paraphernalia, he emerged from the car.

"*Blagodaram*," I said gratefully, using the Macedonian word for thank you.

He grinned from ear to ear, shaking my hand vigorously. He was a tall, thin figure wearing dark trousers held up by a belt pulled to its tightest hole. His white shirt was neatly tucked in at the base but open at the neck to reveal the curve of a white vest beneath. On his head sat a dark coloured beret covering short grey hair which poked out from the edges. His hands were weather-beaten, and his face was carved with the deep lines of life. Declining my offer of a coffee, he shuffled off with a wave to rejoin his friends. Wistfully I dragged my rucksack up the steps to De Niro's reception, wishing momentarily I would be meeting friends here.

———

B itola, with its many consulate buildings, has a wonderful feel of faded grandeur about it. In the past, the city has been at the forefront of many wars and been occupied by Greeks, Serbs, Bulgarians and Germans, to name

but a few. However, after World War II the town became part
of a newly formed Yugoslavian state, Macedonia, with Skopje
as its capital.

Bitola's centre is somewhat jumbled, the only defining
lines being the River Dragor, with boulevards running down
either side of it, and Maršal Tito Street, with its pedestrian
zone filled with all ages taking the air on a Friday evening.
When I visited, there were people drinking coffee and
smoking in the many bars and cafés that spilled out across the
pavement. The Turkish, British and French embassy flags
were very evident but other former embassy mansion houses
were less visible, tucked behind flowering gardens, and
dwarfed by concrete apartment blocks. The old bazaar, with
its many small shops and market, closed in the early evening,
creating an almost ghost-like atmosphere. My gaze strayed
across the river to the only pool of light on the quiet street. It
came from a barber's shop as he gave his client a traditional
cut-throat shave. Back on Maršal Tito Street, the children
powered up and down on toy cars, bicycles, roller blades and
scooters followed by concerned young mothers. The mood
was relaxed as everyone paraded slowly up and down,
walking, talking, meeting neighbours and friends and
enjoying the cool evening temperatures.

It was a pleasure to watch this social evening activity
which included everyone. Although most people in the
Balkans now wear Western-style clothes, some older women
wear long dark-coloured skirts over balloon-legged trousers
and scarves on their heads, while men wear hats of differing
materials and shapes symbolising their religion, whether
Orthodox or Muslim, dervish, or a pilgrim to Mecca. It is a
custom dying out among the younger generation who seem
to favour anonymity, following European fashion rather than
religious persuasion. These are changing times and I wonder
if this is a recent trend spreading across the Balkans as each

country turns more towards Europe for a new modern identity.

It was early but I headed back to the hotel and gladly climbed into bed. It had been a tiring although rewarding day with a staggering one hundred and ten kilometres covered as well as a mountain pass conquered. With the windows firmly closed against the decibels of Friday night's music, I crawled under my duvet and very quickly fell asleep to the hypnotic sound of the whirring fan and fin flips of the air-conditioning unit.

- Bitola/Border Control (16km) -

Ever conscious of avoiding another petrol incident, I refuelled on the outskirts of Bitola. The garage seemed to be a magnet for a whole cross-section of the Macedonian communities. 4-wheel drive Porsches swept in, followed by the local farmer on his aging light blue tractor; a boy racer roared in on his cool motorbike while a family of four in a run-down beaten-up car of no particular description blasted exhaust fumes over us all. A man cycled in to talk to the farmer, and in amongst this gathering sat Tito, the only Zastava to be seen for miles around, or so it seemed. I made the unexpected discovery of a compact fire extinguisher in the garage shop and we left the forecourt ready and road-legal for Greece.

Signs to Heraclea were tempting me to visit the amazing archaeological site of mosaic floors and stone remains dating back to the 4th century BC, but I had my first border crossing to tackle with the slightly worrying thought that perhaps I would not be allowed to leave Macedonia with a Zastava that did not officially belong to me. Resolutely I applied my journey mantra of "*keeping things simple*" and pressed on to the Greek border with the words of advice imparted to me by Veton, my Pristina hairdresser, clearly in my mind, "Don't be in a hurry, Emma. Give one document at a time."

I joined a queue of five cars at the border Medžitlija-Niki, the outside temperature rising by the minute. I opened my passenger door in the hope of trapping some cooler air into the car. Was lunchtime a sensible hour to cross a Macedonian border? Would the heat make the customs officials irritable? I did not know. The queue moved fairly quickly and we were next. A couple of border police peered curiously at Tito and laughed amongst themselves. I got out of the car and walked around to the passport control cabin.

"Dobar den," I said politely, posting my passport through the sliding window.

"Car documents," came the gruff response.

I offered them to him. The officer nodded with a bored expression and glanced over my shoulder towards Tito. He peered at me again with a look of astonishment. Eventually he spotted the obvious. My passport name did not correspond with that on the vehicle papers. He shuffled forward in his chair, fully awake now, and pointed at Liljana's name and then at the car.

"Ah yes, sorry," I said with a half-smile, playing Veton's game perhaps a little too slowly. Casually and carefully I passed through the Authorisation Agreement which Liljana and I had signed in Skopje, authorising me to drive the car. The Agreement was only in English because, as John had sagely pointed out, once one leaves Macedonia, international law applies and English is an international language. The passport officer inspected the Agreement upside down, then turned it around and shot me a look to see if I had noticed his mistake. Meanwhile, two customs officials sauntered over, their curiosity aroused by the delay. There was a great deal of talking, and a computer check was run. They all stared at me, and then at the car. A telephone call was made and yet another official squeezed his way into the already full booth. My heart was racing but I waited patiently and pretended to be unconcerned by their heated discussions. They demanded the "Green Card". This I handed over and, with every second that ticked by, I became more nervous. Were they going to let me through? It seemed they were not sure. Then the word "Fića" was mentioned, followed by great guffaws. I relaxed slightly. Whatever had been said, it persuaded the passport officer. He stamped my passport. "Ok."

He handed back all my documents with a casual wave of dismissal in the general direction of Greece. Trying not to break into a run back to the car, I started the engine and drove the few metres to an eagerly awaiting customs officer.

"Where are you going?" he asked.

"Greece," I said rather obviously, trying to maintain my composure. He ignored my response and waved me through.

The Authorisation Agreement had worked. We had left Macedonia! Now we had the Greek border authorities to overcome. Only then could I claim our first border crossing a victory.

GREECE

THROUGH A LAND OF MANY FACES

- Medžitlija-Niki Border Control/Edessa (100km) -

"Passport please."

The passport control officer eyed me suspiciously and slowly drew a cigarette from a half-empty packet lying on the desk. He lit up and exhaled a large puff of smoke, regarding my passport cover with irritation. Through frequent use the poorly embossed British Nationality insignia had been totally erased and, in effect, where I came from was anyone's guess. He fanned through the pages to the back. A flicker of disappointment registered across his face. "You are British?" he asked.

"Yes," I replied. He handed back my passport and, with a bored look, waved me through to the customs police.

"Insurance." I handed over the Green Card that Liljana had bought for the car. He nodded and glanced at Tito with a smile. "Ok."

I kept my composure until we rounded the corner and disappeared out of view. I was through! "We're in Greece!" I shouted out loud in delight.

Although probably an insignificant event in most people's

lives, successfully crossing my first border with Tito was a moment of triumph for me. In my eagerness to share it, I pulled over into the shade and texted all those I knew who would understand my excitement. I popped a *Werther's* toffee into my mouth in celebration as my Nokia phone beeped repeatedly, delivering enthusiastic replies. Although travelling alone, I was but a text away from sharing these moments with friends. A comforting thought.

It was two o'clock and the temperature was hurtling towards forty degrees once more. With the window down, the quarter light fully extended and my straw hat angled firmly over my left shoulder against the burning sun, I drove along, marvelling at the geographical change a border crossing can bring. The world was opening up in front of us, as wide as it was high. A bright blue sky soared upwards like Nature's own domed cathedral – so vast and light and different from the world we had just left behind kilometres away. I proposed to stop for lunch in Florina – a small town only 16km away – but after a few minutes I realised the road signs were all in Greek Cyrillic with only the occasional Latin translation. This was possibly going to be more difficult than I had thought. I stopped the car and studied the lettering. Luckily, my map had the place names in both the Cyrillic and the Roman alphabets and before long I was deciphering the unfamiliar symbols into recognisable words with some confidence.

We made it to Florina and, after a brief lunch stop, we were now on a main road driving east towards Edessa. Large European Union signage boards informed those driving past that it was responsible for the funding of the current road system on which we were now travelling. However grateful the Greeks may be, I was not. At every possible opportunity we were guided onto the "new" old road heading directly to Thessaloniki, and the more scenic rural route, which I had been hoping to take to Edessa, proved very difficult to find. It became clear I was not the only disgruntled person. Greece's more radical artistic element had been out in force, objecting in their own way by embellishing the EU signs with graffiti or street art wherever possible. Along the route, some buildings were adorned with the Greek flag but more often than not EU flags readily outnumbered Greek ones. I found this rather unnerving or perhaps I had misunderstood the whole concept of being European – perhaps it was not a question of diversity but solidarity – although it appeared to me to be wholly intrusive, as though Greece was losing its identity rather than having that identity enhanced. Was I in Greece or a new country called the European Union?

Despite the EU signage upsetting my mental equilibrium, it was not after all such a difficult journey to Edessa. The town itself was set above the plains, providing spectacular views of where we had just been and to where we were eventually heading: Thessaloniki. Very few people here seemed to speak even a smattering of English, yet I eventually navigated us into the old quarter of Varosi, squeezing our way up its narrow lanes between crumbling and fragile timber-framed houses to a pension with flowers tumbling over the balcony. Leaving Tito in a little square surrounded by stone houses in various stages of repair or dilapidation, to gurgle, bubble and generally cool down after his day's exertions, I took the last available room at the pension. The friendly hosts invited me to join them on the front terrace to eat sun-ripened grapes from their own vine and drink coffee – an offer I could not refuse, especially as I had not spoken a word to anyone that day except the border crossing official. I flopped down into a big comfy chair under the shade of a large white canvas sun umbrella. The afternoon air was still; cicadas sang loudly in the heat and, as I was soon to learn, the Greek summer siesta is a lengthy affair – I was more than ready to adopt this lifestyle.

The buildings in Varosi, the old quarter of Edessa were in a parlous state. Some were shored up with large chunks of timber which, if removed, would surely cause the buildings to collapse. Old homes sat alongside churches of varying sizes and, in many cases, over-sized banners displayed the amount of EU funding being invested. Some of this funding had seemingly created an interesting collection of atelier workshops but on closer inspection it seemed that they were already lying sadly neglected, which raised the question of how much local interest and support had been secured before the money had been spent. Whatever the reason, the stark reality of broken windows and yet more graffiti indicated a sense of failure, however interesting and exciting the initial vision had been.

Evening arrived, bringing cooler air. I headed into the town centre in search of Edessa life. Children cycled through the narrow lanes in the fading light and young and old ambled along arm-in-arm talking and enjoying a respite from the day's heat, just as the people had done in Bitola. Was this a ritual that could arguably link the Greeks to the Balkans as well as the Mediterranean?

A gigantic plane tree dominated the main square, its enormous branches spreading outwards. Underneath, candlelit tables softly illuminated the faces of the coffee drinkers, their voices competing with the loud high-pitched chirping of little birds flitting about in huge numbers in the branches. As night fell, the birds became silent but the people talked on. By nine o'clock I was famished. It seemed I was the only one. Ten o'clock chimed and still no one moved from the coffee tables. Bewildered, I headed back up the hill in search of somewhere to eat. All the restaurants were empty and I went to bed wondering when, if ever, anyone ate.

- Edessa/Thessaloniki (69km) -

The pension breakfast more than adequately made up for the previous evening's unexpected fast. Filled to capacity, I packed up and headed out to the square. Two young boys were peering in through Tito's passenger windows and shouting excitedly back to their parents. They walked shyly away as I approached and watched from a distance as I loaded my luggage onto the backseat, pulled up the engine door to test the levels of oil and water, and then emptied my full five-litre jerry can of petrol into the tank under the bonnet. Apparently, it was forbidden to carry containers of fuel in Greece. More disconcerting was the fact that Greece has the highest death rate in Europe caused by reckless overtaking – or so my guidebook claimed. Not a very comforting thought.

———

I t had rained briefly but the sun was out, although the air felt uncomfortably muggy as we headed east out of Edessa in the direction of Pella – the birthplace of Alexander the Great. This renowned figure and hero had been the King of Macedon, a kingdom which lies on what is today divided between Macedonia and Northern Greece – the territory which Greece also calls Macedonia. It is a political dilemma for both Greece and Macedonia. Greece vehemently claims Alexander the Great as being Greek and a part of its heritage, arguing Pella lies in Greek Macedonia, the hero's birthplace. This is of no consequence to the 'former Yugoslav Republic of Macedonia', which considers him to be Macedonian and a part of its history also. Since 1992, they have laid a claim to a share of Alexander the Great's legacy. On top of all this, Macedonia's official name, the 'former Yugoslav Republic of Macedonia', quite regularly abbreviated to FYROM, is a title which raises the hackles of both the Greeks and the Macedonians. The former insist the name Macedonia should be changed to something other than that which is associated with their region of Northern Greece, while the latter are not happy with having the 'former Yugoslav Republic' tagged on to their country's name. It is all, you might say, a real mess. As I headed towards Pella in the Macedonian region of Northern Greece, I wondered if the issue would become any clearer on my arrival. (Note: Since this journey was made in 2009, the two countries agreed in 2018 to a renaming of FYROM to the Republic of North Macedonia. This new name came into effect in February 2019.)

After our descent from Edessa the route was flat and traffic-free. Tito puttered along happily and before long we arrived in Pella. It was Sunday, and Pella seemed like a ghost town, a town waiting for something to happen. I speculated whether the MK (Macedonia) sticker in Tito's back window and his Skopje number plates would raise a few eyebrows but no one was there to care. I parked beside a sign indicating 'Alexander the Great Square'. In the half-hour I stayed to drink a *Schweppes* and cool down in the shade nothing moved.

The archaeological site of Pella turned out to be equally empty, interrupted by a few standing stone columns, an ultra-modern 21st century designed visitor centre and a few impressive mosaic floors carefully protected from the midday sun by concrete canopies. Within this bleak, vast landscape I tried to imagine a thriving city with Alexander the Great running around as a young boy but the hot oppressive atmosphere proved too much. To whom this hero's legacy belonged would not be solved today, and certainly not by me. It was time to head to Thessaloniki in search of coastal air and a sea breeze.

———

The rhythmic sound of Tito's indicator was a kind of pacifier. We were turning left. I built up courage and counted the ticks: *One, two, three, four...* Gritting my teeth and with my foot flat to the floor, we accelerated across the road into a gap between two vehicles. The morning's traffic-free roads were no more and for the first time we were driving amidst fast cars and wild, spontaneous manoeuvrings. Where had they all come from? Children's eyes opened wide on seeing us and they swung round in their seats to get another look at Tito through the back window. From the frenzy of the single lane E86 road, we were pulled into the melting pot of a dual carriageway, and then dragged into the terrifying inferno of the A2 motorway leading towards Thessaloniki. Cars screamed past and juggernauts loomed towards us with seemingly unstoppable power. Just when I thought we would be crushed, these huge monsters would swerve out and overtake us, sucking Tito's lightweight frame towards the juggernaut's underbelly. Whilst I was struggling to keep control of the steering wheel, I found another unexpected challenge facing us as the car's slim wheels were drawn into the deep-ridged tyre tracks carved out by these heavily laden juggernaut beasts. With a judder and a sudden wrench to the right, I took the slip road to Thessaloniki city centre. The juggernauts ploughed on eastwards towards Turkey as we lurched over the tarmac ridges and onto an equally large but thankfully smooth three-lane highway surprisingly devoid of traffic. I breathed a sigh of relief and regained my composure. *Oh my God, never again!* We were unscathed but Tito was wheezing, coughing and spluttering, loudly protesting against what I had just put him through.

The sea front appeared. Thank goodness we were entering the city on a Sunday. A motorbike pulled up beside us with a powerful, deep-throated, ticking engine. The driver peered out from under his raised helmet visor with a look of amazement, then smiled at me, and started to rev his engine in mock anticipation of a race. I laughed and he grinned back. The traffic lights turned green, he nodded farewell and the girl riding pillion turned her head momentarily towards me in amusement; then, with a stream of long-flowing hair, they were gone.

- Thessaloniki -

Thessaloniki had a laid-back atmosphere but behind the surface it revealed to me a city of two halves; a well-dressed bordering on the pretentious class of person, and a most definite visibly under-privileged second class. The waterfront was where the "lovely" people sat to watch and be watched, reclining on exclusive pavement furniture in full view of the trendily dressed pedestrians. I could not help but marvel at the superficiality of it all when only one or two streets back there was a somewhat different, more down-to-earth world, as well as poverty and begging Roma children. Hard-working individuals manned the vibrant food markets through which large determined Greek women forcefully jostled with enthusiasm; Roman, Byzantine and Ottoman cultural attractions drew some tourists, while others drank coffee, musing a while over Thessaloniki's future. The city has been a victim of war, fire and forced cultural shifts. Pick up any guidebook and you will be fully immersed in the city's intriguing, colourful, dark and dramatic past. It is a subject that I could not even attempt to explain here and as there are many who do so, and do so well, I recommend you seek these out.

On impulse, I phoned Stefanos, whom I had met while working in Kosovo. He was a Greek archaeologist living in Thessaloniki. In his early 30's, he was slim with the typical dark hair and dark eyes of a Greek, and skin that tanned a golden brown the minute it was exposed to the sun. Just back from his holidays and full of post-holiday euphoria, he happily agreed to meet me.

"Let's catch up this afternoon for coffee, say around 7.30?" I laughed.

"The afternoon? It is summer!" he exclaimed. "In Greece we make two days out of one! That means a long afternoon and a very late evening but it is too hot to sleep. It is not like in Britain."

We met at a café and he introduced me to the fashionable delight of summer iced coffee – the frappé and the freddo – iced instant coffee and iced espresso, both refreshing and totally addictive. I was curious to learn more about the Greek way of life, and it did not take much to get Stefanos talking of the difficulties of living in today's Greek society, caught between traditional family values and the desire for a more modern and independent lifestyle. He spoke of the older generation, who had been unfairly denied the right to follow certain professional careers because their fathers had been communists. He spoke of a need for change, and for the older generation to wake up and embrace new ideas, new technology and new ways of presenting Greece to the world.

Stefanos was a man already breaking with tradition by not living at home, as many unmarried sons and daughters are still expected to do. He told me about his worry over the corruption, the misuse of money and the underhand way in which government institutions were run. "Everything is politically motivated," he said in exasperation. He spoke of the rising racial tension between minority groups and the Greek population, particularly in respect to the number of Albanians living and working in Greece. The thriving, colourful Thessaloniki waterfront was, as I suspected, just a façade hiding the reality of Greek life, its problems bubbling barely beneath the surface. However, on this warm evening with everyone enjoying the summer Mediterranean temperatures, and Stefanos and I with them, we were blissfully unaware of the financial crisis Greece was about to face, and Europe with it. (A decade later, the migrant/refugee crisis would be yet a further challenge for a country grappling with financial, political and social hardship.)

- Thessaloniki/Kavala (187km) -

After a water top-up from one of the multitude of half-empty bottles now piling up on the floor of the car, I checked the oil, filled up with petrol and focused on following the Cyrillic signs out of Thessaloniki eastwards in the direction of Kavala. Stefanos had suggested that on the way I visit the birthplace of Aristotle in Stagira, which lies north of the "third finger" on the Halkidiki peninsula. As well as being a philosopher, Aristotle had been the teacher and mentor of Alexander the Great, and like all Greek men, Stefanos greatly admired this hero but was fed up with the rhetoric from both the Greek and Macedonian politicians. Quite sensibly, he had refrained from being drawn into a discussion with me on the topic.

"You must feel like an ant amongst a herd of elephants!" had been Stefanos' exclamation on seeing Tito yesterday evening. He could not have described it better and, as we headed towards the maniacal racetrack A2 road, I cursed the EU signs which insisted on directing us onto their modern but frightening road systems with no option of a B-road escape route. To a delicately-framed, slow-moving vehicle like a Zastava, it is nothing short of hair-raising and as we suffered another thundering, terrifying trip down the motorway, I cried out pitifully, "There has to be an alternative!"

After twenty-five kilometres, a slip road appeared and I took it regardless of where it might lead. We passed through the hamlet of Profitis. Miraculously I had found the minor road and we bounced along this quiet, seemingly unknown route with a feeling of freedom and adventure, and as Tito regained his composure, I attempted as ever to find a comfortable position between the protruding seat springs.

Stavros lies on the east coast of the Halkidiki peninsula and appears to be a place where many Greeks holiday; today it was seething. We continued a further thirteen kilometres down the coast to the small town of Olimbias and up a steep hill hugging the coastline to Stagira. The expectation of gardens and tranquillity in the land of Aristotle's birthplace was met with anti-climax and disappointment. The gates were firmly padlocked. I pulled over into the shade and got out to peer through the iron railings. The land went out like a promontory into the sea and was densely covered in trees with the hint of a track weaving its way down to the point, idyllic but unattainable. It seemed learning more about Aristotle and Alexander the Great would have to wait for another time.

Aware that my days by the coast would be numbered, I headed back into Olimbias. The sun continued to shine and although a strong wind was blowing off the sea I chose to ignore it and reclined like Cleopatra on one of the opulent beach sofas and breathed in the sea air. Although Stavros was busy, there were no people here; just the wind, sea, sand, sun and the gentle sounds of South American music drifting out from a nearby beach bar. What would Aristotle have thought of all this lounging about and salsa vibes? Probably not very much, I shouldn't doubt.

———

The A2 motorway snaked its way alongside us. Like a cunning predator, it tried to lure us onto its track by momentarily merging with our minor E90 road in a confusing manner and then breaking off again. I stuck determinedly to the philosophy of following the road closest to the coastline and by doing so we were not drawn into the mouth of the A2 motorway but instead we enjoyed a calm, trouble-free journey east into Kavala.

- Kavala -

Kavala is the stepping-off point to a number of the Greek islands, with a bustling harbour front filled with tourist buses and disorientated people. We navigated our way through them all to the ferry terminal. My idea was to take a ferry to the island of Samothraki, stay the night and then take another one on to Alexandroupoli, situated further along the mainland coast, and by so doing, give Tito a rest. However, my plans were scuppered. The ferry to Samothraki no longer operated from Kavala. We would have to stay here tonight.

Kavala's old quarter of Panagia is topped by the Imaret Hotel, formerly a Medressa and school for teaching young students Islam in the early 19th century. It was built by Muhammad Ali Pasha of Egypt and the complex consisted of a school, hammam and small decorated mosque. Ali Pasha donated the Medressa to the town but with the collapse of the Ottoman Empire in the early 1900s, the buildings fell into neglect and were finally abandoned. Today, they have been renovated and turned into a luxury hotel with rooms and suites located within four courtyards linked by old stone paved colonnades. Each courtyard was as tranquil and enchanting as the next.

One night's stay cost a fortune but the intoxicating scent of olive, orange and fig trees and the soft sound of water fountains was irresistible, and with Tito parked appealingly outside between a Porsche and a Mercedes, I found myself able to negotiate a discount.

———

The old quarter of Panagia is a place for wandering, an interesting mix of three- and four-storey stone houses, small lanes, colourfully painted doors and windows, balconies dripping in flowers and the chatter of voices emanating from open windows. People were taking their evening stroll, and drinking coffee in one or other of the tavernas or cafés down near the waterfront. The Greeks were enjoying the warm August air and I wondered whether here they considered themselves more Balkan than Mediterranean.

A scene of decadence welcomed me on my return to my hotel room. Finger bowls of water with floating rose petals had been set on a table, while soft flickering candles threw their shadows across the domed ceiling. I bathed my feet in a footbath of cool lavender-scented water and clambered into bed to eat crème anglaise with blackberry and raspberry fruits, which had been left as a nightcap on my bedside table. Chocolates lay on my plumped-up pillows; it was a luxurious moment and so, fully indulged, I fell into a deep, relaxed sleep.

Suddenly, I awoke with a start. The telephone was ringing, cutting through the night calm like a shrill siren of urgency. It was the middle of the night. Hesitantly, I picked up the receiver. "Hello?" I said in a half-whisper, fearful of the response.

Nothing. I replaced the handset. My heart began to pound as I realised I had not been in touch with friends or family today. No one knew where I was. The phone rang again. I hid under the sheets – then leapt out of bed and put a chair up against the locked bedroom door. The ringing stopped. I stood, wide awake in the middle of the room, not knowing what to do. The sound of footsteps grew louder: leather sole on a worn stone surface. There was a sense of urgency in those steps, a quiet confidence. I put my ear to the door and listened. I played out my imminent murder in each footstep. But then they stopped; there was a sense of hesitation in the air and I held my breath. A soft click of a door followed, then silence so loud it was deafening. I felt vulnerable in spite of my luxurious 5-star surroundings but refused to succumb to panic. Instead I tiptoed back into bed. *It was nothing*, I told myself. Another door clicked shut in the courtyard. I pulled the sheets tight up around me and eventually fell into an uneasy sleep.

- Kavala to Alexandroupoli (178km) -

It was good to be back with Tito. Inside his compact frame and back behind the steering wheel I felt strangely safe and secure. Today we were heading for Alexandroupoli and the challenge was to try to avoid the A2 road... although, according to my map, this might be impossible.

Passing under the arches of Sultan Suleiman the Magnificent's impressive Ottoman stone aqueduct, we left Kavala behind us. Timber boats raised high on wooden stilts lined the route. Men industriously scrubbed their wooden underbellies while others painted the newly smoothed surfaces. It was an unexpected sight and equally distracting. As I regained my concentration on the road, I gasped as the A2 almost had us forever in its left lane grasp. I steered dramatically into the right lane and onto the parallel road heading to Xanthi. We were now leaving the northern Greek region of Macedonia, and entering the eastern region known as Thrace.

———

The old rundown Turkish quarter of Xanthi was brimming with activity. I parked beside a kebab shop. The chefs stared out through the open window at Tito in disbelief and then smiled. Muslim women, wearing headscarves and long flowing dresses, hurried past. I was taken by surprise to see a Greek town inhabited by a Turkish Muslim community. I wandered up through the streets to above the town centre. Old Ottoman houses had survived the test of time and had been transformed into modern homes, and an Orthodox chapel accompanied this scene. Ironically, what had once been the opulent Turkish quarter of Xanthi, inhabited by rich Turkish families, was now the home to Greeks, and a much smaller Turkish Muslim community lived in the less affluent part of town below.

Xanthi is but one example of what happened in towns and villages in both Greece and Turkey during the population exchanges of 1923; the fortunes of those affected changed forever, and with them the demographics of the region. Directly below, cafés lined the street, pumping out modern pop music to the appreciative young, who drank coffee and sheltered from the midday heat.

I walked back into the Turkish quarter and found myself drawn to the end of a queue which snaked its way into a pastry shop selling the largest variety of baklava I had ever seen. The line slowly dispersed and soon I was the only customer. The man standing behind the counter fixed me with a sparkling pair of clear blue eyes.

"Where are you from?" he asked.

"The UK. Scotland," I said.

"Ah, I used to live in Liverpool! My son, he is at Manchester University. How do you like Xanthi?"

As I opened my mouth to respond, he continued.

"You know, Xanthi is a very special place." I waited as he paused for effect. "Xanthi is a town of a thousand faces." He extended his arms in an arc to illustrate the importance of his statement and beamed knowingly at me. "You look, you will see. The Greeks, the Turks, the Egyptians, the Jews; we are all their descendants here in Xanthi."

Indeed, I had noticed the faces of Xanthi and in particular people's eyes, which ranged in colour from the darkest brown, to an incredible grey-blue, and an amazing light green. He chatted on and it was a pleasure to listen to someone who was willing to tell me something about his Greece.

Until now it had been surprisingly difficult to communicate in English with anyone, apart from Stefanos in Thessaloniki. We discussed the baklava business and he introduced me to his specialised world of this delicious honey and nut-filled delicacy which, I now learned, consisted of many varieties. I bought five different finger-sized slices of oozing delight and felt the immediate need for a coffee to accompany one of them. Could he direct me to a café that made traditional Turkish coffee? Of course he could! However, his directions had me walking around in circles twice before giving up; instead I settled for one tucked up a side street. I sat down in relief, out of the heat and the sun.

"Turkish coffee?" I asked.

"*Nay*, we do Greek coffee here."

"Ah, then I will have a Greek coffee, thank you." By the mere turn of a corner I had walked out of the Turkish area and into the Greek area and by so doing the coffee's origins changed name although the process appeared to be the same. It certainly tasted just as good and happily I sunk my teeth into one of the honey and nut-filled baklavas – glad to be in Xanthi.

––––––

P erhaps it was a baklava sugar rush that was responsible for the loss of my navigational ability. The intention had been to head inland to Komotini but when we reached the sea, I realised I had gone wrong somewhere. We were in a small deserted fishing area. Tito's slim tyres had masterfully coped with the sand track down which I had inadvertently driven us. I was so disorientated that I initially thought we were looking at a lake, but no, this was definitely the sea.

The area had formerly been an attractive place but now only a restaurant building lay abandoned with all its windows smashed in. Tempting though it was to park Tito and dive into the sea, the air of desolation filled me with doubt. I certainly did not want the car or my belongings stolen while I was swimming in the ocean. Slightly disappointed by my lack of courage in not throwing caution to the wind, I followed the one Cyrillic road sign back up the sandy track and unwittingly stumbled into a village fishing port with a restaurant full of laughing, eating, singing Greeks. This I could not miss. Tito's bubbling and gurgling brought the singing to a momentary stop while they all gaped at him and then me walking towards them.

"Only one?" the waiter asked quizzically. How I hated the sympathetic tone in which these two words were always uttered and I shuffled from foot to foot feeling distinctly inadequate while wishing I did have a companion with whom to share the experience. Yet hunger drove me to answer brightly and with perhaps a slight edge of dignified defiance.

"Yes, only one."

As a lone traveller, eating times were never my favourite part of the day, though necessity forced me to stop. Self-consciousness and at times intimidating surroundings would sometimes prevent me from eating at all. Ridiculous as it may seem, I came up with the idea of creating friends in the form of a book or a map which I would pretend to study earnestly to overcome these moments of awkwardness. I soon learned to select a table where I could observe but not be so noticeable as to be observed back. Here in this little restaurant, however, everyone was having such a good time and the air was so relaxed, I almost forgot I was by myself. I tucked contentedly into a large plate of grilled calamari accompanied by a generous bowl of Greek salad on top of which an enormous hunk of feta cheese balanced precariously, and enjoyed the party atmosphere into which I had unexpectedly landed.

Relocating myself on the map, I steered us away from the sea northwards towards Komotini across a long causeway which stretched the length of the estuary into which I had accidentally navigated us. Still managing to avoid the now E90/A2 motorway, we drove through Komotini – a town of mixed architectural influences embracing the Ottoman, the Greek and, most recently, some ultra-modern 21st century glass structures. The road continued eastwards through the small town of Sapes and then southwards onto the E90 which, although multiple-laned, was not a motorway but a dual carriageway.

I took a deep breath and eyed the road in front of us with some trepidation as it swept upwards – this was going to be tough for Tito. Averaging a speed of 30km/h with some momentary spurts of 40km/h, we began a slow agonising climb.

"Come on, Tito, you can do it!" I said encouragingly, as we headed up a second gradual ascent. There was less traffic than I had predicted and as we climbed slowly and steadily up this vast isolated expanse of tarmac road, I questioned whether it was really such a good idea to be driving alone. I would not want to break down here, or have some hulking great Greek man force me off the road (of course, in my imagination everything was totally over-exaggerated!). All I had were the two bricks under the bonnet as my defence. I fixed my eyes on the empty road ahead, willing Tito to the top and consoling myself with the thought that those of the population whom I had come across and who also drove old cars like myself, seemed rather polite and would be a friend rather than a threat. It was only the minority rich set whom I eyed with some suspicion. They drove fast, air-conditioned and expensive 4-wd vehicles, and in my view seemed rather arrogant. However, it was unlikely they would even deign to acknowledge me, let alone drive me off the road. My misgivings were unfounded, or so I told myself as my fingers curled more tightly around Tito's slim steering wheel as the presence of something more real, and thus more immediately threatening, came into view.

Ahead, a bus had pulled into a kerbside parking area, and out of it young teenagers were emerging. As Tito and I ploughed up the hill towards them in third gear, the teenagers' eyes seemed to lock onto us. They moved closer to the side of the road to watch our progress up the hill.

"Oh no, I'm going to be attacked by teenagers!" I gasped, clenching my jaws together tightly in readiness (for what, I wasn't sure) but as we got closer they began to cheer and, lifting their fists, the boys punched the air repeatedly in encouragement as we advanced up the hill. I began to laugh. They were not jeering; they were cheering. As Tito neared the top of the hill, I was won over by their genuine support and enthusiasm, and waved self-consciously – my faith in human nature restored, and all thoughts of being overwhelmed by large Greek men evaporated. Tito had survived the agonising ascent and the turn-off for Makri appeared. Gratefully, we could leave the E90 route for a pleasant, and gently undulating coastal journey to Alexandroupoli.

- Samothraki (by boat) -

Alexandroupoli is a bustling port town with ferries taking passengers and cars out to the Greek islands. It was eight o'clock and the waterfront was alive with the hustle and bustle of life. The big SAOS ferries were powered up ready for departure; a market next to the port entrance thronged with people while cars edged down the harbour road in search of a parking place, avoiding, where possible, the people weaving in and out of the traffic, laden down with bags of just-purchased market produce. It was a town in motion and from my first-floor breakfast balcony I had the perfect view to watch it all going on. The sky was already an intense "Greek blue" promising another hot day. I headed down to the port past the bustling market, booked a foot passenger ticket to the island of Samothraki – giving Tito the day off – and boarded one of the ferries.

———

S amothraki was once home to an ancient league of Greek gods who were, it was believed, sensible and serious in contrast to the gods of Olympus, who were considered frivolous by their Samothrakian counterparts. Remains of their ancient site the 'Sanctuary of the Great Gods at Paleopolis' still exist. Tucked away in a dip on the upper reaches of a hillside, it is surrounded by barren, starkly beautiful steep mountains which rise like phantom protectors, invoking a sense of dramatic expectation. Religious and spiritual ceremonies took place here over a thousand years ago, attended by Alexander the Great himself. I don't know whether it was the searing heat, the invisible cicadas singing furiously in the grasses or the intense colours of the landscape which heightened the sense of a powerful spirituality in the place, but it lingered over the site, a silent force which could not be ignored. It is said that the great gods of Samothraki were thought to be stronger and more influential than their Olympus counterparts. At this moment I could well believe it as I stood in front of a replica cast of the *Winged Victory*. Its height and majestic grace combined in a striking image of empowerment and for anyone entering the Sanctuary for the first time, it must have filled them with a sense of awe and wonder.

———

Hora, the historic capital city of Samothraki, lies inland with spectacular views down to the island's coast. It was after two o'clock and I appeared to be the only living soul wandering through the town's narrow cobbled lanes from one pool of shade to the next, passing old white-washed stone houses with colourfully painted windows, doors and shutters. Each rooftop was a mass of interlaced half-moon-shaped terracotta tiles on top of which rows of large stones had been painstakingly placed – I presume to prevent the tiles from blowing off in the wind. Today it was calm and quiet except for a fountain pouring quantities of cool clear water into a large stone bowl. A Byzantine tower dominated the skyline; beside it a little café was serving cold drinks and offering expansive views out to sea.

I wandered back down the hill and found a family-run restaurant with a terrace offering shade under a trellis of climbing plants. Dining on beans baked with herbs and spices, a Greek salad and later a dessert of chocolate mousse cake drowning in chocolate sauce topped by a large dollop of almond and vanilla ice cream from allegedly the best sweet shop "anywhere", I was enjoying my day off from behind the wheel more than I had imagined.

- Alexandroupoli/Provatonas (44km) -

It was bound to happen. I even expected it, but not quite so soon. We had been heading north through Thrace's most eastern territorial towns and villages and I was hoping to reach Turkey by evening when my luck ran out. I suppose I should have recognised the signs. Earlier, the wire connecting the release handle to the bonnet catch had snapped. A helpful garage attendant in Alexandroupoli had spent twenty minutes with a pair of pliers trying to tease the coiled wire straight so he could pull it and release the bonnet hook, grinning with delight when eventually the bonnet popped open. Having refilled the petrol tank, he delicately clicked the bonnet lid shut and, in his enthusiasm to be the model garage attendant, he had then helped me refill the oil and water filters.

Further down the road, I had stopped at a second mechanic's garage hoping to buy some pliers, as without them I would be unable to pull on the dangling wires to open the bonnet lid. The mechanic inspected the wires, shook his head and instead took it upon himself to repair the problem properly. Tito was driven into his workshop and, wielding a large flame-throwing implement, he got to work, stopping momentarily to place a fireproof board over the petrol tank when I had frantically tugged at his arm to point out that the large brown object around which those naked flames were licking, was actually highly flammable. The job was masterfully completed and I hit the road once more, only ten euros the poorer but with a bonnet that would easily open and close without the need for pliers.

Skirting the boundaries of the Evros Delta – a well-known migrating stop in the bird world – I bid a joyful farewell to the E90/A2 racetrack leading eastwards into Turkey. We joined the quiet E85 road, leaving the sea and the coast firmly behind us, and headed for the northern border with Turkey beyond which lay the town of Edirne, an apparent forgotten gem I had been told not to miss.

To one side of us acres of sunflowers were lowering their heads with the weight of seeds and to the other, the land rose up to the mountains. Hot air was rushing through the windows as I took a large swig of water from the coolest of my pile of half-empty water bottles. Tito hiccupped and lurched unsteadily forward. Startled, I lifted my foot slightly off the accelerator pedal. He hiccupped again and we moved forward in unpredictable spasms. I lifted the choke to see if that would help and viewed the road ahead. I could see a set of traffic lights but on arriving at them there was nothing but a crossroads and a large church on one corner. Beyond, a garage sign signalled that help could potentially be at hand. We staggered our way in and stopped.

"*Auto mechanic*?" I asked hopefully. The elderly petrol attendant was sitting in the shade on an old beaten up chair. He shook his head and began speaking rapidly in Greek. "English, *Deutsch*, *Français*?" I asked hopefully.

"*Ja, ja*," he said animatedly in German. "*Semaphora, links, links*," opening and closing both hands like blinkers to illustrate the traffic lights. With a mixture of thanks in German and Greek, "*Danke, efharisto!*" we kangaroo-hopped violently back down the road to the traffic lights. "Come on, Tito!" We made it into the left-hand turning lane just as the traffic lights went defiantly to red. "No!" I groaned and braked.

A transit van pulled up on our right and three sets of eyes peered at us from their elevated position. I looked back at them in accusing despair as Tito stalled. I turned the ignition key and pumped frantically at the accelerator with my right foot. Nothing happened. I lifted my foot and the pedal went limp, sinking to the floor. The peering eyes were joined by three large grins and a bellow of laughter from the driver. Two men leapt out of the van and as the traffic lights turned green, they got behind Tito and pushed him with such force that before I knew it, we were hurtling forward at speed. I made the left turn with a grand sweep and a gasp. The men waved farewell and ran back to their vehicle as Tito and I continued to free-wheel down the road for a couple of metres, coming eventually to a graceful stop.

Two men sitting in the cool shadows of a closed terraced bar had been idly watching the drama unfold but as we had glided to a stop in front of them, they had become instantly absorbed in their newspapers. I got out of the car and addressed the two raised newspapers. "*Auto mechanic*?" Both men shook their heads and continued to read. I could almost hear the tumbleweed rolling down the street of this one-horse town. Where was I, anyway? *"Auto mechanic?"* I said again in the hope of engaging at least one of the raised newspapers.

It worked. A pair of eyes appeared above a gently lowered newspaper and I offered him my best "damsel in distress" look. With eyebrows raised in feigned annoyance, he picked up his mobile phone and made a call.

Five minutes later, a super-sonic exhaust-propelled red car arrived on the scene, skidding to a halt. A young Greek mechanic with hair swept back in a ponytail stepped out wearing army fatigue trousers and a sleeveless bright red t-shirt revealing big muscled biceps and, sadly, just the hint of a growing paunch. At the sight of Tito, he lowered his sunglasses with a look of *"Oh my* God, *what is that?"* He then walked oh-so-coolly towards the car and rapped assertively on the bonnet. I pulled the release lever at the same time, indicating rather pathetically and in no particular language that the engine was actually in the boot. Realising his mistake, he strolled nonchalantly to the other end of the car and raised his sunglasses in disbelief as I lifted the engine door. Despite his ultra-cool approach, it was clear the mechanic had no idea how to fix a Zastava.

"Kaput!" was the only word the mechanic could utter, shaking his head. I suppressed the urge to start laughing while I watched him remove and unscrew various parts of the engine, examine them and place them on the tarmac. Tito's innards were now laid out on the side of the road like a dying hero.

"Of course he's not *kaput,"* I murmured to myself. *How can something as simple as a Zastava engine not be fixed?* My young, hulking Greek rescuer with his swept-back hair and rippling biceps was not acting like a true life-saving knight. He made a phone call. More help was on its way!

Masquerading as my back-up hero, a man in blue dungarees on a phut-phut of a moped appeared through the afternoon's shimmering heat. This man exuded an aura of practical assuredness, which made me believe there was hope – he even spoke a few words of English. However, it was now Friday afternoon – the end of the working day. Saturday was a holiday. Sunday they were closed. Tito was pushed off the road. I should come back on Monday. I had no option but to decant all my belongings and hand him the keys. Signalling to me that their garage was about two kilometres up the road, which apparently I could not miss, they both departed.

Feeling like the sole survivor of a shipwreck, I picked up my baggage and staggered across the road into the only visible eating establishment. Despite the lack of customers, there was much cooking underway. It transpired there was a large demand for home delivery and takeaway. A simple menu of falafel, pitta bread, sour cream and sauce, it was the best I had ever tasted, and while I sat looking at Tito abandoned on the other side of the road, I felt remarkably calm, almost relieved at the prospect of a weekend's rest. I unfolded my map of Greece across the table. The major silk manufacturing town of Soufli lay about 20km north of where I was currently stranded. That was as good a place as any, I decided, and loaded down with all my worldly belongings, I shuffled down the road towards a sign that read 'Taxi'.

As I reached the 'Taxi' sign, the man who had been the more helpful of the two newspaper readers – and who had even valiantly attempted to translate the ever-so-cool mechanic's Greek to me – wandered slowly across the road towards the same spot. He, of course, turned out to be the amenable taxi service to Soufli.

- Soufli -

Soufli has many interesting brick buildings resulting from the once affluent town's silk factories, but these now lie in a very sorry state of dilapidation. I visited the local silk museum and met the director, who explained that the recent meteoric rise of cheap silk exports from China had destroyed Soufli's silk trade and with it the fortunes of the town. Residential homes of all sizes, showing a strong Ottoman/Turkish influence, now lie vacant, and in many cases, near collapse. Many have been replaced by modern Greek homes with their marble-stepped entrances and beautifully manicured green lawns, but the character and identity of Soufli are being swept away. I walked around the suburban streets feeling deeply disappointed at what was happening. There was an opportunity to regenerate something quite special in Soufli as silk production has existed since Alexander the Great's time and was something unique in Greece. Surely there was a way with some EU funding or outside investment to kick-start a project which could boost the local economy and perhaps save a community currently hanging on by the skin of its teeth but slowly dying?

———

I found the ritual evening stroll more of a seated experience in Soufli. Old men sat in clusters on wooden chairs by the side of the road, playing distractedly with their strings of worry beads, while women appeared either to go to church or sit in their own groups. The younger men and women drank café frappés and lattes in mixed social groups of ten or twelve. I wandered up and down the main street watching them, watching me, watching them. I was, it seemed, a novelty in the town and all eyes followed me wherever I went. It was rather disconcerting and I could read the speculation in their eyes. *What is a foreign woman doing here in our town – alone?*

There were only two tavernas and I chose the one which seemed the more relaxed and conspicuous. It had tables on the pavement beneath the trees. The location was a popular choice and I squeezed my way to the only vacant table. The restaurant was under the watchful gaze of two stray dogs, one large and one small. They sat in the middle of the street ignoring the traffic, which was obliged to weave around them. The customers of the taverna would lob food across to the other pavement in an attempt to get them off the road but the dogs knew what they were doing. They had worked out their strategy to perfection and were reaping the benefits of plentiful food. As I watched them defiantly return back and forth to the centre of the street, I realised I needed a strategy of my own for the weekend while Tito lay abandoned 20km away awaiting attention. Soufli had limited attractions so it was time to try out Greece's public transport system and visit some other local sights.

- Soufli/Didimotiho/Pithio (by train) -

"You want to take a train? A Greek train?"

I nodded at the hotel owner's sons, who were both in their early 30s and very willing to try out their English skills, but at this point they could find no words as they looked at me in complete amazement.

"I would like to go to Didimotiho and then to Pithio, if possible?"

They continued to look at me in stunned silence. Then one of them shook himself out of silence and said he would call the train station in Soufli. It turned out there was a train to Didimotiho in 45 minutes, but he confided, "This is Greece. Trains may come early, or late, or maybe not at all."

Despite his lack of confidence in the Greek railway system, I decided to risk it and indeed I was not disappointed. The train arrived on time and was extremely modern, although I seemed to be one of very few passengers to appreciate this fact.

The train route hugs the borderline between Greece and

Turkey. Raised lookout posts dot the landscape on both sides of the border allowing the Turks and Greeks to eyeball each other with impunity. Didimotiho is a small town with an army barracks, an array of coffee shops providing shelter from the sweltering heat and a surprising mix of forgotten cultural heritage wonders, from the remains of a Byzantine cathedral to (apparently) the largest, and certainly very impressive looking, mosque in Greece with its unusually designed pyramid roof. Thick stone Byzantine defensive walls enclose the upper part of the town, which has remains of catacombs and wall paintings, as well as several old Turkish houses, which like everywhere else, are falling into ruins.

Pithio, a bit further north of Didimotiho, boasts the oldest remaining part of a Byzantine castle in Greece although the two kilometre walk from the train station in the blazing heat was an unwelcome endurance test, made more unbearable when I saw the inhabitants of Pithio sitting in their shaded gardens eating, drinking, chatting and peering at me as I walked by. From the castle ruins there is an uninterrupted view across a flat landscape several kilometres into Turkey.

It was difficult to believe that I was standing at the very edge of Europe; the vast stretch of land in front of me, a no man's land. The scene of many desperate attempts by Iraqis, Afghans, Georgians, Iranians and others fleeing their countries and attempting to cross into Europe where, they presume, a better future awaits them and their families. As I looked from my vantage point, it just seemed a huge uninhabited agricultural space but looks can be deceiving and it is believed to be a terrain peppered with landmines, against which the desperate, undeterred, are prepared to pitch their wits and their lives.

Pithio had one café. It looked more like a university bar than a café with a well-used billiards table, a table football game and a number of darts boards. The place was deserted except for a teenager playing an internet game and who, with great difficulty, tore himself away from it to make me an Iced Nescafé. Within ten minutes a crowd of youngsters had arrived, revving their scooters for effect. They were the local racing scooter group, some of whom were eager to try out their English on me. They boasted of speed and I asked them whether it was possible to accidentally cross the border into Turkey from here. They all laughed. "No. It is one kilometre away and the river is the boundary line." That was all they wanted to say, or perhaps all they wanted to tell me.

I said my farewells and walked the two kilometres back to Pithio station in the hope of a return train to Soufli. The station was a ghost town apart from a pair of stray dogs who clearly thought of this as their territory. Fighting off their boisterous welcome, and wondering whether I should have had a rabies injection after all, I retired to the waiting room with dirty paw prints all down my white shirt. After five minutes I peered out to find them both sprawled out, patiently waiting for me to reappear. Their earlier excitement at having a visitor had dissipated and they trotted along beside me like old companions. The train station was devoid of human life and I began to wonder if I might have to spend the night here, when out of the stillness two bright yellow headlights appeared down the track. The train crawled slowly into the station and as the engine passed by, the driver leaned out of the window and gestured to ask whether I wanted to get on board. A request train stop perhaps? I nodded emphatically, and although not sure if that meant yes in Greek, he gave me the thumbs up and stopped the train. Leaving my four-legged friends to their station patrols, I climbed aboard.

- Soufli/Feres (by bus) -

After our successful English communication, the hotel owner's sons were eager to stretch their vocabulary at breakfast the next morning. We discussed the declining economy of Soufli and its decaying buildings; the issue of Macedonia being a country when in their opinion it was really a region of Greece, the fact that the town of Edirne where I was headed next was actually ancient Adrianoupolis and had also belonged to Greece, and indeed that the town of Plovdiv, one of my intended destinations in Bulgaria, was actually called Philippopolis and also belonged to Greece. After a thoroughly biased Greek history lesson, which avoided more recent sensitivities such as Cyprus, or Greece's relations with Turkey, I headed for Soufli bus station.

A large clock tick-tocked loudly in the old-fashioned waiting area. An iron stove dominated the room from which pipework ran across a ceiling of peeling paintwork, venting to the outside. Wooden chairs lined the perimeter of the room but the space lay empty as I entered and bought a ticket to Feres. Outside, old men sat on chairs removed from the waiting room and peered in at me from time to time, the click of their worry beads slapping together as they talked. The bus arrived. It headed south through the villages and, without warning, we swept past Tito still lying abandoned by the side of the road in Provatonas. Tomorrow I would be reunited with him and I hoped for a mechanic's miracle fix. To pass the time, I was on my way to visit a 12th century Byzantine church, and, by all accounts, a miniature version of the Hagia Sophia in Istanbul. I had my reservations, but I was happy to have a distraction for the day.

- Tihero/Kastanies Border Control (88km) -

Tihero lay a kilometre or so beyond Provatonas. Here was the mechanic's garage and a hive of activity. The usual banter and guffaws of laughter, which seem to exude from all mechanics' garages, were certainly flowing freely here. A pair of blue dungarees reversed out from underneath Tito's steering wheel and a head emerged.

"I go to town to find bicycle wire for accelerator. Maybe not find," the mechanic warned.

He showed me the snapped cable, which had been the cause of the accelerator pedal going limp. I had a sudden flashback to John's crash course on car mechanics in Skopje. He had given me a running commentary on every item that had been stashed under Tito's bonnet by the previous owner.

"I think I have one!" I said excitedly and began rummaging under the bonnet. Triumphantly, I pulled out some coiled wire from under the spare tyre. "Is this what you are looking for?" Taken aback, he inspected the wire and grinned acknowledgement. In this moment I gained the respect of the garage and was justly rewarded with a privileged invitation into their kitchen to make myself a coffee in the oily kettle – an offer not to be refused.

———

Tito was successfully repaired and the costs calculated. I held my breath, expecting the worst. At least in the hundreds, I thought. The mechanic apologetically turned his calculator towards me. 45 Euros! I nearly kissed him in relief and paid hastily before he changed his mind. Breaking down did not entail my financial ruin after all.

It was exhilarating to be back on the road. Tito seemed to be fine but I took it slowly, aware that it might not be so easy to get the car fixed in Turkey. The mechanic had explained something about the oil and water mixing in the engine but, as the saying goes, it was all Greek to me. I was just happy to be back on the E85 road heading northwards to Edirne.

———

The fierce wind from yesterday had eased but the temperature was on the rise both outside and, more worryingly, inside the car. A hot stream of air seemed to be blowing in over my feet from that still unidentified hole in the floor. As the kilometres went by, the intensity of heat rose to an unbearable burning pitch across my right foot. The handbrake was scalding. Something was wrong. I turned off into the town of Orestiada in search of another garage. The mechanic came out, looked at me, and called another who then hollered loudly up to the window above. A young man's face appeared.

"I speak English, I will help you."

Tito straddled the garage pit. Everything was fine. "No need to worry," the mechanic said comfortingly.

"But the handbrake is scorching hot. The air off it is burning my feet. It wasn't like this before. Are you sure it is ok?"

He regarded me less confidently and moved the two floor mats to cover the now identified hole in the side of the gearbox.

"No problem. It is your free car radiator! The mats will provide temperature control. Leave like this in summer. Take them off in winter!" He grinned at his ingenuity. I was not entirely convinced but I wanted to believe him, shrugged my shoulders and with a sigh headed back on to the road heading for Turkey.

The Greek border village of Kastanies was surprisingly quaint. *But where was everyone?* I presumed this to be the lesser-known route into Turkey as the border post was practically deserted but for a garage and a telephone box. I refuelled Tito and, after a spontaneous but unresponsive attempt to call home, I drove up to the passport control point.

"Ok." The official dismissed me with a desultory wave in the direction of his colleague the customs officer, who smirked and said, "Skopje?"

I nodded as he looked casually at Tito's documents. He handed them back and pointed towards the narrow lane ahead. It looked rather sinister and not at all welcoming but I had no choice but to set off down its heavily fenced route, leaving Greece behind us.

TURKEY

A TASTE OF THE EXOTIC

- Pazarkule Border Control/Edirne (8km) -

With rising apprehension we travelled down the imposing track. I felt acutely claustrophobic. Trapped within a tunnel of chain-linked fencing. Eventually the lane opened up to a water dip. A *'STOP'* sign stood in front of it, on the other side of which, and perhaps two metres back, stood two armed Turkish soldiers. There was no vehicle in front to follow so I stopped, not knowing whether to wait for a signal from them to advance, ever wary of anyone with a gun slung over his shoulder. They continued to stare at me as I eyed the water dip with trepidation. It looked ominously deep.

A group of four young people appeared from the Turkish side. They walked past the soldiers without a backward glance. They had towels slung over their shoulders and were dressed as if on to the way to the beach, although the coast was some distance in either direction. Noticing Tito, they approached and asked where I was from. Was I Macedonian? And why had I stopped? Feeling a little foolish, they told me to ignore the soldiers: "no problem" they said. So with a wave of farewell and bolstered by their advice, I headed for the water dip, subconsciously holding my breath as we entered its depths. No water appeared to seep in under the doors and nor, thankfully, did we stall in the middle. I continued down the high fenced lane, throwing a fleeting glance at the composed stares of the two soldiers, and turned the corner to where the border post of Pazarkule nestled in an area of pine trees. A young and hugely delighted soldier came running over and patted Tito's roof. He enthusiastically offered to stand guard while I took my documents to the control point.

Customs and passport control seemed to have merged together behind four numbered glass-fronted counters, of which the windows marked 1, 2 and 4 were currently manned. Those trying to enter Turkey were battling for attention against those who were trying to leave and enter Greece. As a result, all three windows seemed to be dealing with exit and entry requests at the same time. Passports and documents flew backwards and forwards while two officers sat glued to a computer checking car registrations and ownership.

Entering into the general free-for-all spirit, I presented my passport to window 4, and was directed to hand my car documents to window 1. Somehow, they came together at window 2, where the moment of truth was revealed on the computer. 15 Euros were demanded at window 4 for an entry visa stamp and I saw my passport being passed from window 2 back to window 4 and returned to window 1. An entry stamp was emphatically smacked into my passport at window 1 but window 2 objected when they realised my passport name and the car documents did not match. Window 1 was in trouble for stamping my passport before window 2's approval had been given. I passed through the magic Authorisation Agreement signed by Liljana, which, with some reluctance, they accepted. I received back my documentation along with an extra bout of intense scrutiny as

I battled my way out of the scrum of arrivals and departures thrusting documentation over my head to window 2 and under my arms to window 1.

My smiling soldier proudly welcomed me back to a waiting Tito and with a friendly wave we sailed under the rising barrier post into Turkey, heading for Edirne, the most north-western town in the country.

We drove in regal fashion down a wide, straight, tree-lined avenue, the old cobbled surface creating a soft rumbling sound under Tito's tyres. Street hawkers sold fresh fruit piled high on their carts. Everywhere people seemed to be pushing or pulling old wheeled wooden contraptions, riding bicycles or just sleeping in the shade away from the afternoon heat. We had entered a totally different world of sights, smells, bustle – it had a touch of the Orient about it – but nothing prepared me for the view that emerged. Majestically piercing the sky with delicate points like fine needles, the minarets of grand white mosques dominated the landscape against a backdrop of azure blue, and an alluring prospect of a city brimming with the architectural wealth of another era.

An elegant stone bridge lay before us, appearing to hover in space, as it rose and fell spanning the Meric River and then the Tunca River, and into the city. I could not believe this was the entrance into Edirne, nor that we were expected (or indeed allowed) to drive over such a seemingly fragile historic structure. Veering away from it along the cobbled road towards Istanbul, my mouth open wide in awe, I could not believe this was still Thrace; admittedly Turkish Thrace, yet worlds apart in look and splendour from its Greek counterpart just the other side of the border.

I managed a U-turn without any noticeable consequences and drove up to a group of young men who were tending their horses and carts beside the bridge. I wound down the passenger window and said, "Edirne?"

They looked at me, scanning my car full of luggage and

empty water bottles with curiosity. They did not seem to understand my pronunciation of Edirne. I tried again and was met with another blank look. At that moment a car mounted the bridge. Even if this was not the entrance to the city, I felt compelled to follow, just so as to drive across the bridge, if nothing else.

The structure was narrow, barely wide enough to accommodate a horse and cart – or Tito. Like an intrepid explorer, aware that I was entering something quite new and exotic, I journeyed across the bridge wondering how many other Fićas had ventured this way. Was Tito the first? Ahead lay the town centre and the many minarets that I had admired from the cobbled avenue, but pushed along by the traffic and before I could do anything about it, we began to head away from our goal and down a three-laned street of buses, cars, horses and carts, bicycles and hand-pushed wooden barrows all vying for their share of the road. Unable to understand the road signs, I pulled into the first petrol station in the hope of finding help. Plenty was at hand, with Tito being the main point of interest. Three policemen, the garage manager, and the petrol attendants all gathered around my car in a mixture of childish excitement and genuine disbelief. They had never seen a Zastava.

Cameras appeared and photographs were taken, the policemen staying away from the photographs but involving themselves in the discussions. With some difficulty I managed to understand from our combined words of German that the old town was back in the direction from where I had come and not far away. I thanked them in my best German, at which they smiled and waved me off like a long-lost friend, uttering the Turkish "*Tesekkurler*! *Gule, gule*." ("Thank you! Goodbye, goodbye").

I am not sure how we managed the next part of the journey; it was a blur of cars, traffic lights, an enormous roundabout, road police and revving engines. Somehow we survived and as I made it back up the hill, past the mosques and minarets, I turned right into what I thought might be a hotel car park but which was in fact an army barracks. A young soldier strode over with a smile, ready and eager to help, but he was reprimanded by his superior and told to tell me to move on. I left none the wiser as to where I was or where I would find somewhere to stay. It was all rather overwhelming. Eventually I spotted a sign to a hotel car park and pulled in. The Sultan Hotel was perfectly located, just a stone's throw away from the old town. The excitement of being in this unexpectedly beautiful city encouraged me to stay two nights – and with Tito safely stowed, the exploration could begin.

- Edirne -

There was never a greater contrast between the dying town of Soufli, the elite coffee-drinking set of Thessaloniki and now the vibrancy of this alive and colourful city of Edirne. It was like being hurled back in time to when the town was Roman, Ottoman, rich, royal and a capital city. The Ottoman Empire's final decline in the 1900s was the last defeat the city has had to overcome. The Edirne people have adapted themselves, accepting all that remains of the city's magnificent buildings and crumbling ruins into their everyday lives. Yet the old mansion houses, with their intricately carved and decorated interiors reflecting the glorious and rich lives of the Ottoman Empire in Edirne, are sadly of little interest to today's inhabitants. Their historic significance is seemingly unappreciated as they gently fall apart in the back streets of the town.

Edirne's popularity and development has been influenced by a staggering mix of peoples, including Jews, Armenians, Bulgarians, Greeks and Romans. In today's society, the diversity of the ethnic mix has been largely lost, but the dynamism of those who remain brought Edirne alive. Street corners were filled with fruit sellers – carts piled high with a colourful mix of Turkey's summer crop. Bazaars, full of small kiosks selling modern clothes, fabrics, shoes and electronic equipment, sat amongst traditional jewellery stores and tourist gift shops. The peaceful atmosphere of a restored caravanserai, formerly a resting house for travellers and their animals, was shattered by the voices of French and American students sitting in groups chatting loudly to one another, yet out in the streets their voices could not be heard over the daily bustle of life.

As the sun disappeared and early evening approached, the city was dominated by the muezzins' call to prayer. With so many mosques in the centre, the calls seemed to bounce off the minaret towers, fusing the voices into an engaging chant that sent shivers down my spine. I sat in a square surrounded by young and old Turkish men and women who also seemed hypnotised by the plaintive sounds filling the air. As the calls to prayer ended, a general hush fell over the city as though it was physically relaxing. Evening had arrived, the temperature cooler and the day's work over for many. As in Macedonia and Greece, the familiar evening walk, talk and socialising could now get underway.

————

There are four prominent mosques right in the centre of Edirne, each as outstandingly beautiful as the next, the oldest dating back to the 12th century. The largest, the Selimiye Camii, was where I witnessed my first Muslim ceremony. The synchronised movements of prayer – from standing to kneeling, to leaning forward onto their foreheads and then back again on to their heels – were mesmerising. I had never before experienced the symbiotic power and unity of prayer as I did here in Edirne. The muezzin's call, heralded by the human voice, the ritual cleansing of hands and feet, and the slow and rhythmical movements of devotion, all were conducive in promoting a natural sense of harmony, well-being and inner calm.

Continuing my wanderings, a half-demolished brick building with fireplaces clinging to the outside walls caught my attention. At its base, an old woman sat on an equally old wooden chair in the shade, eating fruit. With her one free hand, she beckoned me over and offered me the uneaten half of a plum. Thanking her, I shook my head with a smile and pointed to the inside of the building. She took hold of my arm and we walked round to an entrance. It was an old Turkish bathing house, a hammam. A young man got up from his chair and explained to me in English that the old lady wanted to invite me inside the hammam for a full wash, massage, scrub and hair wash. She named her price and then instantly lowered it.

"Ok," I said, nodding my agreement.

Her face lit up and before I could change my mind, I was whisked back round to the ladies' side of the hammam, which discreetly segregated male bathing from female bathing.

We entered a large domed room, which had seen better days but still showed signs of the magnificence it must have once had. Her elaborate arm movements made me realise I was being asked to remove all my clothes and follow her. With flip-flops protecting the soles of my feet from the intense heat of the stone floor, I tentatively walked into the bathing room, nude and distinctly self-conscious. It was wonderfully hot inside and instantly I could feel the heat relaxing my muscles after all the driving of the past two weeks.

For the next half-hour, I was washed, soaped and thoroughly scrubbed by this old lady as she talked about her life, probably telling me all sorts of secrets and interesting things which sadly went straight over my head along with the hot water which was poured over me at regular intervals from a bright pink plastic jug. A large warm marble table dominated the central space of this vast and once majestic central bathing room with its high domed ceiling and filtering light holes. Our voices echoed loudly, muffled only slightly by the humidity and heat of the room. Soaped from head to foot, I slid and glided across the marble table, quite unable to stop. Laughing, she grasped my ankle and pulled me in a soapy slick back towards her, so saving me from landing unceremoniously on the piping hot floor on the other side of the room.

Undeterred by my lack of Turkish, the old lady continued to chat away. Somehow, I managed to understand that she was married with five children, and that she was in her sixties. She had the face, arms and hands of someone who had seen much outdoor labour. They were leather-brown while her body was alabaster-white. It was as if I was looking at two bodies as she sat in her large white cotton knickers, more holes than cloth, her hair piled high up on her head and held together by a plastic clamp, scrubbing away at my skin.

The scenario was rather surreal as, lathered in two inches of thick creamy soap, I listened to her merry chatter. After a while, the soaping, scrubbing, massaging of hands and feet and rinsing down was complete. She washed my hair with a psychedelic pink shampoo and massaged my head until I was unable to think straight. All the stories I had heard about hammams, the heavy-handed neck manipulations and bone crunching had, until now, deterred me from visiting a Turkish bath. But this lady, for all her sixty years, had provided me with an unusual, but I am sure, truly local Turkish hammam experience.

As I admired my soft and gleaming skin, three Turkish ladies arrived and I wondered how she was going to cope with all three of them at one time. It was clearly of no concern to her. I was instantly forgotten as she raced over to embrace them and they her. The latest Edirne gossip was waiting to be shared. As I said my farewell, the old lady rushed back to complete the final hammam treatment – running a fine-toothed comb through my not-so-fine and decidedly knotted hair. I escaped this painful procedure as politely as possible and with many thanks, made a bolt for the door. My body felt so relaxed, smooth and squeaky clean, it was quite a shock to leave the calm of the hammam for the midday sun and dusty atmosphere of the city. In my chilled-out state, I took myself off to the nearest café with wide comfy seating and sun umbrellas, and ordered the ubiquitous sweet black tea.

- Edirne/Kapikule Border Control (8km) -

I filled Tito with petrol and took a last lingering look at the city's skyline of minarets. Opposite the petrol station an old Ottoman bridge sat almost forgotten by today's world. I had discovered a gem of a place, a place to return to one day, and with a contented smile I turned my back on exotic Edirne and headed northwards towards Bulgaria – a mere 28km away – wondering what would be next.

The road from Edirne to the Kapikule border crossing unravelled like a ribbon through the Turkish countryside until it hit the O3 motorway. Either we were just being incredibly lucky or, perhaps, being August and the summer holidays, the normal levels of heavy traffic had evaporated in the heat. I did not know the real reason but Tito and I were happy to putter along the empty O3 road in what was effectively no man's land between Turkey and Greece while the sun blazed and Tito's engine bubbled gently in the back.

We were met with a barrage of smiles at the Turkish border post and an exit stamp was punched into my passport with none of the chaos we had experienced on entering. With Turkey behind us, we were now heading towards our third country, Bulgaria.

BULGARIA

A LAND OF SELF-SUFFICIENCY AND KINDNESS

- Andreevo Border Control -

W e joined the queue denoting EU citizens. A Bulgarian border control officer paced up and away, and back again.

"*Makedonski*?" he enquired.

"No. *Engleski*," I responded. He hesitated, walked away again and then came back for a third time.

"Car documents. *Makedonski*, yes?"

"Yes, but me, *Engleski*," I said with more emphasis.

Cars were beginning to stack up behind us as Tito and I crawled forward in the queue. The officer walked away and joined his colleagues, who by this time were gathering to discuss the situation. Tito's Macedonian number plate was causing great confusion and I had a feeling this border crossing was not going to be so easy.

"OK, you must go to the control point over there."

"But I am from the EU," I protested.

"Yes, but your car *Makedonski*, you must go over there."

It was futile arguing the point and I drove us to a white hut away from all the other queues, including one marked non-EU, along a lane signposted in Bulgarian, which seemed to apply only to us.

The cabin window was slid open and I handed over my documents somewhat distractedly as Tito began making a strange sound. I switched off the engine and we waited while a woman busied herself checking, cross-checking and entering data into her computer. Holding up a USB memory stick, she said, "You must hand this to the border customs police."

I nodded, staring apprehensively at the half a dozen customs police waiting for us to advance. I took a deep breath and turned the ignition key. Nothing.

"Please don't break down here Tito!" I muttered and smiled apologetically at the lady.

"Take your time. Do you need some help?"

"No no, thank you. It'll be ok." I counted to ten and tried again. Tito sprang into life and with my heart thumping we inched hesitantly towards the rugby scrum of customs police, who by this time were flexing their fingers as if psyching themselves up for some sport.

"*Dobur den,*" I said politely (being careful to pronounce the words in as Bulgarian a manner as I could, which differed ever so slightly from the Macedonian "*dobar den*" and the Serbian "*dobar dan*").

I presented my passport and the USB memory stick into the impatient grasp of an officer's large hand as it appeared at my open driver's window.

"*Dobur den*" came the gruff response.

The officer regarded my well-worn passport cover with interest and raised eyebrows. Throwing me a suspicious look, he began to flick slowly through the pages. It was so hot in the car that I got out, but left Tito's engine running for fear he might not start again. "You are English?"

This was not a moment to be specific and say, 'Well, Scottish actually.'

"Yes, I am English," I said, trying to sound matter-of-fact.

"Car documents."

Remembering Veton's advice on border control tactics while he had cut my hair in Pristina on the penultimate day before my departure from Skopje, I handed over the minimum documentation. The officer observed me again but said nothing.

"Green Card." Slowly it was delivered into his waiting hand. "Hmmm," he said. "the car is from Skopje, Macedonia. And you, you are British? Why are you driving this car?"

I suppose it was a fair question. I handed him the Authorisation Agreement, my trump card, saying innocently, "Oh I'm sorry, I forgot this."

My documentation and USB memory stick were carried off swiftly by one of his junior officers.

"We need to look inside," he said ominously.

"Of course," I said, standing back out of the way.

One rather plump customs officer had already tilted the front passenger seat forward and in the process of climbing onto the back seat had become wedged in the narrow space. As he shifted from one leg to the other in an attempt to free himself, Tito rolled backwards and forwards and I stifled a laugh. Another officer peered under the bonnet, while yet another leaned behind the driver's seat and began to gently knead the backseat with the palm of his hand. Tito's engine continued to run, slowly engulfing us all in an intoxicating cloud of exhaust fumes. The young officer returned with the USB stick, and my documents were placed back into the outstretched palm of his superior. All was in order; nothing untoward had been unearthed during the heavy-handed search of Tito, yet my passport remained hostage, held firmly in the officer's large hand. He asked again what I was doing in Bulgaria.

"Well, I'm on a journey. Through the Balkans." Patiently, I expanded my explanation. "I began in Skopje, have come through Macedonia, into Greece eastwards across Thrace, and into Turkey – to Edirne – and now I am heading to Sofia to visit friends and then..." "Greece!" he said emphatically. "You have been to Greece?"

Unsure whether this was an accusation or a trick question, I answered, "Er, yes – wonderful country."

He seemed somewhat reluctantly impressed. Why, I was not sure; I could only deduce that Greece, like Bulgaria, was part of the European Union, and if I had managed to enter and leave Greece with Tito, there should be no problem in his allowing us to enter Bulgaria. Whatever the reason, his other officers were getting bored. They had had their fun. They had not found anything remotely suspicious and had inhaled more than enough of Tito's noxious exhaust fumes intensifying under the canopy of the carport. He eyeballed me fiercely for one last time, handed me my passport and spat out a rather ungracious, "Goodbye."

I was in the car as fast as possible. The charade of handing over the USB stick continued through two further checkpoints until finally I could relinquish it, and as the border post disappeared from view I declared out loud, "Tito, we are in Bulgaria!"

- Andreevo Border Control/Plovdiv (122km) -

In front and behind, cars were being beckoned over by men and women waving tickets in the air. They had satchels slung across their shoulders and it seemed as though everyone was stopping to buy one. The young ticket seller watched us approach but, with a dismissive wave, looked over Tito's roof to the next car. Whatever it was, he clearly thought we did not need to purchase one. Giving it no further thought, I thrust my sun hat firmly over my left shoulder against the burning midday sun and headed along an old country road to Svilengrad for a much-needed coffee.

———

The young waitress bore her tall, elegant figure effortlessly around the shaded patio in staggeringly high-heeled shoes. She glared at me furiously, flicking her head aggressively upwards in response to my request for a cappuccino and shaking her head rudely at me when I asked for the bill. Her response both surprised and puzzled me, especially when an espresso and the bill arrived seconds later. There was, of course, a simple explanation. In Bulgaria the flick of the head means "no" and the shake of the head means "yes" – simple, unless you have spent years following a custom which means quite the opposite! The Greek culture, although similar, seemed softer and less aggressive than this Bulgarian version, or perhaps my Svilengrad waitress was just having a bad day. In any case, it was confusing and I doubted whether I would be able to relearn my 'yes' and 'no' after years of doing the reverse.

———

My aim was to make it to Plovdiv, where possibly I would cross paths with two friends travelling east through Bulgaria on holiday. Losing my way out of Svilengrad, I stopped to ask directions from a green-painted wooden caravan, patriotically flying a large Bulgarian flag on its roof. A dog lunged out from the shadows beneath the wagon, barking ferociously. Perhaps not. I hastily U-turned and went back to the garage we had just passed. Here at least was a welcoming face. He appeared at my open window. Blonde-haired and blue-eyed, resting his well-toned forearm on the window edge. His eyes had an instant hypnotic effect on me.

"Is this the road to Plovdiv?" I asked distractedly.

"Yes," he replied pleasantly. "You are travelling alone?"

His English was effortless and in my surprise, I nodded and then shook my head. Did that mean I had said no then yes, or yes then no? I was not sure and blushed ridiculously.

"Well, you should use the highway; it is much safer." And then, "Are you married?"

His directness, although not an uncommon trait among Balkan men and women, appeared almost matter-of-fact and as I floundered with an appropriate response, he continued, "And you have come from Skopje in this car?"

To this at least I could answer with conviction, laughing at his genuine astonishment.

"And now I'm on my way to Plovdiv to meet up with friends."

"Ah, of course," he responded casually. "Well, you must go straight, then turn right onto the motorway; it is safer and quicker than the old road." He straightened up from his crouched position and I indulged myself with a final look into his deep blue eyes, my impression of the Bulgarian species much improved.

The road took us westwards past the towns of Harmanli and Haskovo. I stayed away from the motorway. Our experience in Greece had been a salutary lesson and Tito was moving along very happily. At times a stream of powerful, sleek, black cars, all with smoked windows and aero-dynamic luggage boxes clamped to the roofs, would glide past with a strong 'whoosh'. Their number plates suggested origins in Switzerland, Germany, Austria and Italy, and like an army of "Imperial Storm Troopers" from *Star Wars*, they moved with incredible speed, expressionless beasts with not a flicker of life coming from within. We were on one of the European arterial routes which run between Turkey and Western Europe. The road, although single lane, was easily wide enough to accommodate Tito and a "Storm Trooper" side by side. Tito, although unable to impress these modern machines with his speed or technological capacity, was stealing the show as the most popular vehicle on the road. Local cars would pass and we would be hailed with waves and smiles from the children, the adults turning their heads for another look. A Zastava in Bulgaria was a novelty and the spectacle was being thoroughly enjoyed, with friendly 'toot-toots' of approval from drivers passing in both directions.

W e had been on the road for a couple of hours; I was hot, thirsty, and numb from the pressure of the seat springs digging into me. I pulled over to a timber-clad café and parked Tito in the shade. A volley of protests erupted from behind the engine door – he definitely needed to cool down.

Lunchtime was over but I was able to order a bottle of *Schweppes* and enjoy the cool, calm tranquillity of this Swiss chalet-style café. The cook, waitress and cleaner sat perched on a wooden bench glued to a Bulgarian soap opera on the television. It appeared to be a very dramatic moment and before long I too was drawn in. We sat in a collective, mesmerised silence. Although I could not tell who any of the characters were or what the story was about, I found myself equally gripped until the commercial break shook me out of my trance. Re-energised by the stop, and the minor distraction of foreign television, I was ready to hit the road once more.

It seemed some distance away but a vast curtain of rain was spreading across the landscape towards us. With my foot firmly down on the accelerator, I focused on getting us to Plovdiv as quickly as Tito's small wheels could turn. A car packed with people began to overtake and all heads turned to look at us. We smiled at each other as they passed, admiring our respective vintage vehicles in the process. As they moved back into the lane but now in front of us, a muscular brown arm appeared from the driver's window; it unravelled full stretch and a large thumb was extended upwards. I was left in no doubt of his admiration for Tito.

A relentless swathe of expressionless "Storm Troopers" swept past and I marvelled at the contrasting pace of our two journeys: theirs fast and focused on an end destination; whereas ours was an easy-going ramble in comparison, with the end destination not necessarily inevitable, although for now Tito was going well and continued to charm everyone who clapped eyes on him. Despite his lack of electronic controls and air-conditioning, except for the open window; despite the rising springs of the car seat, and the criss-cross rubber floor mats which regularly slipped out of position to allow a stream of scalding hot air to scorch my feet, I was suffering no real discomfort. In fact, it seemed to heighten my enjoyment of travelling with him. He was one of former Yugoslavia's almost-forgotten treasures and I could quite understand why.

The skyline was dominated by high-rise apartments intermingled with tall, red and white painted industrial chimneys, from which smoke streamed upwards. My expectations were initially deflated by this sight but as I was soon to realise, most cities in the Balkans followed a similar pattern – a style reflecting a Stalinist ideology of socialist realism which artistically glorifies the poor while ensuring the communist doctrine was practised through architectural form. We headed into the centre but the forceful flow of traffic found us travelling through an underpass system and out the other side of Plovdiv. The sky turned black, the wind picked up and threateningly large drops of rain began to fall. I pulled into a petrol station to ask directions. I was pointed back in the direction I had just come, where a left turn would take me into the old town of Plovdiv. Taking a look at the leaden sky, the garage manager scuttled back into his office and I made a dive for Tito.

The traffic flow had eased and we found our way to the old town. Three men sat, watching with interest from the pub's veranda as Tito carefully negotiated the large irregularly bedded stone surface and into a parking bay. I switched off the engine. They looked expectantly at me but no one moved. After a moment's hesitation, I opened the driver's door and stood up stiffly. One of the men got up from his chair and enquired if I was looking for somewhere to stay. He was the owner of the hotel next door, a recently restored old house dating back to the 18th century. I needed no further encouragement and gladly pulled my rucksack from the backseat.

After a long cool shower, I came out to find the impending rainstorm had evaporated into thin air and in its place, pillars of white cloud hung dramatically in a blue sky. As the sun set, rays of light filtered through and around the clouds, a magnificent light show for all who had time to look upwards. Night fell quickly and the old town was soon plunged into darkness. I headed into the widely lit boulevards of Plovdiv's more modern town centre as a text message came through on my phone. My friends were not going to make it to Plovdiv, it seemed.

'Sorry! We are still in Greece!! We will meet you in Samokov in two days!'

It was a lively scene and my social moment of the day. Evening strollers, coffee drinkers, ice cream lovers and window shoppers were admiring the latest fashions. Others hovered under a canopy boldly flashing *'Casino'* pondering whether to try their luck. Children raced around on bicycles or stood entranced by the impressive fountain which dominates the large central square. Their parents sat and chatted in one of the many terraced cafés. It was the usual evening activity to which I was becoming accustomed, whether it be Macedonia, Greece, Turkey or Bulgaria, and a moment to push away my faint disappointment at being on my own and just enjoy.

- Bachkovo Monastery/Plovdiv (54km return) -

Bachkovo Monastery and its location within the Rhodope mountains was too good to miss, particularly on a hot summer's day, my Dutch hotel host had insisted. We travelled south from Plovdiv to the town of Asenovgrad, from where the road winds slowly and narrowly upwards to Assen's Castle – a slight diversion *en route* to Bachkovo. I parked on the steep slope, put Tito firmly into first gear, and hastily placed my two trusty bricks behind each back wheel. It was a mountain goat climb up roughly hewn steps in the bedrock to reach the 11th century chapel and ruins of Assen's Castle perched high in the Rhodope mountains. Despite the perilous scramble, a steady flow of Bulgarians were paying their respects, lighting a candle and leaving money at the chapel.

The merciless summer heat was made bearable by a strong wind, although its gusty strength made it difficult to remain upright. I scanned the scenery, from Asenovgrad's industrial chimneys in the valley to the wild beauty of the mountains and back to the chapel. A larger-than-life Bulgarian flag flapped vigorously above my head, clanging noisily against a well-anchored flagpole. A young couple shouted over to me to ask if I could take their photograph. Surprised to find I was not Bulgarian, they asked in stilted English why I was in Bulgaria. The wind whipped our words away, but their concern was visible.

"You are alone? This is brave to do. We would never do such a thing! Are you not scared?"

My assurances did not appear to convince them, but nevertheless they wished me luck for the rest of my journey. I picked my way back down the rocks to Tito, trying to ignore the sudden rush of doubt. The weaving road soon needed my full concentration and I pushed any developing fears to the back of my mind.

———

S talls selling a combination of tacky tourist souvenirs, dried herbs, spices and home- produced jams and chutneys lined the pedestrian route to Bachkovo monastery. Founded in the 11th century by the Georgian politician and military leader Grigori Bakuriani, the monastery has survived through many centuries of war as well as numerous manmade alterations. Its buildings are a huddle of two churches in separate courtyards, a refectory building and monks' sleeping quarters. The smaller church was closed to visitors, as was the refectory. However, it seemed I was the exception to this rule: for a small visitor's fee I was ushered into the gloom of the old dining quarters.

"No photographs!" the official warned me sternly, turning to leave and firmly bolting the door behind him.

My eyes becoming accustomed to the dim light, I stepped through a stone doorway where a barrel-vaulted ceiling rose gracefully over my head. A long table stretched almost the full length of the room. It was made from large square pieces of smooth white marble, interlocked with one another and supported on short stone pedestals, an object not to be moved often, if at all. On the end wall, three painted religious figures gazed down at me, while the other walls and curved ceiling of the room were covered in brightly coloured scenes illustrating stories from the Bible. I turned to study the ones behind me. They depicted a tale of decapitated sinners being swept to Hell on a river of blood, followed rather gruesomely by their heads. My stomach churned uncomfortably – scenes to put all but the hardiest off their dinners.

The bolt slid open at my knocking on the refectory door to *"let me out"* and I gladly stepped into the summer sunshine, leaving the cold, damp room and its gory illustrations behind. I quickly warmed up in the fierce midday heat and headed for the cool of the main church. A queue stretched from just inside the entrance before disappearing through a pair of carved wooden doors. Curious, I followed the snaking line of bodies to where the revered icon of the Virgin Mary Eleusa was displayed, positioned high on a platform. A makeshift staircase, wide enough for only one person to climb at a time, rose up to the 14th century relic. The pilgrims kissed the icon, prayed and descended the steps as the next eager devotee squeezed past in their haste to offer a bundle of money clutched tightly in their fist. Although the figure originates from Georgia and not Bulgaria, she had no shortage of visitors and the reverence paid to her image seemed to me quite astonishing, as did the thick wodges of money being donated to her in the belief that the Mary Eleusa would help them to overcome their health and general difficulties in life.

Swept along by the moment, I climbed the steps and stared into the eyes of her delicate long face, hoping for Tito's and my continued well-being on our journey. I offered what I hoped was an appropriate bundle of Bulgarian Leva notes and in return a monk handed me a large pile of slim yellow candles. The candleholders were square trays of sand. I found enough space to thrust my fragile burning stick lengths into them. They leaned this way and that; as I watched them burn, they were unceremoniously swept up by another hovering monk, blown out and dropped into a metal bucket swinging from his arm. As others turned their backs to leave, their burning lengths received the same fate, religious reverence snuffed out by a realistic fear of fire or perhaps a better awareness of smoke damage. The wall paintings covering every inch of the interior were barely visible through layers of black dirt. Centuries of candle burning had reduced many of the religious figures to shadows, a practical issue for the monks, since it is a particular expression painted on a saint's face which invokes prayer, or so I had been informed by an Orthodox bishop while working in Kosovo. No wonder a monk had been elected as "candle snuffer" although perhaps he could have been a little more discreet!

————

I t was three o'clock and excruciatingly hot. I had returned to Plovdiv, to the old town, and scuttled along the semi-cool lengths of shade created by timber-jettied first-floor balconies of grand Ottoman housing. Many are painted brightly, and some very elaborately with floral or geometric designs. The effect is stunning, an open-air architectural gallery reflecting a time of wealth and success for the middle-class Bulgarian as Ottoman rule had relaxed to allow Bulgarians to trade in the mid-19th century. This greater freedom from suppression evolved into the *Bulgarian National Revival* era, which influenced the development of elaborate external and internal decorative design styles which, amazingly, have survived to this day.

In contrast, as I walked up the narrow streets, I encountered another time in Plovdiv's history. An ancient Roman amphitheatre sits in surprisingly good shape at the top of one of the six hills that surround the town. It was remarkable that old Plovdiv (Philippopolis, as I would have been corrected by the Greek brothers from Soufli) had, to a large extent, been spared from communism. Rows of tall apartment blocks interspersed with towering brick chimneys could be seen in every direction – a powerful statement reflecting a confidence in the communist ideal – bold and strong, on an architectural scale reminiscent of, yet far more prolific than, the socialist housing of 1960s Britain, though they had been built around the old town, rather than over it.

- Plovdiv/Samokov (114km) -

Samokov, once a renowned centre for literature and art, as well as iron mining, lies 100 kilometres west of Plovdiv. I did not expect it to be a strenuous day for Tito except for the last part, which involved a steep ascent to the Borovets, a popular ski resort in the Rila mountains, and then an equally steep descent down the other side, but nothing was going to stop me from getting there to meet up with my friends and have a much-needed social with familiar faces.

As Tito and I left the city, we passed a young Roma boy sitting in the shade of some street bins, his back leaning against the rear of a brick building, reading a newspaper. His slight frame clothed in tattered garments, his bare feet, grubby hair and face heightened the sad dichotomy of his life, as he sat perhaps dreaming of another destiny beyond the one in which he was currently trapped through the mere consequence of birth.

Despite being on a minor road, a regular flurry of "Storm Troopers" streamed past, taking the toll-free route as they headed northwards returning from holidays in Turkey. *Why would they not stick to the E road like everyone else – surely they could afford it?* For the main part, it was a quiet journey with only horse and cart, tractors and slow moving four-wheeled Dacias from Romania, our nearest rival in the classic car domination stakes.

Enticed by the piles of colourful fresh fruit for sale along the route, I stopped at one of the many huddles of roadside stalls. The sellers looked at me in fascination, then, with whole-hearted delight, began to compete for my attention. Unable to refuse any of them, I walked away weighed down with peaches, grapes and a super-sized melon, overwhelmed with heady sweet scents of ripe fruit. In high spirits, I overtook a horse and cart, raising Tito's success tally to at least six horses and carts, eight bicycles, four tractors (admittedly two of which had been stationary) and one over-loaded lorry – *not bad for a thirty-one-year-old Fića*, I thought.

The road rose gently. I kept Tito at a steady 40km/h. Above us, the Rila mountains loomed, filling me with some misgivings, but we had come this far and with any luck my friends would be waiting on the other side. They were on their way, coming from the opposite direction. As long as I did not look up, I was sure all would be well. The route wound in and out through small pretty villages, the landscape green and lush and, for a moment, I almost felt I was in the English countryside.

The road should not have been unduly taxing for Tito; it was still relatively flat, yet he was not happy. I pulled over but I was too late. The temperature gauge shot up to red. "No!"

I leapt out and threw open the engine door. A full orchestral sound erupted from inside, accompanied by a spray of sludgy water bursting out on one side, engine steam hissing from the centre while burning oil bubbled out the other side. This did not look good. Cars went by and a number of enquiring faces followed my moves as I grabbed a half-empty water bottle and a rag in readiness to refill the water tank as soon as the engine had cooled. I checked the oil level; it appeared normal. Gritting my teeth, we set off once more. To this day I am not quite sure how Tito managed to get to the top, but he did and, lurching to a stop in Borovec, the temperature gauge hit red for the umpteenth time. Smiles emerged on the faces watching us from a roadside kiosk serving coffee. A couple of young lads sniggered as I walked away from a parked and steaming Tito but I was proud of him. Perhaps my stolid confidence in him was going to get me into trouble at some point, but not today.

———

It was downhill all the way to Samokov. We set off at a cautious pace in low gear, weaving our way past ski chalets and small groups of summer walkers. With a considerable amount of pressure on the brake pedal, my arms could remain in control of an otherwise wilful steering wheel. My right calf muscle began to ache as I held a constant braking pressure on the juddering pedal but I dared not alter my position for fear of losing control. Braking in a Fića is, at times, an alarming experience; the connection between foot, brake pedal and wheel is unnervingly direct, uncannily similar to that between hand, bicycle brakes and wheel. The connection seemed fragile and hugely tenuous as we negotiated the hairpin bends. I clung tightly to the steering wheel, my body tense with concentration as I physically had to wrench it left and right to prevent Tito from heading over the mountain edge. As the road straightened out, we could free-wheel, albeit hesitantly down towards Samokov, where I eased my right foot off the pedal with relief and stretched my calf muscle, feeling rather smug. 2500 metres – not bad, Tito!

———

My first mistake was to switch off the engine while I went to ask for directions at the garage shop. My second was to urge Tito back to life with too much enthusiastic choke action. My third and final mistake was to ignore the warning sounds emanating from the engine as we crossed the bridge into the town centre. Halfway over, the engine failed. "Oh no, Tito, not now, please!"

I tried frantically to restart him as cars honked behind us and we slowed to a limp stop on the crest. Shuffling forward in my seat was enough to take him over the crest and miraculously the car gathered enough momentum for us to ceremoniously glide over the remaining half of the bridge (ignoring the red traffic light), negotiate a right turn and come to an abrupt standstill in the shade of a large tree at the pavement edge, allowing a stream of cars to pass. A mechanic was required once more!

I got out, stiff from the tension of the last few hours, and surveyed the street. On our side it was just trees, grass and river with an old lady hurling remarks at me or Tito, or perhaps both. Across the road was a shop selling car accessories. Perfect. I ambled over and tried my "Auto mechanic?" line once again. It did not work and the man looked blankly at me. I pointed across the road to where Tito was parked but he just shrugged his shoulders in response. Hopeless. I wandered back out into the street. A man in blue dungarees was getting into his car. He had to be a mechanic!

I walked up quickly and through his half-open window asked, "*Auto mechanic*?"

A pair of scared big brown eyes looked back at me.

"*Engleski*?" I asked with a hopeful smile.

He raised his eyebrows, shook his finger at me emphatically, and drove off. How odd. Perhaps wearing blue dungarees was not the mark of a car mechanic in Bulgaria? I wandered down the road to a shop sign which read 'CHANGE' – an English word at least.

———

It seemed Viktor's reputation as a good mechanic was well known to everyone in the town, including the foreign exchange bureau. The added bonus for me was that he could speak English, with German words thrown in.

"*Ich bin* very busy, I coming soon, thirty *minuten*," said the voice at the end of the phone.

"OK that's fine, I will wait for you," I replied.

Meanwhile, I decanted my luggage from Tito into a patiently waiting taxi and went in search of the hotel where my friends were also staying. My relief at seeing Anke and

Johann was immense and they were instantly drawn into my breakdown drama. We returned to the scene where Tito had come to a grinding halt and Anke "ooh-ed" and "aaah-ed" over him with the admiration of a protective mother hen. What a shame she would not be able to drive him!

Yes, well this might be the last time I, too, would drive him, I thought as a car drew up and a man in blue dungarees got out. This was Viktor and not – thankfully – the man I had scared off earlier.

With a grave glance at me and much tutting and scratching of his head, Viktor poked and prodded around Tito's engine. I stuck my index finger into the water tank and pulled it out, all oily and black, just to show him how, somehow, oil had got in there. This merely increased his concern; he was not sure whether he would be able to fix it.

"Emma, these cars not in Bulgaria. *Keine* (no) parts and you need new head gasket; it is ripped."

"Oh," I said glumly, "but Macedonia is not very far away; they have many Zastavas, perhaps I could go back and buy the parts?" I suggested optimistically.

Viktor looked at me, undecided. He made a phone call. "*Mein freund* coming. He take you to his garage. No room in mine. I look your car at weekend."

"Thank you," I said appreciatively, hoping that Viktor could and would do all that was possible.

"The problem is trying to find a towing point on the car which is not rusted away," Viktor explained in German to Anke, to which she laughed loudly in delight, thoroughly enjoying the unexpected situation of witnessing a "real" Tito breakdown.

A secure point was found and the tow rope attached. With that, we were slowly towed down the main street of Samokov by Viktor's friend – as tall and skinny as Viktor was short and plump – leaving Anke and Johann to revel in the comical spectacle of Tito being pulled by a 4-wheel drive jeep double his size through the town, behind which a stream of Samokov traffic followed, and pedestrians stared in amazement at the unusual sight.

My foot hovered over the brake pedal while I desperately tried to focus on the seriousness of my predicament and not make matters worse by inadvertently careering into my rescuer through lack of concentration – as, without doubt, Tito would come off the worse. I sobered up when I realised we were heading out of town towards the mountains and still not stopping. Viktor and my friends were nowhere in sight, while Tito and I remained completely at the mercy of this thin dungareed man in his 4-wheel drive vehicle. Just when I thought I was being towed away, never to be seen again, we veered right, down what was probably the last side street in Samokov, through a set of gates, into a vast emporium of smashed-up cars, vans and army tanks of differing origins and ages. We came to a standstill beside what I considered the best of a bad bunch; an American Cadillac. The tall, silent man indicated that I should leave the keys with him and then, still silent, he drove me back into town and that was the last I saw of him.

- Samokov -

The strong, black coffee that had followed me through Macedonia, Greece and Turkey, was also prevalent here in Bulgaria and restored the energy we all needed to agree a strategy for Tito's recovery. Viktor had brought along an English friend, whom he solemnly introduced as "Jim from Swindon", and I had "Anke and Johann from Germany" with me. So with coffee and the brainstorming of five of us, we concluded that the mechanical parts must be brought from Macedonia. The details were left to Viktor, as he seemed to have connections in every town in Macedonia and Bulgaria, all of whom appeared willing to do him a favour. The planning was formidable and I could only watch and listen in awe as Viktor seemed to mobilise the whole of the Balkans to ensure the right Zastava part was identified, bought and transferred to Samokov without delay.

For the second time, Tito had broken down on a Friday afternoon. Today was Saturday and there would be no delivery of parts until Monday. In the meantime, Samokov became my home. While Anke and Johann were off walking in the Rila mountains, Viktor and his wife Tsveta whisked me off to the village of Dragoshinovo to witness the annual soup festival. This particular local harvest festival seemed to involve the whole village. The inhabitants chopped, cooked and stirred a meat-based soup in an enormous cauldron in the local church. Traditionally, the cooking takes all night, and the following day each family brings a bucket and receives a full portion of soup to be eaten at home with friends. After lunch, the villagers of all ages descend on the village square to eat popcorn and candy floss, and sing traditional Bulgarian songs accompanied by a live band.

The music blasted out at full volume from powerful speakers while the resident village storks stood in their enormous nests perched precariously on rooftops and telegraph poles, furiously bashing their beaks together in protest – no one took any notice. The songs brought a smile to everyone's faces and I could not help but feel a strange sense of kinship with this traditional music full of pathos and lost love.

Meanwhile, the new Zastava parts miraculously arrived at midnight on Sunday evening from Macedonia. Exactly how, I was not sure and decided it was best not to enquire too closely. The main thing was they were here, and with any luck Viktor would be fixing Tito on Monday and I would be on the road again bound for Sofia.

———

"You stupid, stupid girl, what do you think you are doing driving a Zastava? It is so stupid, why are you doing it?"

I grinned down the phone. I had met Rosa on a number of occasions in Kosovo and she had become a great ally. Her immense knowledge and experience in the field of cultural heritage was fascinating and although strongly opinionated, she conveyed her arguments with such good humour and energy she was a breath of academic fresh air. Now, finally I had an opportunity to visit her in her hometown of Sofia, as soon as Tito was fixed.

Rosa's exasperation came from her concern for my safety, and putting my ear back to the phone I said, "I know Rosa, but this is something I have wanted to do for a long time. Don't worry, everything will be fine. I have found a great mechanic. If I break down again, I can always give up and continue my journey by train or bus."

We both knew, of course, that this was not an option. She sighed and with a small laugh said she would book a hotel for me in Sofia for Tuesday evening. "Just wait at the Pliska Hotel. You cannot miss it; it is easy to find and you can park. Try to be there by 5 o'clock and I will come and find you."

Viktor had been so busy he had not had time to fix Tito.

"Tomorrow it will be done, I promise."

Johann and Anke had headed off on their travels and with my friends gone and Tito out of action, I felt rather lost. With one more day on my hands, I pulled out my guidebook for inspiration. Rila Monastery, a renowned UNESCO world heritage site run by the Orthodox Church, was not too far away. Curiously, it was also the burial site of an Anglo-Irishman, James David Bourchier. Whoever he was, the Irish in me felt inclined to pay him my respects, as I doubted he would receive many visitors.

Apparently it was possible to stay overnight at the monastery. Although the accommodation phone number did not answer, I decided to chance it and jumped on the next available bus to Dupnitsa, from where I could catch another one up to the monastery. The road followed a flat plain before rising and then falling steeply down to the town. The journey was slow, the bus lurching its way around and into the numerous potholes which covered the poorly maintained road. The driver deposited me by the side of a busy dual carriageway rather than at Dupnitsa bus station itself, and with a wildly pointing finger, he indicated the general direction in which I should walk. It was all a bit vague but before I had time to protest, the doors closed and the bus full of passengers set off. I crossed the double-laned highway at a run and headed down some steps into an empty piece of land. A gate at the far end led out to a one-pump garage. *If in doubt, ask at a petrol station* was my motto. I was directed in a mixture of German and sign language to turn right at the traffic lights and follow the road for fifteen minutes. I arrived at the bus station hot, and decidedly out of sorts. A group of travellers sat on their rucksacks in the shade. There would be no bus for a few hours, no return bus that evening and no connection back to Samokov until tomorrow afternoon.

"Take taxi," said the bus information official, pointing towards the line of parked taxis, their drivers patiently reading newspapers and chatting amongst themselves. They appeared an intimidating bunch of old men and although it was clearly obvious I was the only potential customer, no one was in any particular hurry to leave the comfort of the shade.

———

Complicated negotiations continued the full length of the half-hour journey to Rila Monastery, involving frequent phone calls to the taxi driver's English-speaking relative who could act as interpreter. There were three possible deals on the table. To return me tonight to Dupnitsa;

to pick me up in the morning so I could catch the bus back from Dupnitsa to Samokov; or, to return me tonight to Samokov. By the time we arrived at the gates of Rila Monastery, a fog had descended over the mountains, it was raining heavily and I was feeling car sick from the looping turns up the mountain road, but the sight in front of me was spectacular.

Rila Monastery was like no other place I had ever seen. Its colourful façades of red and white, black and white striped and diamond shapes; its carved wooden roofs fanning out into the courtyard; its stone passageways and timber stairs leading upwards in tight landing turns to dizzy heights; stone-columned arcades; and brightly coloured wall paintings adorned the exterior walls of the church. I walked amazed across the courtyard to the lodging office. A long-bearded Orthodox monk, dressed in the usual garb of flowing black robes, appeared to have had enough of his lodging duties, tourists and rain for one day.

"No, we are full," was the blunt unsmiling response to my polite enquiry into accommodation for the night. With barely a look in my direction, he closed the register book loudly and ignored me. Apparently, I was dismissed. My taxi driver hovered expectantly in the background. We would be driving back to Samokov that evening.

Despite the scale of this 14th century Rila Monastery complex, it was blissfully peaceful except for the odd camera click from a tourist, the noise of scuttling feet across the rough cobbled courtyard from an elderly nun, and the sound of falling rain. Climbing the hillside behind the monastery, I found Bourchier's grave, the once well-known Anglo-Irishman who had apparently been respected by Bulgarians across the social strata, from King Ferdinand to the country people. He had been buried close to a place dear to his heart but sadly whatever respect he may have enjoyed while alive had paled considerably after death. The graveside was being used as a discreet toilet stop by those too desperate to wait and find modern facilities. The heavy rain, the damp air and this graveside scene chilled my bones. It was time to leave.

"Zdravco."

"Emma."

We shook hands amicably and I was upgraded to the front passenger seat next to Zdravco for the long taxi journey back to Samokov. Zdravco was a big man in his 50s who, because of a heart problem, was having to eat healthily. He had a wife and children and we talked in a sort of stilted pigeon German, laughing when we could not understand each other. He insisted I ate the remains of his "healthy" packed lunch, which his wife had given him that morning. A newspaper was spread across my knees as I bit into the ripest tomato I had ever encountered. As we approached the village of Rila in the valley, Zdravco stopped the car and rushed off, returning within minutes with a large bunch of herbs that he had picked from the bank on the opposite side of the road.

"*Name ist 'Zdravco',*" he said proudly, as he handed me the powerfully smelling herb. It never became clear what I was supposed to do with the herb but I was happy to inhale the intoxicating scent and feel healthy.

A dark night sky replaced the gloomy afternoon, the wind picked up and the rain threatened to follow us as we weaved our way out of the Rila mountains up to the Kilsurski Pass, and across the flat plateau towards Samokov, dodging the deep and numerous potholes.

Zdravko muttered, "*Sehr losho, sehr losho*" in a strange mixture of German and Serbian ("very bad, very bad").

It was late when we arrived back at the hotel. Zdravco declined the offer of coffee and, with a shy smile and nod of farewell, my brief acquaintance with the mild-mannered Zdravco from Dupnitsa ended; he went back to his life and a regime of healthy eating, and I prepared for tomorrow – onwards to Sofia.

Viktor had informed me Tito would be ready by 2 o'clock. I sat wondering how I should pass the morning when my eyes settled appreciatively on a painting in the breakfast room.

"Beautiful, isn't it?" the hotel owner said, noticing my interest.

"Yes, it is. Is the painter from Samokov?"

"Ah, he is no longer alive, but his son still lives here. He is our friend. I will call him. You have time?"

Before I could protest, he was dialling the number and ten minutes later a clapped-out old car arrived at the hotel entrance driven by a middle-aged man with an amazingly thick beard and dark brown eyes. This was Radko.

Softly spoken, fairly small in stature, wearing a pair of shorts and a t-shirt which had seen better days, his feet clad in a pair of grey socks and trainers, Radko was also an artist. His parents, Christo and Zlatka, were famous in Bulgaria and he was ensuring their legacy lived on. He drove me a couple of blocks away and parked midway down a tree-lined residential street.

The house – a typically rundown Samokov-style town house with discreet decoration to the façade and ornate timberwork at roof level – had certainly seen better days. There were ominous signs of structural cracking and peeling paintwork, unsteady-looking brick chimneys and an overgrown garden, all indicating that house maintenance was not his strong point. To one side of the house, an extension was underway; a new gallery in which Radko was planning to exhibit his parents' paintings and woodcuts. His father, Christo Neikov, had been best known as a book illustrator, having illustrated politically motivated books about the Ottoman conquest of Bulgaria but which, at the time, could not be released publicly for fear of retribution. His wife,

Zlatka Dabova, had been more the artist, developing her own particular spiritual yet traditional style, which was greatly admired by many in Bulgaria.

The house inside was dark. The rooms had timber-panelled wainscoting and large old wooden floorboards; an antique dining table dominated one of the rooms. It was a hidden treasure waiting to be revealed but Radko liked things just the way they were, with piles of books toppling over and curious looking artistic objects perched everywhere. The attic space had been converted into a light, bright artist's studio accessed by a makeshift staircase which creaked and wobbled as I climbed. Paintings, sketches, lithographs, woodcuts and illustrations were bundled higgledy-piggledy within large timber chests. He pulled out works which both his mother and father had created, explaining in stilted English that one day he would sort everything out properly. But today, as he reminisced, I almost felt the presence of Christo and Zlatka there with us in Radko's studio.

- Samokov/Sofia (60km) -

I found Viktor's garage – a car-port at the side of his father-in-law's house with a pit, over which a Land Rover was precariously straddled. Tito was parked out on the street. Viktor was not happy.

"Why do you want to go to Romania?" he asked ominously. Whatever he knew about Romania, he was not willing to tell me in any detail, but he was obviously keen for me to give it a miss. Perhaps it was the mountains that worried him.

"Emma you only use second gear uphill, you not to go to third, ok? 20km/h is maximum speed, ok? You break the filter if you go faster."

I promised that I would be very careful from now on and do as he advised. Before I could leave, I was invited to eat tomatoes and plums from his father-in-law's garden. It was not an obvious combination but they tasted so good I had trouble in stopping myself. I was handed a large bag of plums for the journey to Sofia before Viktor would allow me to pay him what I hoped was an honest and fair fee for his work.

I was sorry to say goodbye to Samokov. I had been welcomed into the homes of some of the nicest people I had met so far on my travels. They had assured me this was the Balkan way – the Bulgarian way – and for them it seemed important to include me in their lives, even though I was a complete stranger.

"Don't forget, second gear!"

And with a final wave from Viktor, I headed off on the road towards Sofia, knowing I would always have fond memories of the people and my time in Samokov.

We took the road north, following the Iskar River across a flat plateau before gliding on down towards Sofia and joining a fearsomely busy dual carriageway into the city centre where everyone, except us, seemed to know exactly where they were going.

They had the advantage of understanding the Bulgarian Cyrillic hieroglyphics, which differ subtly from Macedonian and Greek Cyrillic – not that I had mastered either of these. Two policemen stood monitoring the traffic flow. Tito and I cruised slowly past. They looked on in astonishment and through my rear-view mirror I could see them both laughing. Distracted, I overshot the exit to the Pliska Hotel but, hoping for the best, took the next right turn. We negotiated our way through some heavily potholed residential backstreets and miraculously popped out by the hotel car park. Under the shade of a café's sun umbrella I waited for Rosa and watched as Tito became an object of fascination for everyone who walked past. First they would spot the Skopje registration plate, then peer in through the windows, and finally look around to see where the owner might be. As the least likely suspect, I could remain anonymous and enjoy the attention my Zastava was receiving with impunity.

"No, I don't need any help thank you, and yes, I do want to ride in your car," Rosa said firmly. A lady of great dignity and determination, she confronts life's challenges with effortless fortitude. She is a realist, a no-nonsense lady with a sense of humour and a directness which could never be considered rude because it is always delivered enquiringly, and with the expectation of being enlightened.

It was a pleasure to see her again. I stacked her walking sticks on top of my luggage on the back seat and we drove off, her light-hearted infectious laugh making us both laugh as we sat crammed side by side in Tito's small interior. Rosa was my first female passenger since I had left Skopje and it was fun to have her experience the great spirit of adventure I felt every time I started the engine. This particular adventure only took us 500 metres around the corner to a distinctly more affordable hotel than the Pliska but it was fun anyway. With Tito safely parked under a large overgrown bush – the only car parking space the hotel had to offer behind locked gates – we dined at the local *'Bears'* restaurant, which Rosa described as being a "democratic not autocratic" place. The restaurant was attracting a wonderfully eclectic cross-section of the local population of Sofia; both young and old, from all walks of life. Sipping the popular summer soup, Tarator, a refreshing combination of cucumber, yoghurt, garlic, dill and crushed walnuts – a dish the Bulgarian government recommends its people to drink every day during the hot weather – we discussed the differences between the Balkan and British mentalities and she quizzed me on the British psyche. It was an evening of revelations and for the first time I began to better understand the complexity of the Balkan mind and its culture.

- Sofia -

Arriving back in a large capital city was a shock to the system. I had forgotten how loud, polluted and full of people they were, but Sofia had a certain fascinating buzz which intrigued me. Everyone seemed to be going about their business but there was always time to stop for coffee. Rosa arrived with one of her PhD students, who had been appropriated away from her studies to act as chauffeur. In one day it was not possible to see everything Sofia had to offer, but Rosa was determined I should see what she considered the most important things first. This included the UNESCO-listed site of Boyana Church, situated just outside the city. I was given a full morning's tuition on Byzantine wall paintings – an intense and entertaining experience – whereby Rosa tried to fill my brain with the knowledge she had acquired over the past forty or fifty years, while I did my best to keep up.

Sofia is an architectural tour through the centuries, from Roman times right up to the 21st century. Everywhere I looked, something caught my eye. The golden statue of Saint Sophia stood high on a stone pedestal, dressed in a flowing black dress with a black owl balanced on one arm and a black wreath in the other hand. She had replaced a statue of Stalin, and did so with great presence and striking beauty. I could not imagine Stalin ever providing anything near the same effect.

Wide boulevards and squares dominated parts of the city centre, huge Stalinist-type stone buildings topped by graceful figures carrying the familiar communist symbols of hammer and sickle. Narrow, more intimate streets were filled with small cafés and restaurants, the signs of capitalism evident everywhere, with small businesses sitting comfortably next to European retail stores. Then there was the TSUM building – the previously state-owned department store, now re-vamped with small boutique shops selling extremely expensive articles. As I sat drinking an over-priced coffee in the large and not-surprisingly half-empty coffee shop, I watched three women with long soft scissor actions mop the already polished and gleaming walkways of the store in continual synchronised sweeping motions up and down, up and down. Despite progress, some things will never change.

- Sofia/Vratsa (105km) -

Despite the temptation to stay longer in Sofia, it was very hot in the city and I felt a desire to be on the road while the weather remained sunny. Perhaps it would still be fine when I reached Croatia but that seemed a far-off aspiration, when there was Romania, Serbia and Bosnia yet to cross. It was the last week of August and for the first time I began to wonder how long the summer would last. It had been almost perfect until now. Would September be as good? More importantly, how would Tito fare in wet weather?

We had completed only one-quarter of our journey's circle. There were some large Balkan mountain ranges to conquer, whichever route we took. Two breakdowns had sobered me up to Tito's capacity when it came to ascents of any kind. The time had come for a bit of damage limitation. If we were going to make it full circle, I had to reduce our climbing adventures wherever possible, and that meant taking our route through Romania across the western plains; crossing the Danube River onto its north bank, to reach Romania, rather than driving several hundred mountainous kilometres east so as to cross into Romania while still south of the Danube. It was a compromise that had to be taken and Rosa was all for me making at least one sensible decision on my journey.

With a wave and a "*Merci!*" to Rosa (a word the French shared with the Bulgarians), we headed northwards to the town of Svoge and then northeast towards Vratsa. Mountains were unavoidable whichever route we took through Bulgaria but, heeding Viktor's warning to stick to second gear, we weaved our way onwards. It was a thrilling journey, with the Vraćanska mountains and national park on one side and the Golema mountains on the other – rising walls of magnificence stamping themselves on the landscape, from forested green slopes and mined escarpments to chalk white cliffs and craggy outcrops. The contrasts were breathtaking. As high as the mountains rose, the potholes in the road ran as deep. Slaloming our way around their vast cavernous depths, we arrived in the town of Vratsa and entered a low-ceilinged, concrete underground car park manned by a highly excitable old Bulgarian who could not believe that we had come all the way from Skopje.

In ironic contrast to the car park attendant's energetic and open-hearted welcome, the hotel receptionist's bland and unfriendly response to my enquiry for a room was followed by a brusque demand for my passport and immediate payment. Perhaps my wind-blown appearance as a result of a day's natural ventilation from the open windows, unglamorous attire and well-travelled rucksack initiated this cold attitude, matched only by the temperature in the building. For whatever reason, the hotel's indoor temperature was at freezing point. I pulled out every available blanket from the drawers and layered them on my bed, hoping I would survive the internal arctic conditions while outside the temperature remained at a steady 30 degrees centigrade.

The hotel overlooked Vratsa's main square, dominated at one end by a statue of Hristo Botev, who had championed (albeit unsuccessfully) Bulgaria's independence from the Ottoman Empire in the late 19th century. Despite a badly planned and poorly supported uprising, which ultimately failed and ended in his death, Hristo Botev is revered for his revolutionary and patriotic spirit. His poetic rather than fighting background seems to have made him all the more popular. A commanding statue of Botev provided an awe-inspiring backdrop to the rising chalk cliffs behind, particularly at sunset when the light streamed over him to dramatic and colourful effect.

In true Balkan style, the town came alive with the evening strollers. Old ladies sat on the pedestrianised high street selling small piles of vegetables and fruit, which I supposed had come fresh from their gardens. They did not have much, but what they had spare was being sold. It was a stark reminder that European Union membership did not necessarily bring the anticipated change or wealth to some people's lives, particularly in rural towns and villages where the quality of life and economic security of its citizens was yet to improve. In striking contrast, an enviable horde of gold and silver treasure was revealed in the Vratsa Museum. Originally belonging to a 4th century B.C. royal Thracian family living in the area, it is thought the family was forced to flee and hastily bury its magnificent wealth from the then invading forces. Today, the museum proudly displays the Rogozen Treasures; an exquisite collection of beauty and intricate craftsmanship.

- Vratsa/Čiprovci/Belogradčik (113km) -

Although I had eaten my way through the mass of grapes and most of the peaches I had bought from the fruit sellers on the road between Plovdiv to Samokov, I still had to tackle a large, and by now, very ripe melon, emitting a strong smell from the back seat of the car. Its overpowering perfume billowed out from Tito's interior as I opened the car door to repack my luggage. I was not sure when I would eat it, but it should be done sooner rather than later, I thought, waving farewell to the Vratsa car park attendant and heading northwards in the direction of Belogradčik.

The E79 road to Montana was conspicuously undulating

but Tito's engine sounded fine; the water container still looked clear, as did the oil cylinder. Viktor's work was holding true despite our mountain climb of yesterday. We crawled steadily up the hills and free-wheeled happily down the other side as cars and trucks tore past heading for the industrial town of Vidin. Although this was to be our eventual destination too, I had been lured by my *Bradt* guidebook into the idea of visiting Čiprovci, 'an enchanting and old-fashioned' village 'famous for its carpet weaving.' A detour was necessary if only to see some domestic architecture and perhaps observe some traditional culture. We sailed downhill into the town of Montana, past a police car, surreptitiously parked near the bottom of the beckoning downhill slope, on the lookout for the speed junkies who could not resist such an invitation – something we could never emulate, even with a strong wind behind. Discreetly set back from the road, a stone memorial listed the names of many who had fought for the Partisan cause during World War II. It sat largely unnoticed by the world, as did a similar memorial I had spotted on the road to Bitola in Macedonia a few weeks before – unsung Balkan heroes from a former age, quietly remembered by some but largely forgotten by most. The road took us westwards into a green valley between the Široka and Jazova mountains before veering left into the very foothills of the Jazovas, whilst another set of mountains rose up like a barricade – the Berkovska range, on the other side of which lay Serbia.

Tito drew a small amount of surprised attention from the villagers of Čiprovci as we came into – and then, just as quickly, shot out the other end of – the village, completely missing the unassuming signpost directing us to the *'Centar'*. The centre was in fact no larger than a postage stamp; a piece of grass on which two donkeys nonchalantly grazed. It was early afternoon and extremely hot. I peeled myself out of the car and observed the scene. A village famous for carpet weavers had conjured up in my mind a picture of a modest cottage industry lining the street, with perhaps some wool dyeing and people bustling about, but the only activity I could see came from the grinding jaws of the two donkeys.

I peered in through the windows of a café. I could not face the melon. The café was deserted apart from two women deep in conversation. They looked at me compassionately as I tried to make myself understood, but with pointing as the only alternative to Bulgarian, even this was not getting me very far. One of the ladies beckoned me to follow her. We walked back down the street past Tito and stopped to unlock the door to the *'Turist Information'*. With great presence of mind she opened up a translation programme on her computer. The connection was a faltering one but eventually my request was understood and we set off back through the village, into the garden of a traditional house, past a table crammed full of men deep in raucous conversation, and with much ceremony she ushered me triumphantly into the gloom of a small restaurant.

Emilija, who just happened to be on holiday here from Sofia, spoke fluent English. Soon I had a large bowl of salad in front of me and an invitation to a tour of the village when I had finished. There seemed to be no question of refusing. "It's no bother for me and it's good to speak English. My grandmother is weaving just now, it might be interesting for you."

Emilija was a confident young woman who worked in Sofia. She was casually dressed in shorts and t-shirt and looked relaxed and sun-tanned. She had spent the last two weeks in Čiprovci staying with her boyfriend's family and seemed very much at home. The house was like many traditional timber structures in the village, with flowers and vegetables growing in the garden; green, yellow and red peppers laced together and hanging from the fence posts to dry in the sun; drying red chilli peppers hung from every convenient post or hook. Two cats lay stretched out together asleep on the path; there was hay bulging out from the upper level of the timber-posted barn and everywhere a sense of organised self-sufficiency prevailed in a ramshackle but orderly way.

A river gurgled along at the bottom of the garden and above loomed the steep slopes of the Berkovska mountains, forming a natural boundary between Bulgaria and Serbia. The only stress seemed to be emanating from a large wooden hut in which a huge dog was pacing up and down, barking angrily at our presence. Emilija was as wary of the dog as I, and following her lead, we took off our shoes and retreated into the house. Katina, the grandmother of Emilija's boyfriend, was weaving industriously in the corner. With a huge smile she stopped momentarily to welcome me. I watched in wonder as the patterns slowly emerged on Katina's loom set in a large sturdy oak frame, apparently generations old.

The afternoon went by in a blissful haze of being part of a family. We sat and drank coffee in the garden and relaxed to the sound of the fast-flowing river, donkeys braying, and chickens glorifying the arrival of their freshly laid eggs. I listened to Emilija's stories of wolves and other wild beasts to be found in the mountains, in between taking large bites from a fresh peach plucked from their garden tree, and watched peppers drying in the sunshine. On this hot summer's day, it was difficult to picture how harsh the life would be in the winter away from all the comforts we take for granted in a modernised, western society. Although I envied them this idyllic location, I knew I might not find it so appealing in the depths of winter.

It was a struggle to tear myself away but realistically I needed to get to Belogradčik before dark. Tito was admired as I departed the village with a wave, the strong-smelling melon now safely in Emilija's custody – I only hoped she would not wait too long before eating it. For me, it had been a great privilege and another happy and unexpected encounter, whereby a family had not thought twice about welcoming me into their home and allowing me to be a part of their life for an afternoon – Bulgaria was fast becoming my favourite Balkan country.

The road to Belogradčik continued along the valley between the Jazova and Široka mountains. As we reached a T-junction, the landscape suddenly changed radically; strange pinkish gnarled rocks sprouted up from out of the ground. The signpost directed us left – another 17km away. At 40 km/h, we successfully took on a horse and cart carrying a large load of cut grass. Our overtaking tally had risen beyond a respectable count of ten horses and carts but any thoughts of Tito being "King of the Road" were short-lived as I changed down into second gear for the final slow ascent into the town. It was a twisting road overshadowed by large trees. There was a backlog of five cars behind but no one seemed to mind or tried impatiently to overtake. With no map of Belogradčik in the guidebook I was, as usual, instantly lost and headed for a helpful-looking petrol station. A polished old red Trabant, pulling a trailer behind it, drove in next to us and a happy-faced family peered out from their ageing yet still stylish Romanian classic vehicle; on seeing Tito, their smiles widened. The attendant filled up the petrol tank, made a telephone call and handed the phone to me. It was the owner of a hotel in town telling me to stay right where I was; he would come and find me. Bulgarian hospitality knew no bounds! As I waited for my escort, I nodded to the family, wondering, as they drove off still smiling, how many of these ageing classics from Romania had filtered across the border to become four-wheeled Bulgarian favourites.

Unfortunately, the hotel in town was full and I politely declined the owner's enthusiastic offer of a room at his other hotel 10 kilometres out of town. It was almost dark and I did

not want to risk driving much further. Instead, I noticed a
discreet sign advertising a guesthouse close by. It led up a hill
to the outside of a small store. A plump middle-aged lady
shot up from her chair on the neighbouring balcony and
cheerily came out to meet me. This was Sasho, who ran the
very popular, well-stocked but miniscule local food store in
the basement of her house, above which she rented out
rooms.

She clapped her hands in pleasure at seeing Tito, who was
making a fair amount of noise after the exertions of the steep
hill. I was swept off upstairs and proudly shown into a large
brightly decorated room with bed linen covered with a design
of large psychedelic blue, pink and white flowers. Perfect! It
was a home, not a hotel, and I loved it.

- Belogradčik/Vidin (65km) -

A Roman citadel loomed high above the town of Belogradčik
with a magnificent set of timber doors set within its walls.
These, however, were the firmly locked back doors. I was
obliged to take a bush scrub walk around to an equally
impressive front entrance. Inside, natural stone shapes rise
high above the walls and have been nicknamed "the
Madonna", "the bear", "the monk" and "the camel" by the
locals – according to legend and tradition. It is considered a
site of natural beauty in Bulgaria and was recently put
forward as a candidate to become one of the new natural
wonders of the world. It was designated fourth within the
Balkan Regional nominations. The winner was a site in Serbia
although no one seemed to know what exactly it was or
indeed even where it was. For now the citadel remains
something to be enjoyed and clambered over by all willing to
take on the challenge. Its precarious surfaces and wobbly,
unstable staircases were an equal match for the high-heeled
shoes of Bulgarian woman, digging up the stone's surfaces as

they climbed. I had to admire their fortitude, although most were clinging to a large, brawny Bulgarian male. The heat was oppressive, the step ladders shaky and, in some cases, downright dangerous but the views were stunning for miles around and certainly worth the effort.

It was another steaming hot summer's day as Tito and I left Belogradčik. The aim was to reach Vidin, the northernmost town of western Bulgaria, by nightfall, but first there was a two kilometre-long underground cave to visit known as the Magura Cave, which apparently had spectacular rock paintings dating back to Thracian times. Tito managed the wildly bumpy and potholed back roads with ease. I was chewing on a *Trebor* soft peppermint, my *Werther* toffee supply having long run out, when we were overtaken by an old Dacia brimming with people. Tito was in a perky mood this morning and so I could not resist the impulse to overtake them back with a wave of triumph. On the next hill our 20km/h pace brought much hilarity from the occupants of the Romanian classic car which, in no time at all, overtook us again. Viktor's 'second gear ascent' survival strategy for Tito could not be ignored, even if it did mean I lost to the Dacia!

The parking at the Magura Cave was chaotic. Vehicles spilled out from the car park down a narrow tree-lined lane. I found a space and Tito slotted into a space in which most other cars would not have stood a chance. I gathered up a cardigan and laced my walking boots for what I supposed would be quite a cold underground adventure. People smiled at Tito, and some remarked quizzically, "Ah Skopje?"

"Da, da," ("Yes, yes,") I said in response, feeling extremely proud of Tito's achievement in having got this far. Some would try further conversation; "Sorry, *Engleski,"* and they would raise a hand in friendly but disappointed defeat and we would just smile at one another.

The Magura Cave is an amazing, softly lit labyrinth of

many caves, both wide and deep, filled with stalactites and stalagmites. Whether in high-heeled shoes or walking boots, we all had the same concern – trying to remain upright for 2km on an extremely slippery surface with handrails that did not always guarantee stability. Cave bats flew around and lights illuminated our path but, try as I might, I was never quite sure whether I actually saw any Thracian wall paintings. Sliding and gliding along, down, through, and up into each cave needed great concentration. A guide appeared from nowhere and encouraged some of us down into an unlit cave. Mobile phone lights and my pocket torch provided some assurance for the few who followed him. We did not go far before turning back. Letting the others go ahead, I stood for a second and turned off my torch. It was blacker than black. I could see nothing and my huge respect went out to all those cave explorers, geologists, potholers and indeed miners who dared to map, explore and work in these dark underground halls so deep below the earth's surface. I would surely go crazy or panic from claustrophobia. I clicked the torchlight back on and, before I lost sight of the dim gleams of those who had already turned back, I followed at a slightly quicker sliding pace until I was back in the comforting glow of the main trail.

Emerging into the afternoon Bulgarian sunshine was a pleasant relief and as my limbs began to warm up after the damp cold of the caves, I peeled off my cardigan and began the 2km walk back to the car park. Tito was being admired by a stream of fellow Magura Cave walkers. I smiled politely and laughed as some exclaimed, "Ah *bijou*, *bijou*!"

Despite my inability to communicate, their friendly acknowledgements were comforting and I realised how much Tito contributed to my own sense of security. I felt uniquely accepted in a way which was to give me the continued confidence to travel alone through this remarkable Balkan land in a Zastava – feeling strangely at ease, or possibly too caught up in Tito's well-being to think of anything else.

We drove across the old cobbled streets of Dimovo town and onto the E79 route to Vidin. The vast Bulgarian mountain ranges were behind us to be replaced by an open, flat plain. After the relaxed beauty of the countryside, Vidin jarred and jolted me into another Bulgarian reality. Everything looked rundown and shabby with towering grey apartment blocks but it was from here I caught my first proper glimpse of the River Danube.

Mighty, incredibly wide and most certainly (from a visual perspective) powerful, the River Danube moves at a slow, soundless pace. I stood in awe at its size, amazed at how the same river could display so many different faces. In Vienna, I had seen this very same river, quiet and unassuming; in Vukovar (Croatia) I had seen it, some years ago, a tumbling, raging tiger where giant-sized mosquitoes had mercilessly attacked any exposed piece of skin; and here, today, the Danube resembled a relentless, grey warhorse, commanding and unstoppable. Most surprisingly, no one else seemed to be paying it any attention; the Danube existed as an intrinsic part of their everyday lives and their evening strolls.

- Vidin/Border Control (7km) -

It was Sunday morning and Day 25 – almost the end of August. I was awake early and having breakfast with two heavily smoking Bulgarians. I beat a hasty retreat back to my room, packed, paid and headed to the garage to refuel Tito. The garage attendant looked at us with surprised delight as we motored up to the petrol pump.

"Skopje?" he said.

"*Da, da,*" I acknowledged, laughing, "and today, Romania."

"Romania? But why not stay here in Bulgaria?" he asked indignantly.

"Ah, but I have been travelling through Bulgaria and now it is time to go to Romania," I said firmly.

He smiled and shrugged his shoulders. "Then we must prepare!" He filled the petrol tank, while I checked Tito's oil and water levels. He washed the windows and then, looking at the tyres, exclaimed, "You need air!"

I had not even thought about Tito's tyres since I had left Skopje – thankfully, at least someone was thinking of them on my behalf. Tito, it appeared, was being prepared for the journey of his life and I did wonder for a second whether I should be worried about what lay ahead.

"Good luck!"

The garage attendant waved me off and I took the deserted road eastwards towards the border control point. It was still early but already a line of articulated lorries lay ahead of us. We joined the queue feeling dwarfed by their size. A man waved excitedly and beckoned us over. He grinned at Tito and motioned for me to show my documents to the passport control officer, who was also grinning widely. Clearly, exiting Bulgaria was going to be a lot easier than entering.

"Ok, no problem."

I drove on down the dusty road to the next kiosk where a lone customs officer said, "Where your vignette?" pointing to my windscreen.

"My what?" I wondered curiously, staring at him blankly.

"Your vignette. Where is it?" he asked again, slightly exasperated by my ignorance. It was then the penny dropped. That's what everyone had been buying from the young satchel carriers at the Andreevo border.

"Oh! Do you want me to buy one?" I suggested, not really knowing what else to say.

"Where is it?" he insisted.

"I can buy one?" I repeated rather lamely. He sighed deeply.

"Never mind. Goodbye."

I joined a line of two cars. A man with a battered old leather bag slung across his shoulder came over to me and I bought a ferry ticket. This was it. We had left Bulgaria and there in front of us across the River Danube lay Romania. Two rather desolate looking wheel ramps lay abandoned three-quarters of the way down the concrete slipway, but there was no boat in sight. The wind had picked up into powerful gusts, and the Danube was no longer the peaceful, strong river of the evening before but a choppy, fast-flowing band of water. The queue of large articulated lorries began forming behind me and I started to have serious doubts about what kind of floating structure would be strong enough to carry us all across the river – these trucks were huge. *Had they been weighed? Was I about to sink in the Danube?*

A small metal raft-shaped vessel appeared, chuntering sideways towards us with a full load of lorries on board. Watching it fight against the downstream current of the Danube, my fears only heightened. Apparently, there was to be a bridge built soon but so far as I could see, they had not yet even started. I watched as the ferry docked and an alarmingly large number of vehicles disembarked. Two portly women, who had boarded as foot passengers on the Romanian side, staggered up the concrete slipway dragging and pushing enormous amounts of luggage. All the men watched from their lorry cabins but no one made the slightest attempt to help. The women seemed to be rowing as they struggled and we all became transfixed by their raised voices and expressive arm gestures as they stopped to catch their breath.

Our attention returned to boarding the ferry as the two previously abandoned wheel ramps were dragged into position, providing the link between concrete slipway and ferryboat. They were spaced apart for a normal sized modern vehicle. I launched Tito tentatively onto the ramps, hoping they were close enough together for the width of his narrow wheels. The ferrymen sniggered and one of them gave me the thumbs up – I exhaled in relief. As more and more vehicles drove on board, I could feel the ferry lowering with the weight. A siren signalled our departure. I stood at the ferry rails, ready to jump if necessary. The ferry began to reverse slowly off the slipway, suddenly stopped and then moved forward again. A sleek-looking motorbike roared on board with its two equally sleek-looking trim leather-clad passengers and then we were off, heading full steam across the choppy waters of the Danube towards a seemingly continuous wall of green forest, and Romania.

ROMANIA

AN EXPERIENCE OF EXTREMES

- Calafat Border Control/Baile Herculane (141km) -

From the moment we boarded the ferry, we became instant heroes; Tito for being a four-wheeled curiosity from Macedonia and by far the smallest and oldest car on the ferry and myself, because I was the woman driving him – alone – through the Balkans.

The leather-clad good-looking Romanian couple with their powerful top-of-the-range motorbike could not sustain the interest of the truck drivers for long. It was Tito who stole the show. One driver was pushed forward as spokesperson and between his small amount of English and my small amount of German, mixed with an even smaller amount of Bulgarian, he asked questions and translated my answers back to the expectant group of large, rugged-looking, fat-bellied and round-eyed "truckies". It was a comical moment. They asked to look at his engine and while some peered underneath Tito to inspect his suspension, others got into deep conversation about Tito's back wheels which, characteristically for a Zastava, angled inwards. They smiled at me and made a joke which, probably for the best, I did not understand but their conclusion was a thumbs up. Tito was *"bijou"* and "retro" in their opinion. We returned to our vehicles as the ferry reached Romania, any thoughts of sinking or drowning during the short twenty-minute journey across the Danube having disappeared.

As the trucks throttled into life with a roar, revving their engines in anticipation of a swift disembarkation, my apprehension increased. They were so immense beside Tito – the ant leading a herd of elephants off the ferry. Unwittingly, I had been directed to park in such a way as to make it necessary for Tito to disembark first. As the wheel ramps were shuffled into position, I was beckoned by one of the ferrymen to advance. They looked at Tito and then at the two ramps they had aligned for us to cross. There was a look of hesitation and then concern as, in some trepidation, I edged Tito forwards. One man got down on his knees to size up Tito's width and stood up quickly, raising his hand for me to stop. The revving juggernauts waited patiently for the ramps to be realigned. With a smile and a wave from the ferrymen and a toot of congratulations from one of the trucks behind us, we successfully negotiated the ramps and headed for the border control point.

A slim police officer with a kindly face and twinkling eyes raised his arms in surprise, saying, "You have come from Macedonia?"

"Yes," I answered proudly and handed him my passport and car documents. He looked at them and continued to chat to me in a friendly, relaxed way – a far cry from the welcome I was expecting, based on stories I had heard about Romanian police and border control practices in the past.

He handed back my documents and said with approval, "So you go through Romania, that is good," and almost in the same breath and with no change of tone he asked, "And do you have any ammunition or narcotics with you?"

I hesitated for a second, wondering whether I had heard

him correctly. "Er, no?" I said, slightly amazed at the perfunctory delivery of this loaded question.

"Ok," he said mildly, "Have a nice trip in Romania."

I drove forward a few paces to the next waiting official holding a wallet stuffed full of bank notes. I paid a small fee for something; I was not quite sure what, but it seemed to be some kind of entry or eco tax.

The man waved a bank note in front of my face and said with great concern, "Is this legal?"

Instantly recognising the Scottish Clydesdale Bank ten-pound note, I laughed.

"Yes, it most certainly is."

"Can you take it please?" he said.

"Well yes, but I can only give you Bulgarian Lev in exchange."

This did not seem to appeal and he sighed resignedly and waved us through.

The road led through the small town of Calafat. I stopped at a cashpoint. An armed guard stood nearby, which made me feel more nervous than secure. I hastily withdrew some Romanian Lei and headed off, wondering whether Romania would prove to be a dangerous place to be on my own. I had decided to make for the town of Drobeta-Turnu Severin, a route which followed the Danube River for a short distance before the 56A minor road took us across country while the Danube looped westwards. We would then rejoin it 10km before the town.

For the first 40km the road was like silk – courtesy of European Union funding. After the potholes of Bulgaria, it was a refreshing luxury and several trucks from our ferry overtook us at speed through one of the villages, taking full advantage of the smooth surface. With a resounding deep-throated blare of their horn, the grinning drivers looked down at us and waved in friendly recognition as they swept past. Through each village, children waved, old people stopped mid-conversation to stare and follow our path past them, while others beckoned us to pull over so that they could take a closer look. The number of horses and carts, or donkeys and carts we overtook rose so significantly I soon lost count of Tito's overall tally. He was storming along now. The road was flat or mildly undulating in between the villages and it seemed we were the only car on the road – possibly because it was Sunday – but the welcome and attention Tito attracted was heart-warming and I found myself waving back to people, astonished and amused by our overwhelming popularity.

I could not believe that crossing a river could change everything so radically – Romania was a different place altogether. The houses in each village were architecturally simple, and a pleasure to admire. Although mainly square-shaped, single-storey buildings with pitched roofs, the level of external decoration and detailing was extraordinary; each house differed from its neighbour. In every village, there was generally one building larger and more ornate than the others and I assumed this to be an institutional or public building. On each side of our super-smooth tarmac road lay dirt tracks or cobbled lanes. Each house had a garden plot and from first appearance it looked as though great care and attention had gone into them, but the resurfacing of the road was having an impact on village life. A good quality road, and the only main route for trucks, juggernauts and fast cars resulted in a racetrack, splitting villages in two, leaving children, families and old people marooned on one side or the other, unless they were brave enough to take on the juggernauts in order to cross.

The road rejoined the Danube at Hinova and at this point the quality of the road changed dramatically. I had dangled a pair of miniature Macedonian leather shoes around the arm of the rear-view mirror – a good luck present from Tomi – and they began to dance a jig as we rattled and bumped our way into Drobeta-Turnu Severin in search of a café.

A large brick 19th century water tower stood impressively as the centrepiece of a roundabout, around one side of which lay a café, but the blue-and-white painted curb signalled that I should not park and with a police car idly circling I decided not to risk it. Lost in the grid-like side streets, I found a bread shop kiosk. A young girl reading a newspaper was perched on a stool. There was no door to the shop, just a sliding window. She leaned down from her elevated position and smiled at me. The smell of freshly baking pastries wafted through the window in intoxicating waves. I bought a chocolate croissant and sat in Tito contemplating my next move while devouring the best croissant I had ever tasted.

With the pleasant chocolate rush re-energising my thoughts, I decided to keep going and head for the inland spa town of Baile Herculane. I circled Drobeta-Turnu Severin one last time, heading for the river's edge where large amounts of road reconstruction seemed to be mixed in with an archaeological restoration project. There was nowhere to park and it was so windy I decided the Roman remnants of Trajan's Bridge, which once spanned the mighty Danube, would have to wait for another time. I found my way back on to the pitiful, almost non-existent surface of the E70. Queues of cars and trucks crawled in front of us. The road was under reconstruction while we were still expected to drive on it and its connecting sections of dangerously weak-looking concrete bridges. Gritting my teeth, we ploughed across these perilously fragile surfaces held miraculously together by corroded reinforcement bars. Traffic lights had been set up to restrict vehicle flow to a single file over the bridge sections. A well-loaded lorry followed us closely and I could feel the impact of its weight on these fragile bridge sections shudder under Tito's wheels. The strong wind whipped up gusts of construction dust and dumped them on the windscreen. I could not wait to get away from this precarious, dusty scene.

An impressive looking hydro-electric dam spanned the Danube ahead. I pulled off to the left into a motel car park to get a better look. This was the Portile de Fier dam stretching across the mighty river between Serbia and Romania and controversially responsible for the flooding and loss of a huge area of natural beauty as a result of its construction. Standing out by the Danube with the wind gusting around me, and the clouds scudding across a not-so-blue sky, it felt for the very first time that autumn was on its way. Tomorrow would be the last day of August but the temperature was still a high 20 degrees – surely summer could not depart overnight?

With relief we peeled off the tremulous traffic-filled E70 road onto the 67D towards Baile Herculane. As the road moved inland and away from the Danube, the landscape changed dramatically from small dome-peaked hills into craggy-looking cliffs with pine trees perched at precarious angles along their ridges. It was a striking backdrop to our next stop – an old and decaying spa town – Baile Herculane. The towering sad-looking communist-style apartment blocks were a shock, as were the staggeringly deep potholes. We snaked our way beside the fast-flowing River Cerna to Hercules Square, leaving the tower blocks behind us, and were confronted by grand and highly ornate Hapsburg buildings. Although now sadly abandoned, these grand spa buildings symbolised a town that had once been a glamorous and sophisticated place.

I booked into the Hotel Ferdinand, the one renovated Hapsburg building in Hercules Square. It boasted spa baths as part of the hotel package and as taking the waters was one of the reasons why people come to Baile Herculane, I thought I should try them.

Engulfed in a complementary fluffy white bathing robe over my swimming costume, I went to investigate. The signs led me into the mineral smelling depths of the hotel basement down a steep, narrow staircase with high walls towering ever higher above me as I dropped deeper underground. It all felt clinically humid and oppressive and I began to feel strangely nervous. A white-coated spa attendant greeted me with an extended fat-fingered hand and a sardonic smile, a brown and rather too shiny wig on his head adding to his creepy appearance. Here was a place that reputedly contained naturally occurring mineral waters heated to varying degrees which could cure all kinds of disorders, but I felt as though I was entering some kind of psychological thriller. The spa attendant, in his white coat, quietly answered my questions while fixing me with an intense expression, his eyes drilling through his glasses into mine. I felt a rising sense of panic. *Was I going to be trapped? Imprisoned down here in the depths of the hotel and left to go stark raving mad? Would anyone find me in time?* I was directed to a large spa bath of murky-coloured water through which a young boy was being swirled by his mother. The spa attendant left the room and I relaxed slightly.

The spa waters of Baile Herculane are supposed to be therapeutic and were apparently the most fashionable baths in Europe during the 19th century but I did not feel able to enjoy the experience in this high domed echoing space, which lacked any kind of warmth or architectural charm. A space so out of proportion to its height, made one feel strangely claustrophobic. I felt vulnerable, defenceless, subdued and completely ill at ease, despite the laughs coming from the boy as he was spun back and forth across the pool by his mother; this to me was not a place of healing. I could take it no more and I hurried back into the comfort of my oversized white robe, making a bolt for the staircase, back up the mountainous steps to safety. It was with a sense of contained relief I re-emerged into the hotel lobby once more.

A plate of polenta with sour cream, and cabbage leaves stuffed with rice, meat and herbs, respectively known as *mamaliga* and *sarmale*, did much to revive me. Nothing much was happening at this end of the town in Hercules Square; all the other buildings were redundant. I headed for my room and an early night. Peering out of the bedroom window to check Tito was still parked outside, I observed two men standing behind the car. They appeared to be discussing his back wheel design. One was illustrating to the other with his arms the angles of the wheels, while the other nodded and bent a little closer to look. Tito had a pulling power all of his own and I felt hugely proud of him as he continued to bring a smile to people's faces – most of all, to mine.

- Baile Herculane/Lugoj (107km) -

I felt uncomfortable in this spa town and after a fitful night's sleep I was glad to leave. Behind the fading architectural grandeur of Baile Herculane there lurked a sad, depressed and slightly sinister atmosphere. The tired, track-suited figures I saw walking drearily up the street or sitting rather dejectedly on wooden benches all seemed lost in an aura of hopeless despair. Where was the energy, the revived spirits which must have existed here in the golden days of the Austro-Hungarian era?

The only building in decent repair was the Romanian Orthodox Church. Perhaps financial investment will be found one day to restore Baile Herculane's architecture to its former elegance and beauty, and bring with it renewed hope and prosperity. For now, the communist-style tower blocks in their stark, grey multitudes cast a deep shadow of gloom over the town.

As the high forested escarpments disappeared behind us, I flicked open the three-quarter light and wound down the window. Breathing in the warm air, we headed back onto the E70 road that would eventually lead westwards to Timisoara. The road carved a route through the Timis valley between green and pleasant hillsides dominated by haystacks looking more like sentries or sculpted figures marching up the newly cropped slopes. The wind from yesterday had eased substantially into a soft breeze and white fluffy clouds drifted across a blue sky. As a result, the temperature was rising again and the sun shone strongly. Tito was feeling fine and as we cheerfully motored along admiring the makeshift kiosks selling mounds of red apples and other recently harvested produce, the eerie experience of Baile Herculane drifted away. This harmony with nature did not last when we hit the first stretch of kilometre-long roadworks of the day. Between temporary traffic light changes the traffic drove cautiously across hacked-up road surfaces now also rutted with dusty wheel tracks. The experience was made all the more unpleasant by the inordinate number of lorries travelling too fast, kicking up large clouds of dirt and dust in their wake which then smothered all those forced to follow them.

It was slow going and as the day got hotter my back stuck to the car seat upholstery. Burning hot air blasted over my feet as the rubber mats slipped away from their position across the gearbox hole and I sighed in exasperation. My hair was matted with dust and my mouth felt gritty. A signpost ahead suggested there was a castle to visit. I could see some kind of tower in the distance and impulsively I swung off the dusty road onto a narrow lane leading into a village. The signpost indicated left and I followed it. Villagers were watching with a smile as we went by and out of the corner of my eye I saw a young man dash inside his house. A little way ahead the road turned into a dirt track and I slowed to 20km/h. Ahead, three young boys were staring down the road towards us in eager anticipation, and as we neared they pulled out an assortment of mobile phones and cameras to take a photo of Tito as we drove past, smiling and laughing in their excitement – they had been tipped off. Beyond the village, the road became edged with high grasses and I began to wonder whether I was on a wild goose chase. The tower I had seen from the road had disappeared completely from view. A tractor straddled the middle of the route ahead. As we approached, the farmer turned off his engine and I got out to ask. "Castle?" pointing in the direction ahead.

"*Manastirea*!" he said, smiling and pointing straight on, raising two fingers of his other hand to indicate 2km. Oh well, not a castle, but I would go and look anyway. The road surface was a mass of firmly packed dirt, loose stones and potholes and it was necessary to weave a drunken route to avoid the worst of it. Another car bundled up behind us just as we reached a signpost indicating right to '*Manastirea St.Treime*'. The car edged past and all three occupants turned to look. Well, I may have been in the middle of nowhere but at least I was not alone.

The road led through a small forest and out into an open space of rolling green fields in which there was positioned a sparklingly new church with glistening white walls topped by three red metal roofs shaped like witches' hats. At first sight I was not sure whether this was Catholic or Orthodox but the long single-storey building further up the bank with open balconies festooned in flowers suggested an Orthodox *konak* or guesthouse. Two young women and a young man, dressed in jeans and t-shirts, jumped out of the car I had followed for the last 600 metres and with a slightly curious glance towards me, turned and strolled towards the church. Not really knowing what else to do, I parked and followed suit.

A plump, friendly bespectacled nun dressed in a full flowing black dress and matching headdress came hurtling down the hill from the *konak* to greet us. Her smile at seeing so many visitors clearly betrayed her delighted anticipation of conversation and possibly the opportunity to alleviate the quiet monastic lifestyle in this isolated setting. She regaled the group of three with tales of the church and they all made the sign of the cross at various intervals in front of painted icons, leaning forward to kiss one of them as the nun continued to talk. I stood back and watched, feeling slightly awkward, wondering if I was interrupting some kind of personal ceremony. The nun cast me a curious glance as she led the three young Romanians towards a table selling various crafted religious gifts and candles. Feeling I should contribute in some way, I bought a handmade bracelet of intricately linked small wooden beads deftly fastened by an ingenious threaded push and pull system.

The nun directed a question at me with a smile.

"*Engleski*," I said apologetically.

"Ah," they all said in unison and the young man immediately responded in stilted English that I had been invited by the Mother Superior to join them all for coffee. "*Multumesc*." I thanked her with an appreciative look – the only word I had managed to master in the Romanian language – and she led the way up the bank across the temporary wooden planks which straddled a large trench to the konak building.

A table had been placed in the shade of one of the large trees and I sat in bewildered amusement as coffee suddenly turned into lunch with large bowls of soup being distributed along with bread, boiled potatoes and salad. My companions Claudio and Talida talked in stilted English and we passed a pleasant afternoon in the shade while their other friend, who it transpired had been taught by the cheerful Mother Superior and who was considering joining the religious order, busied herself in the kitchen. A quiet calm radiated out across the surrounding rural landscape although I could imagine this being a very solitary life for the handful of nuns living here, particularly in winter. Apart from a few visitors and the priest who came to take the Sunday service, all they had were four long-eared white rabbits, a strutting cockerel and a mass of free-roaming hens for company and conversation. Despite the

Mother Superior's kind hospitality, cheerfulness and cheeky smile, her suggestion that I should stay the night (or indeed, become a nun and not leave at all) was my cue to make a gracious exit. I climbed back into Tito's comforting interior and we headed off with a wave, lots of thanks and respect for those who choose this monastic life; it cannot be easy.

I drove Tito slowly and carefully back along the thick, potholed gravel road, afraid that the dust particles might choke his engine, through the village where one of the young boys, part of the line-up of village photographers, was crossing the road ahead of us. He smiled shyly and gave us a hesitant, self-conscious half-wave as we passed and headed west back to the E70 main road with its long sections of roadworks. It was now nearly five o'clock and, ever conscious that night falls with a sudden bang in this part of the world, I headed for the next town, Lugoj, in some earnest.

- Lugoj/Timisoara (57km) -

Lugoj is a pretty little town in the western region of Romania known as The Banat. It is predominantly a flat land whose borders lie next to Serbia's ostensibly autonomous region of Vojvodina. The Banat has seen mass migration flows in and out over the last few centuries. The most recent inhabitants were Serbs as well as German-speaking people known as Swabians, both of whom took on the challenge of turning this area of flat marshland into a civilised, sustainable and habitable region. Lugoj straddles the river Timis with, historically, the Serbs living on the west side while the Swabians dominate the east bank. Nowadays, an attractive, grey-blue coloured steel bridge, adorned with flower boxes filled with masses of pink blooms, connects the east with the west and a small plaque attached to the western side of the bridge explains that the communities of this town were once deeply divided.

Lugoj was alive with evening strollers, and I joined them. Despite the dilapidated state of many of the buildings in the town, walking with my gaze angled upwards, I could see the architectural detail was still there: the bow-shaped iron balconies, cornices and pediments, intricate and eye-catching in their splendour. As the sun set, the buildings gave off a warm glow, adding to the fading charm of this small town. Coupled with its architectural beauty, Lugoj had apparently produced many aspiring and talented singers and musicians. I stumbled upon the music theatre clad in timber scaffolding behind which evidence of a new restoration project revealed itself in somewhat startling colours of maroon, peach, pink and white with gold leafing around each window head. I wondered whether these were the original colours of the theatre or whether they were the fantasy of the current owner.

———

I t was the first day of September yet people continued to eat ice cream after a morning's shopping, young and old happily mixing together. A poster of Romania's bodybuilding hero, Florin Teodorescu, was firmly taped to the entrance of a gym. Sporting a red thong and posing in such a way as to ensure that his rippling biceps, triceps and "six pack" were shown to maximum bulging advantage, this bodybuilding image was enough to send me back over the bridge, to pack my bags and get on the road again.

As I headed out of the hotel, a heated debate between the laundryman, the maid and hotel receptionist was in full swing. Piles of crisply folded laundry were being thrown into the arms of one and snatched back by another. Loath to interrupt, I mumbled a goodbye, thankful I had paid earlier. We joined the E70 road out of Lugoj and headed west for Timisoara, the town synonymous with the start of the

Romanian Revolution of 1989, and my proposed final stop in Romania.

The section of road between Lugoj and Timisoara was without doubt the worst we had yet travelled upon. The summer heat had warmed the tarmac to such an extent that the heavy traffic of juggernauts had remoulded the softened surface with their deeply tracked double wheels. Where they had swerved or changed lanes, a criss-crossed pattern of trenches had been gouged and set. Thin ridges rose up between the wheel tracks. They too had hardened, providing the only hope of salvation for Tito and me. It demanded unparalleled levels of concentration to keep his small wheels from being trapped within the jaws of the ruts as we rode the tarmac ridges into Timisoara, fearful that if we did not stay high, the deep, tyre-carved trenches would certainly control Tito's dainty wheels and most probably land us in the nearest ditch.

The outskirts hummed with fast-flowing traffic on two-laned boulevards. I took a wrong turn and ended up in the middle of a large estate of communist-style apartment blocks. My second attempt at trying to find the city's historic quarter was slightly more successful. With the help of two policemen who were idly watching me from the shade of a building, I managed to extricate myself from the narrow streets in which I now found myself and ended up by chance at the barriered entrance to a modest car park. It was early afternoon and extremely hot. I pushed every button I could find on the ticket machine but the barrier remained firmly down. A man watching us from the middle of the car park, as I sat sweltering in the searing heat of the car, headed towards us and asked, "*Makedonski?*"

"No, *Engleski.*"

"Ah, ok. You must wait for a car to leave and then a ticket will come from here and the barrier will go up."

His eyes scanned Tito with interest and he seemed to

hesitate but was driven back into the shade by the scorching temperatures. Finally, out popped a ticket from the machine and the barrier lifted, allowing us to park in the recently vacated space of the otherwise full car park. The man moved from the shade and wandered over to introduce himself. Marku lived in Timisoara and had recently been made redundant. He had a big interest in old cars and in photography. I eyed the large professional-looking camera slung around his neck and, after some hesitation, he asked if he could take photos of Tito.

"Of course!"

Marku volunteered to help me find street parking, which he advised would be far cheaper. I unhooked Sean's passenger door locking device, which was still holding firm, and Marku climbed in with all the excitement of a schoolboy. He pushed and prodded every button on the dashboard with apologetic exuberance and grinned smugly at the car park attendant as we left, Tito once again weaving his magic. It was fun to engage with someone who was clearly enjoying a "Tito moment" and I was grateful for his friendly company. Successfully parked in a more affordable position, Marku thanked me with a huge smile and we said our goodbyes.

I checked into the Hotel Victoria, a renovated old building with enormous rooms, high ceilings and no lift. Once I had successfully climbed the two floors, dragging my luggage behind me, it was a relief to enter my cool room and collapse on the enormous bed. I felt exhausted from the heat and two nights in Timisoara meant I could unpack my bags and relax a little. Although I was not racing around the Balkans (that was impossible in Tito), the constant stimulation and absorption of new sights, sounds and customs, coupled with the fact I was travelling alone, were sometimes more tiring than I realised; for now, I was going to sit in a café and watch the world go by.

- Timisoara -

Timisoara is a city of contrasts; a city moving forward from the revolution of December 1989 at a speed which almost belies belief. Romania is now a member of NATO and the European Union. It is embracing capitalism after years of communism, and, at the time of visiting, this was only twenty years after the revolution. December 2019 marks the 30th anniversary since the revolution, a historic event sparked off by the eviction of Pastor Laszlo Tokes from his home in Timisoara. He was a popular man, strongly critical of Ceausescu and the Romanian government, and his eviction was a catalyst for protestors to hit the streets of Timisoara in their hundreds to air their grievances. President Ceausescu sent in tanks, the army, the police and Securitate to quash the protest. With over one hundred protestors gunned down and many others injured, the tide of support for Ceausescu turned; the unrest spread to Bucharest, and within days the Ceausescu regime fell.

Walking around Timisoara, you find memorial plaques screwed to the sides of buildings to commemorate the missing and the dead from the days of the revolution. Some buildings, particularly in the main square (Victoria Square), were pockmarked with bullet holes. The Romanian Orthodox Church, outside which many protestors gathered and were killed, was constantly glowing with candles lit to commemorate the dead. In the squares, cafés were filled with young fashionably dressed people; the women in summer dresses were teetering on slim high-heeled shoes, the men in linen shirts and jeans. Watching the world go by, it was hard to imagine the town could have been the scene of such atrocities.

Tucked down a side street, I came across the Association to the Memorial of the Revolution. Here I met Ioana, my guide for the visit. The tour started in the chapel built and dedicated to all those who had died during the revolution. She asked where I was from and why I was in Timisoara. I explained about working in Kosovo and now travelling around the Balkans in a Zastava. In her astonishment and curiosity to know more, the formalities of the tour were forgotten as we began to talk of other things. It was as though we had known each other for years. She spoke about herself, her husband and daughter and about Romania's sudden and fast advancement and adaptation to capitalism. She was concerned that a capitalist and European Romania had made some people very rich but equally some even poorer, making them believe that communism was indeed a better way of life whereby everyone at least had a job and food.

Ioana giggled self-consciously as she confided in me the story of her first shopping trip after communism fell. Although it seemed her husband did most of the shopping, on one particular occasion she was in charge. This was the first time she had been to a supermarket since the communist period and on seeing the variety and extent of cheese on sale, her reaction had been to buy as much as possible, in case there would be none the following week.

"This, Emma, was my fear, and my husband laughed at me so much because this does not happen anymore, and I still believed it might. It is difficult to change one's way of thinking overnight but now I too laugh at my reaction."

We moved upstairs to the museum, entering a room filled with empty rows of chairs except for three. These had dummies sitting in them, suited in three different styles of uniform. The walls were filled with photographs and newspaper cuttings illustrating the horror of the revolution and the days of suspicion and fear that followed after Ceausescu and his wife had been caught. Everyone, it seemed, was a target and no one was safe during or after the revolution in the lead up to the new government being formed. I sat and watched a film on the events with my three companions sitting behind.

A short, slimly built man limped into the room supported by a walking stick, giving instructions at the top of his voice to the two men who followed him. He seemed not to care he was interrupting and, giving me a momentary glance, he left the room again. By the end of the film, I sat motionless in my chair, filled with conflicting emotions caused by what I had just seen. How effortless my life had been in contrast! I had never experienced mistrust and fear on this scale; repression; the influence of informers; sudden or unexplained imprisonment; torture or death for holding a political view contrary to the government's; suspicion – and no freedom of speech.

Ioana came back and I asked her how she had managed to live during this oppressive time. She was matter-of-fact.

"I always wanted to travel but we were not allowed; I could not leave Romania. Communism was not all bad; our life was what we knew but food was rationed – a kilo of flour and sugar per month, and a quota of bread each week. You could buy bread in other towns but you had always to prove why you were travelling. There are things today that are worse than before and people have become very greedy."

Ioana's office was filled floor to ceiling with bundles of neatly piled newspapers.

"These we must go through looking for articles on the revolution. Everything must be catalogued and recorded."

The man with the walking stick reappeared from the next room. This was the President of the Association. He looked thoughtfully at me as Ioana explained I was from Scotland, had worked in Kosovo and was interested in cultural heritage. I could sense from his demeanour that he was probably a difficult and unpredictable man with whom to work. He had been shot in the leg during the Timisoara Revolution of 1989 and now walked with a wooden walking stick, the handle of which was topped with a silver eagle. He was gruff, almost aggressively defensive. I could tell he did not want any kind of informal discussion about the weather or the niceties of life – that would surely annoy him. He asked if I could send him any articles on the revolution which had been written in the Scottish newspapers and I promised the next time I was in Scotland I would go and find out what I could. The intensity in his face softened and he gave me a half-smile of appreciation.

The President urged me to watch another film on how he had saved the museum building from being demolished. Leaving me alone once more with the three figures dressed in uniforms representing the police, the army and the secret police, he pointed to them and said, "They must watch the documentary on the revolution every day so they do not forget what they did to us during those days. It is their duty to watch and remember and I make them sit there."

Ioana said she worked at the museum with mixed feelings. "I feel guilty some days. Here I am working, and earning money in a job which only exists because so many people died. It is hard sometimes to believe that this is an honest way to live and earn money."

Indeed, the irony of Ioana's situation is very sad but this little museum has a heart and soul of its own, a human spirit which lives on in the President and Ioana and probably all the other colleagues whom I did not meet. Certainly, for as long as they are there, I am sure the martyrs of the revolution will never be forgotten and I, for one, will never forget the few hours I spent there. As I left Timisoara the next day, the President's gentle appeal rang in my ears: "Please, do not forget me."

- Timisoara/Jimbolia Border Control (48km) -

The sun was shining once more and despite the fact that we were now in September, the temperature continued to remain in the high 30s. Two nights in Timisoara had recharged my batteries and I was ready for the road again. It continued to amaze me how fascinated everyone was by my white Zastava 750. It was not something I had expected; indeed, I had thought the car would have helped me to fade discreetly into the background – it had, in fact, been the reverse. The kind, friendly and sometimes enthusiastic acknowledgement of people on the road continued to make me feel part of their world and I felt privileged.

Today, however, we were heading to Serbia, to the northern autonomous region of Vojvodina and I was feeling just a little bit apprehensive. It probably had something to do with a number of unnerving crossings I had had over the past few years into the south of Serbia from Kosovo. This was the first time I was entering the country with no diplomatic backing. Now it was just myself.

It was a distance of 48km westwards along a flat open road. As Jimbolia and the border grew closer, my stomach churned uneasily. I chewed distractedly on a peppermint, hoping that the vast number of Kosovo entry/exit stamps smattered throughout my passport would not upset the border official. Surely I was being unreasonably scared? I determinedly focused on the road ahead. Two kilometres to go.

SERBIA

HOME TO THE ZASTAVA

- Srpska Crnja Border Control/Subotica (125km) -

A white and red milestone marked the distance. I stopped the car and took a deep breath. Why I felt so nervous I really did not know. It was totally irrational. I captured the moment with a photograph, and drove the last two kilometres at 30km/h in an attempt to calm my nerves and adopt an innocently nonchalant air. True, my passport was peppered with Republic of Kosovo stamps. Would this rile the border officials? In 1999, NATO had bombed Belgrade, Novi Sad and Valjevo as well as Serbian militia headquarters in Pristina in its efforts to end the escalating atrocities being carried out against the Kosovo Muslim population by Serbia under President Milosevic. The war had ended swiftly and a subsequent interim administration of Kosovo was established under a United Nations resolution. In March 2004 ethnic tensions were sparked once more between Serb and Kosovo Albanian communities, which had resulted in the burning of numerous Serbian Orthodox Churches. Then, in February 2007, Kosovo had declared independence; a move that has been welcomed and acknowledged by many

European countries but not enough to make it eligible for membership in the United Nations or the Council of Europe. Serbia had made it very clear that it did not and would not accept Kosovo's independence as this is the historic religious heartland of Serbia.

While I had worked in Kosovo under the "international" banner of the Council of Europe, of which Serbia is a member, I had always had an official letter when crossing between Kosovo and Serbia – not that that had, on some occasions, made things any easier. But today I was entering Serbia solo. No letter; just a car with documents in someone else's name. Would they be suspicious or difficult with me? Would the Authorisation Agreement work here?

The border crossing was deserted. We came to a stop. Almost immediately the door to the passport control cabin crashed open. With his arms raised in disbelief, the border official came rushing towards us, shouting excitedly, "It's a miracle!"

I sat in stunned silence as he took my documents and studied them. It was evident that at this little out-of-the-way border crossing post in northern Serbia they were more interested in Zastavas than politics. "It's a miracle!" he repeated. "A Fića! You are driving a Fića! From Skopje?"

The officer peered at the kilometre dial, looked at the engine, exclaimed from under the bonnet at the petrol tank and then stood back in amazement, unable to stop chuckling to himself. It seemed all my fears were completely unfounded. Serbia was welcoming us with open arms.

By my calculations Tito and I had now made it halfway around the Balkans. We had driven through five countries in four weeks and had broken down only twice. The sudden realisation of Tito's accomplishment hit home. At 70km/h on the straight and 20 km/h on the slope, my four-wheeled vehicle with its bubbling, gurgling engine was still going strong – perhaps it was a miracle!

We were in the home of Fićas; their owners acknowledged us as much as I acknowledged them with a nod or a wave in recognition of our shared Zastava status. My aim was to head to Subotica, the northernmost town of Serbia, lying almost on the Hungarian border. Here, I hoped to catch a glimpse of the Hungarian influence on architecture and design. To get there I needed to head northwest along roads marked as tiny white lines on my map. It was not easy to navigate and my concentration had evaporated with the euphoria over such a smooth border crossing.

Away from the villages, we careered across the open plains of Vojvodina in the heat of the day with not a soul or Fića in sight. Fields of dead sunflowers bowed their burnt heads and acres of cereal crops waited to be harvested. The flat, dry, emptiness of the landscape filled me with unease. It was as if we had unwittingly driven through an invisible door into a world where civilisation no longer existed. Perhaps it was just the heat playing tricks with my mind. I had been told that Vojvodina was a strange place and at this moment I quite believed it. Tito was a lone vehicle travelling along a burrow-like network of lanes edged high on either side with agricultural crops. The narrowness of the roads and lack of signage made me feel increasingly claustrophobic.

Eventually, a road sign to Čoka appeared. I was completely off course but thankful to find civilisation close by. It was a sleepy town with one-storey houses running down either side of the main street, some behind front gardens bursting with flowers. Nothing moved in the intense heat of the day. I was by now very hot, and light-headed with thirst. Serbian time was one hour behind Romanian lunchtime. A restaurant festooned in white sun umbrellas lay empty. Inside, a waiter busily cleaned glasses in the gloom behind a long, high bar.

"*Dobar dan!*" he said cheerily.

Armed with my map, I ventured over to him. He offered me a drink. No money, I replied apologetically.

"*Nema problemo*. On the house!"

I sipped gratefully on a chilled glass of *Schweppes* and spread out my map across the bar. The waiter spoke a little English and German mixed together. He traced the route I should take to Subotica and then pointed to the small town from where he came in Bosnia. He now lived in Serbia with his wife. Here he could get a job and things were easier. He did not say whether he was Bosnian Serb, Bosnian Croat, Bosniak, Croat, Albanian, Kosovar, Roma or Serb but with him this did not arise and I found myself realising how unusual this was in a world where I had become accustomed to everyone identifying themselves through their family roots, their wives, their generally mixed allegiances through marriage, their political alliances or their despair in understanding the very complex world they now lived in, filled with ethnic divisions and political manipulations. But not this man, and I found that rather refreshing.

The bar was cool and the drink revived my waning energy. We communicated in a pigeon language, somehow managing to sustain a conversation about Serbia, Bosnia, roads and Zastavas before he waved me goodbye with a "*Sretan put!*" (good journey). I drove off bolstered by his Balkan generosity and friendliness towards me, a mere passing stranger. As I navigated along the narrow lanes of rural Vojvodina, I began to overcome my fear of this flat rural environment with its strange introverted atmosphere, though I was still glad to join a stream of open-backed lorries piled high with harvested tomatoes and peaches making their way to Subotica.

- Subotica -

The buildings, the colours and the architecture of Subotica were like nothing I had seen in the Balkans. They were bright and decorative – a style apparently referred to as *'middle European secessionist architecture'*, with a touch of *'Art Nouveau'* thrown in. The town emitted a friendly, relaxed air. A fountain in the main square had become an impromptu swimming pool, and in the heat of the afternoon the elderly sat on benches in the shade while others drank coffee in a nearby café, all watching the Roma children as they laughed and dived in and out of the jets of water which would unexpectedly shoot upwards as they swam.

I followed signs on which the words Hotel Gloria had been ornately written. It was not listed in my guidebook – a new hotel. As we emerged into the car park, a group of young men sporting tracksuits with *'Srbija'* written on their backs were deep in discussion with what looked like their team trainers. Looking rather conspicuous in my white Zastava, I parked and peeled my hot, tired body out of the car and into the cool of the hotel reception followed by a trail of curious eyes. I took an attic room with a spectacular view of the City Hall's magnificent clock tower. The daring, flamboyant architecture somehow did not fit in with my perceptions of Serbia.

The evening ritual was a more male-dominated activity in Subotica. The town's inhabitants apparently include an ethnic group known as the Bunjevci, who originate from Herzegovina, of Bosnia and Herzegovina. They migrated to Croatia and then to the Vojvodina in the 17th century. Although often referred to as Croat, they are Bunjevac, one of many minority ethnic groups who live in this uniquely autonomous region of Serbia. It was impossible to distinguish who was Hungarian, Bunjevci, Croat or Serb, not to mention any of the other ethnic groups, as they walked together through the town and drank in the cafés, just as I had witnessed everywhere else in my travels. As the evening light faded, the streets became quiet. The town's lighting was poor. I found sanctuary in a Hungarian restaurant, where the Magyar speciality of the day was catfish served with a selection of sauces and a generous portion of potatoes. A band of middle-aged men set up their instruments and played while a woman with brightly dyed red hair sang at top volume to an audience of three tables. Around one table, four men sat playing cards, becoming progressively drunk on *rakija*. This, the preferred national drink, as well as that of the whole ex-Yugoslav region, is consumed at every opportunity including breakfast – although I have been assured that this is purely for medicinal reasons. Two elderly couples waltzed across a makeshift dance floor in front of the band. The card players' interest in their cards was being distracted by my presence. I ate self-consciously and made a swift exit away from their hazy-eyed glances and into the mediocre light of Subotica's streets.

Shadows can play tricks with one's mind, all at once becoming a threat. It was true that travelling alone did make me feel vulnerable and insecure at times, not helped by the fact that I had no real grasp of the languages. The physical size of both Balkan men and women could be quite intimidating. I quickened my pace back to the hotel. The lift doors were being held for me. As I stepped in, one of these tall formidable types stood looking at me curiously. He was a teenager and already huge.

"Hello," I volunteered courageously, "Are you playing in a sports tournament in Subotica?"

"Yes," the young *'Srbija'* track-suited man replied proudly in carefully pronounced English, "It is the under 19s football. Tomorrow we are playing Israel."

"Ah, and do you think you will win?" I asked.

"Of course!" he said, with such conviction it caught me off-guard. I hid a smile.

"Good luck!" I said as the lift reached my floor and I was rewarded with an unexpected, bashful smile in response.

As I clicked my bedroom door shut, a clap of thunder heralded the beginnings of a thunderstorm with a dramatic display of lightning and torrential rain. Barefoot, I balanced on the arm of the sofa, opened the slanting louvred window and peered out over the rooftops. Poor Tito; I hoped he would be alright. Lightning lit up the clock tower of the City Hall. Was this heralding a change, I wondered? Perhaps cooler, rainy days were on their way.

- Subotica/Petrovaradin (116km) -

I bade farewell to Subotica – a town influenced over the centuries by the Hapsburgs, the Hungarians, Austro-Hungarian rule, Jews, Catholics, Serbs, Croats, and the Bunjevac, to name but a few. What did the future hold for this town? The large Jewish population had been rounded up during World War II and sent to camps where most had perished and those who had possibly survived certainly never returned to Subotica although, ironically, the town's synagogue still stands, elegantly restored, but closed for viewings; many Hungarians had left when Milosevic became President of Serbia and Vojvodina's powers of autonomy were considerably reduced; only the street names written in Cyrillic, Latin and Hungarian seemed constant. An illustrious city of many cultures symbolically defined by their architecture, now disintegrating and, sadly, little money to fix it.

Tito appeared to be no worse from last night's downpour and, apart from a small damp patch on the back window ledge, he was still dry. This was a relief, and we headed for Novi Sad via the 22 road, which runs almost parallel to the faster European network road the E75. The 22 had definitely seen better days. It had been constructed in concrete sections jointed with flexible strips. However, these connections had long perished and as a result we *'clickety-clacked'* our way southwards over the open joints, passing more sunflower fields – here their large heads were gazing happily upwards at the sun – edged with rows of brightly painted beehives.

As the morning advanced into afternoon, the temperature rose and any fears I may have had of inclement weather vanished. The heat became almost unbearable. A burning air streamed through the hole at my feet despite my careful placement of the rubber foot mats while hot air tore through the window, like a hairdryer on my face. As we approached Novi Sad, my thoughts centred on finding a cool place to sit cradling an ice-cold drink. The town, however, seemed impenetrable. Car parks, one-way streets and a pedestrianised zone kept the historic core of the city at an unreachable distance. I would have to abandon Tito if I wanted to see anything. It all seemed too difficult today. Frustrated, I took the road leading out of the city and came up against my old friend the River Danube and a cool breeze wafting gently through the window. I pulled over beside a café and unstuck myself from the car seat. My shorts had suctioned themselves to my legs like cling film and my shirt stuck to my back. I had never felt so hot or uncomfortable in all my Tito voyaging days.

Conscious of my appearance, I walked slowly towards the café trying to capture as much air as possible between my clothes and skin in a vain attempt to dry out. The humidity was unbearable. I made it into a welcoming cool shade and there I sat for the next two hours – the waiter quick to replenish my glass with another fizzing, bubbling bottle of *Schweppes*. I gazed up at the stone fortifications of Petrovaradin's fortress at the base of which the Danube glided past. Here the river was a slow-moving, more docile body of water, *so different from the one we had crossed from Bulgaria into Romania*, I thought, as I looked towards the bridge that would take us back over the Danube River once more; away from Novi Sad, and southwards into the geographical heartland of the Balkan peninsula.

———

B ullets of rain sporadically hit the windscreen. "At last!" I thought, as dark clouds gathered threateningly. A sign pinned to a lamp post read *'Sveti Georgije Hotel'* and then in brackets underneath were the words *'Doss House'* with an arrow to the right. Impetuously, I swung off, amused by the hotel's choice of advertising slogan. A young man sat locked in concentration behind his computer at reception. He looked up distractedly as I pushed open the front door.

"*Engleski*?" I said hopefully.

"But of course," he said with a welcoming flourish.

I was possibly the only guest tonight in a perfectly decent hotel which did not remotely resemble a doss house. At that moment the heavens opened. It rained with such force that the humidity level evaporated almost instantaneously and the heaviness lifted from within my head. A long cool shower and I felt human once more.

A young woman stood talking to the receptionist. No evening meals were being served but there was excellent *domaća kuhinja* (home-cooked food) at a restaurant not far from here. "She will show you the way," the receptionist said encouragingly.

The woman gave me a shy smile and off we set. After a

little hesitation, she decided to try out her English on me. It was, in fact, very good and as we chatted our way down the residential streets, jumping the rain puddles, she confided, "You know, many people want to leave Serbia now but I do not understand this. I love my country and I love Novi Sad; I am happy here and I do not want to go somewhere else."

She explained that she had a job at the local hospital and although she did not have a very high position she hoped that some day she would be a nurse.

"You need to know people to have a chance. If you do not have a recommendation, it is not easy for you. I was just lucky. I am new at the hospital; I have no connections or money to help me but maybe in time I will be promoted."

She did not seem to care that the institutional system in Serbia was clearly corrupt; she just accepted that this was so and hoped things would change in time. Her love for her country was admirable. She seemed unaffected by the war and Serbia's current political dilemmas. Her life was simple. She had a job, she loved her family and her country and she had no intention of leaving.

Her view was in complete contrast to the hotel receptionist's, who could not wait to inform me that everything was a mess. "Have you heard of Serbian spite?" he asked conspiratorially.

"No," I responded hesitantly.

"Well, you need to understand this concept to understand Serbia, the Serbian people, the mentality, the politics." He laughed self-deprecatingly. "We do things to spite ourselves and everyone else and look where we are!"

He did not elaborate but instead changed the topic by announcing that he would not be staying much longer in his country. Like so many young Serbs, he was fed up. "We are all trying to find ways to get out. We are not able to travel. Everything is difficult for us. I want to go to Canada and start a new life with my girlfriend. I have the visa forms and I am studying IT management skills so I can get a job."

He could not care less about Kosovo or the politics of Serbia; he just wanted to live and be free. It was interesting that neither of these young people had any inclination for politics, and whether Kosovo should belong to them; that was for politicians and nationalists. For them, what really mattered was the chance of a better life with opportunities, whether they found those in Serbia or somewhere else.

- Petrovaradin/Belgrade (77km) -

The following morning my *'Doss House'* served me a strong traditional coffee. It was a question of knowing when to start drinking and when to stop. Drink before the coffee has settled properly and you end up sifting ground coffee sediment through your teeth; drink too much, and the sediment is again waiting for you as a thick layer at the bottom of the cup. It was an art I had not yet mastered, but as Balkan coffee tastes delicious, it was well worth persevering.

Fortified with caffeine (and sediment), I set off to find the old fortress in Petrovaradin. A cluster of small lanes at its base contained a mix of stone houses in various states of either disrepair or homely elegance with beautiful ornate façades. Each had a finely carved timber door with intricate plasterwork around the windows; some even had an oriel window, and despite many looking rather dilapidated, they all seemed to be inhabited.

Armed with a pastry from the only bakery shop I could find open, I climbed a mass of winding stone steps, quickening my pace through a darkened tunnel, up to the fortress's heights. The place was deserted. I felt a little spooked. A strong wind blew and dark rain-filled clouds scudded across the sky. I felt cold in my shorts and shirt, hugging myself for warmth, taking a large bite out of my chocolate croissant.

A group of elderly German tourists appeared on the ramparts looking equally chilled but better equipped in windcheaters and armed with umbrellas. They traipsed past looking curiously at me sitting alone hugging my knees, clearly under-dressed in the biting wind, and clutching a half-eaten pastry. How lucky I was not to be one of them; I watched as any strays were quickly shepherded back into the main group and forced to listen to the boring monotonous voice of the group's guide. They shuffled on, leaving me to view the scene alone. The Danube meanders wide and deep, flowing past and beyond a mish-mash of mediaeval red-tiled roofs. Multiple bridges span the river. Many are new constructions following the NATO bombings in 1999 in response to Serbia's military actions in Kosovo. They have been rebuilt and any signs of the destruction have been swept away so, remarkably, it was hard to tell from up here which ones had been destroyed.

———

The bus doors banged open and I climbed the rickety steps. The driver looked at me in surprise and beamed. He was a good-looking man in his 30s with blue eyes and light brown hair.

I said, "*Sveti Georgije* Hotel?" and with my hand indicated that it was straight on.

"Ok, no problem," he said in English, and shook his head when I proffered a handful of dinars towards him for the fare.

The old bus clattered along packed with people all dressed for the weather. I stood amongst them feeling extremely self-conscious in my summer clothing but glad not to be walking the long route back to the hotel. The bus stopped a couple of times and more passengers squeezed on until it was full to bursting. Through his rear-view mirror the driver watched with interest as I peered out to see where I was. I pushed the button for the next stop, climbing over shopping bags and fighting my way past the other standing passengers, who were so busy staring at me they did not realise I was trying to get to the front of the bus.

"*Hvala,*" I said a little prematurely, as the bus drew to a stop at a red traffic light.

The driver looked at me with his piercing blue eyes and said, "Don't go. Stay." And he banged his hand down on the steering wheel for greater emphasis.

The passengers turned their heads expectantly and waited for my response. Embarrassed by his sudden attention, I stared at him, not knowing what to say. Did he mean stay here, on the bus? Here in Novi Sad? Here in Serbia? Or here with him?

"Sadly, I have to go to Belgrade," I said rather lamely, although flattered that this good-looking man wished me to stay.

"Oh well, that is a shame," he said with a smile of regret and I laughed at his response. The lights turned green and the bus trundled forward to the stop. The doors slapped open and I climbed off.

"*Ciao.*"

The bus moved off and the passengers watched me cross the road, their eyes following me back down the street towards the '*Doss House*'.

Halfway down the street garage doors were flung open wide. I stuck my head in for a closer look. A couple of men came out carrying large white buckets back to their cars. A machine stretched the length of one side of the garage and in it mountains of tomatoes were being washed in an elongated stainless steel basin and then pushed through some kind of mashing system. A bright red tomato purée poured from a spout into one of the many waiting white buckets on the ground. The place was going like a fair, with a steady stream of customers filling bottles and buckets with this beautiful bright red liquid. A car backed in too close and a bucket of tomato purée tipped over, its red contents gushing across the garage floor. A volley of protestations were directed at the clumsy customer, who looked on, completely unabashed by what he had just done. I backed out of the mayhem clutching my modest purchase of the red stuff, suitably impressed by this thriving organic enterprise, blissfully unaware that European Union rules would probably ruin its spontaneous existence – although hopefully that was some way off.

———

I sat with my foot on the accelerator and raised the choke lever to full throttle. Tito fired into life and we hiccupped our way past the tomato purée garage and back out onto the open road towards Sremski Karlovci, the summer home of the Patriarch of the Serbian Orthodox Church. I wondered if I should pay an unannounced courtesy call for, although I had never met the man, it was his churches that I and a whole team from Serbia and Kosovo had been repairing in Kosovo for the past five years.

Saturday in Sremski Karlovci was a hive of activity. The sun was endeavouring to come out and the market was in full swing. The gates to the Patriarch's summer palace remained firmly shut and very uninviting, which was perhaps just as well. In contrast, the school, which as an institution dated back to the 18th century, was buzzing with young life. I wandered along the streets of this old town and into the local museum. As I was the only visitor, the museum curator began following me around, a severe frown set firmly on her face. To try to break the intensity of her constant shadowing, I tried a few words of Serbian from my guidebook. With that she clapped her hands together in delight, her demeanour changing instantly from one of cautious communist severity to one of natural grace. We ventured through the museum's rooms with hesitant Serbian and English, laughing as she tried to explain, and I to understand, what some of the exhibits represented – and although I did not leave any the wiser, the engaging personality of this middle-aged lady was priceless.

———

Tito and I continued to jolt down the badly maintained 22 road towards Belgrade passing through small towns, all of which had a statue prominently located in their main streets. These statues date back to President Tito's days and the communist era. They depict men of strength, their silhouettes dominating the streetscape from where they can be seen by everyone. Although most people were more concerned with whether the bus was coming or whether they could get across the road with their grocery shopping, I could not help being captivated by these powerful figures. As I gazed in awe at these visions of muscular strength, I became aware that I was being as closely scrutinised by three young men in the car behind. It was not me but Tito that was fuelling their excitement. One leaned forward with his mobile phone pressed up against the windscreen to take a photo. I waved in the rear-view mirror and they overtook, tooting cheerfully as they did so, staring at my Zastava from Skopje with delighted fascination. The old 22 road led me effortlessly southwards and as I entered Belgrade, I continued to be charmed and intrigued by the diversity of this Balkan world.

- Belgrade -

The buzz and adrenalin of Belgrade was catching: a place I knew vaguely and where I had friends. The 22 road, for all its faults, had led me straight into the centre of town with no navigational effort on my part. Tito was safely stowed in a long-term car park, the sun was shining once more and I was excited to be back in a capital city. For two whole days and nights I would not be a tourist and would not be alone. I could relax without having to worry about a thing.

Dragomir and Nada are two opposites. Dragomir is dynamic, a showman, quick to laugh and tell a joke, whereas Nada is a more careful, thoughtful person. She frowns at Dragomir's flippant remarks, but underneath there is a serious side to him which creeps out when you least expect it. Nada and Dragomir are respected academics, both married with children and have considerable experience in the cultural heritage sector, holding high positions of responsibility. They are sincere people, surviving as best they can in a Serbia in complete turmoil as a result of the 1990s Balkans war; a war which has affected them, their families, their children, their friends and the country they love.

"Everything is a mess," Nada said regretfully, fiddling with her large square-shaped glasses, "All our young and talented people have left Serbia, while the nationalists are still fighting over Kosovo – and it is too late for that! I really do not know what our future will be and it is very sad. We have gone through a very dark period."

Dragomir nodded. He feared for the young. "They do not want to do anything; they are not motivated. I have two sons and they have no energy or motivation and I worry about their future."

It was true: Serbia had many difficult hurdles to overcome, one being to openly accept its guilt and thus allow its people to face the truth. It would take courage to address this.

———

D ragomir pored over my map, his silver-grey hair glinting in the candlelight. Where should I go next? What route should I take through Serbia to reach Bosnia and Herzegovina? I swept up pools of rich pepper sauce with a final morsel of steak and savoured the decadence of my dish, which Dragomir insisted I must have – a speciality of the Royal Knez restaurant – and I was not disappointed. The restaurant was timber-panelled and divided into individual dining niches with comfy banquettes. Politicians still came here for private conversations and good food – if only the four walls, which dated back to the late 19th century, could talk. The food was fabulous, the décor conservative yet elegant. Dragomir felt I should be treated to the best Belgrade could offer; after all, it was not every day a traveller came to town in a Zastava. Nada was equally excited to be there. Her last visit had been before the war and she was wondering what had changed; it seemed nothing had, in an otherwise much-altered world. We turned back to the subject of my next destination. Nada hesitated at my idea of going westwards and across the border into Bosnia through Srebenica. Her professional expertise was in cultural heritage and she was adamant I should see the Drina River by entering Bosnia from the south west of Serbia. It would mean driving across the Tara Mountains. Dragomir agreed enthusiastically. From here I could visit Mokra Gora and then cross the border into Višegrad, the town which inspired the well-known book *The Bridge on the Drina*. They were both in agreement – a more culturally rewarding route. I nodded, grateful for their advice, but decided not to make any decisions that evening.

- New Belgrade -

The "new town" was conceived after World War II and has undergone much criticism. Without doubt it is growing in size, and a place where designers and architects can flex their design skills. Towering high-rise apartment blocks built with the architectural concept of socially mixed communities, not socially separated ones. They dominate the skyline to the south of the city centre, reflecting the communist style. Liked by some, disliked by others, the area houses many and lures many more of Belgrade's inhabitants away from the crowded city centre with the promise of a better quality of living. It seems to have worked.

Dragomir and his family lived on the twelfth floor of one of these blocks. All around were open spaces, the river, bicycle tracks, and an island, Ada Ciganlija dedicated almost entirely to every sporting activity and just a ten-minute ferry ride away, sitting in the middle of the Sava River. People seemed content and an atmosphere of community togetherness prevailed. My perception of tower blocks was limited to the UK experience; the reputation of being associated with poverty, graffiti, unemployment, gang culture and class division. Here in ex-Yugoslavia the concept of social classes was not developed to the same degree.

Every city I had visited in the Balkans had had its fair share of dreary-looking high-rise communist apartment blocks. I had eyed them with uncertainty, curiosity, and always from a distance. Here it seemed apartment blocks did not mean 'ghettos'. The area housed everyone, from the director to the cleaner. Snobbery, whether looking up or down, did not appear to exist in the way I had been accustomed to expect – however much I disliked it. We took the lift to the twelfth floor and I stood on Dragomir's kitchen balcony marvelling at the view of tower blocks, each constructed on a slightly different axis, and reflected on how social integration can work, given the right conditions.

Dragomir pointed to an apartment block. Radovan Karadžić had lived there for two years before being arrested in July 2008, maintaining his anonymity.

"None of us saw Karadžić or recognised him. He was

living under our noses for two years," Dragomir said incredulously.

- Belgrade/Valjevo (85km) -

Belgrade sits at the junction of two grand rivers; the Sava and the mighty Danube. Perhaps it is their combined strength that has created such tall people. They towered over me in huge numbers and Nebojša was no exception. The familiar broad figure strolled amicably towards me. We had not met since his visit to Kosovo two years ago. He had the height and strength to appear formidable yet, ironically, his work entailed intricate delicacy and skill. He was a wall paintings conservator – a master of his craft and greatly admired by his colleagues. I sat with a cup of the ubiquitous traditional Turkish coffee, which in Serbia can also be referred to as a Balkan coffee or indeed a Serbian coffee, depending upon to whom you were talking.

Nebojša laughed heartily at my account of Tito's breakdowns and with a twinkle in his eye said, "Ah the Zastava! You know, Fićas, they will go on forever! You will not have any problem now that you are in the countries of ex-Yugoslavia. Everyone knows how to fix a Fića. All you need is a spoon!"

I believed his proclamation held more than an ounce of truth and strangely this reassured me. It seemed everyone had owned a Zastava at some point and they were all more than familiar with the idiosyncrasies of the car's insides. So as I departed Belgrade with Nebojša's words of comfort ringing in my ears, I felt more certain than ever that perhaps I could make it full-circle to Skopje.

N ada could not resist being a passenger in Tito. As she did not drive herself, she had a driver and he led the way in the official office car out of the city through Belgrade's rush-hour traffic. A Roma boy came up to the window begging for money. Nada shooed him away with a stream of Serbian as we sat sandwiched between vehicles pushing in from all sides, rendered stationary by the roundabout. Giving way to another vehicle was not an option considered by anyone during the afternoon rush hour.

"Emma, you are very brave," announced Nada. "Do you never feel frightened being alone, or scared that something might happen?"

It was not the first time I had been asked this question and not wishing to "jinx" my good fortune, I replied cautiously, "Well, no, not really."

It was true I had been careful never to drive at night. Breaking down had been my only concern and this had indeed already occurred on several occasions but with no catastrophic repercussions. However, I knew the next part of my journey would probably be the most challenging of my trip so far with numerous mountain ranges to overcome across southwest Serbia and through Bosnia and Herzegovina until we reached the coast of Croatia. *One day at a time*, I thought.

Nada's driver successfully guided us through the contorted traffic jams and out onto the 22 road, which would merge with the minor 4 road heading south west to Valjevo. Grateful for the escort through the city, I said my goodbyes. As they turned back towards the city, I faced the next leg of my journey, wondering how long it would be before I would see that buzzing capital again.

The road was mostly flat, passing through villages on the way; I was glad to be on the road again, and in the countryside. The journey took longer than I had estimated and the sun had just set as we entered Valjevo. In the semi-gloom I ended up as usual in a petrol station to ask directions. The attendant nodded towards my car.

"Fića! Skopje?"

"*Da, da,*" I said.

He laughed in disbelief, as did everyone else around him. He directed me to the Grand Hotel with a "*Links, links,*" ("left, left").

"*Hvala!*"

We drove across a bridge and into the hotel car park. I was faced with the bland concrete architectural form of a former communist state-owned hotel. Its wide signature designed entrance, long reception desk, and deserted, faceless atmosphere was formal, functional, dated and over-priced but it would do for one night.

In Valjevo the ritual evening walk was in full swing and as a foreigner in town, I attracted the usual local curiosity. I followed the crowd, ending up in a fast food shop selling hot savoury pastries. The shop assistant handed me a packet of sauce to accompany the tall popcorn shaped-box of pastries she had enthusiastically selected for me and I headed back to the hotel for a bedroom supper in front of Serbian TV, feeling a bit lost at being alone once more after my hugely social time with Nada and Dragomir.

- Valjevo/Bajina Bašta (55km) -

The bass sounds of modern Serbian pop music vibrated harshly through the hotel speakers. A cheese omelette was delivered to my table along with a cup of strong coffee and large hunks of white bread. It was the most delicious yet least peaceful breakfast I had experienced on my travels, but fortified and perhaps now marginally deaf, I was ready to face the day.

Dragomir had suggested I visit his friend and Director of the National Museum. The Director did not speak English but his assistant was volunteered to translate. Although he was busy preparing for a visit from Belgrade dignitaries later that day, the Director was keen to sit and talk to me about Zastavas and my journey. He warned of large mountains ahead but if I should break down, I was just to call him. His assistant translated with mild amusement until it became clear that he would be the one sent to rescue me if I did break down!

With the familiar Balkan courtesy, nothing was too much trouble; I was given a complementary tour of the town's two museums and art gallery, both alive with activity in anticipation of the impending dignitaries' visit. The exhibits portrayed tales of Serbian uprisings against Ottoman Rule and presented Valjevo as a fashionable and wealthy place in times gone by. Today, it was just one of many small towns in Serbia, which was bombed by NATO in 1999 in response to Serbia's military action in Kosovo and, like most in the region, had a struggling economy, post-communism and post-1990s war.

It was September; the summer holidays were over and a new school year had started. Children of all ages mingled in the streets carrying books and brightly coloured satchels on their backs. The sun was out but it was notably cooler and the air was fresh. Autumn was on its way. An elderly man walked down the cobble-stoned street of the old town. He was wearing trainers, thick woollen green socks, baggy green woollen trousers, a voluminous white shirt and a green hat which folded flat lengthways down its centre. A style originating from the 18th century, it was known as a Šajkača hat worn by Yugoslav Partisans, older people in rural villages across former Yugoslavia and more recently associated with Bosnian Serb military commanders during the recent 1990s war in Bosnia. The man was most certainly rural and indeed the first person I had seen dressed in even a remotely traditional way. Over his shoulder was slung a modern black sports bag with the word *'Speed'* written on it. He stopped in front of a café terrace to talk to a couple of men drinking coffee and soaking up the sun's rays. He leant against his two-toned wooden walking stick, smoothing his fabulously shaped cavalry moustache – one to match Vuk Karadžić's. Known for creating the modern-day Serbian language, Karadžić had also found time to grow a fabulous moustache and his figure stood proudly in the main pedestrian street for all to admire.

A row of old houses lined the cobbled street of the old town with timber flowers detailing their quaint windows. Signs of change were definitely afoot. Many of these homes had been abandoned and left to fall down, to be replaced with taller concrete framed structures, thus changing the streetscape forever. It was an increasingly common trend and one dominating the Balkan landscape with no thought or respect for the cultural value of these traditional towns and villages. I sighed at the inevitable loss from another, more charming era.

I filled Tito with petrol at last night's friendly garage and we were waved off with a *"Sretan put!"*

It was early afternoon and the temperature was rising into the high twenties. I chewed rapidly on a peppermint as we headed up the first real hill we had seen since Bulgaria. Tito had had an easy time over the last few weeks with nothing much to challenge him; now things were definitely about to change and I was not entirely sure how he was going to cope. There was only one thing to do – keep going and hope for the best.

We were heading for the town of Bajina Bašta and for the next few hours Tito climbed and conquered the mountain ranges, puffing, wheezing, spluttering and labouring. Still, at our sedate pace of 20km/h and with several rests, he was surviving. Apart from visiting a 13th century monastery and disturbing a sleeping monk, which did not make us too popular, there were little signs of human activity up in the hills. The odd car passed by quickly, leaving us to slowly climb and descend, climb and descend. Rounding one of many gently sweeping corners, I pulled over to give Tito a breather. The road stretched out ahead along the breadth of the mountainside with breathtaking views opening out across the valley below and to more mountains beyond. As I opened the engine door, two cars suddenly swung into view from the other direction and skidded to a halt. Doors flew open and the drivers got out, their bodies a tense mix of agitation and confrontation. I absorbed the scene from behind Tito's engine door with some hesitation. They were a good 700 metres away but it was a bleak stretch of road except for the farm on the corner beside me, but the farmer was herding his goats up the hill. With no mobile phone coverage and a car with no "oompf", any thought of a quick getaway was out of the question. The argument rolled on until one driver got back into his car, did a U-turn up the hill and drove out of sight. The other driver stood for a while smoking a cigarette, looking thoughtfully in our general direction, before he too got into his car, made a U-turn and went back over the hill. All was silent but for the bleating of a goat on the mountainside. I lowered the engine door and climbed back into the car. Tito had cooled and we began our ascent once more through a spectacular landscape of pastoral mountains while I speculated on what this meeting had been about.

———

I was not quite sure why I had decided to stop in Bajina Bašta. I suppose it was getting late in the afternoon and I had had enough of mountains for one day. My guidebook did not say anything about the place except that it presented a good base for exploring the Tara National Park – our next destination. All signs of the sun had disappeared, to be replaced by a low black cloudy ceiling of gloom. I circled the town, trying to spot a place to stay. It was the red brick former communist state-owned Drina Hotel or nothing. The interior did nothing to raise my spirits. I lugged my rucksack behind the hyper-stressed male receptionist who, moving at speed on his long thin legs, assured me that there was a lift in the hotel but just not in this wing. I followed him as best I could down a string of corridors to the room I had been allocated. Everything was decorated in mustard yellow. The colour was replicated on the walls, doors, fixtures, fittings and duvet cover. I felt faintly sick. The bathroom was in need of considerable modernisation although it was clean – relatively speaking – and the room did have a double aspect view, but I slumped down on the bed feeling unusually deflated despite Tito's heroic conquest across a challenging set of mountains.

From my bedroom windows I could look down on the residential street below. A man on crutches made his way slowly down the street and entered a house. He only had one leg. Had the town been affected by the war? There was but a passing reference to Bajina Bašta's proximity to the Tara National Park and it being a 'pleasant border town' in my guidebook, nothing more. As evening fell, lights began to come on in every house. I put on a cardigan and made my way back along the hotel corridors, most of which stood in darkness. It was like something out of the film *The Shining*. I left my key with the receptionist and went out in search of coffee. The usual evening ritual was underway, with young and old walking or sitting around, but the atmosphere was very subdued. Tito sat outside the hotel, the only car in the street, and I wondered whether he would be safe. I walked along the streets of Bajina Bašta, intrigued by the shop window displays. Everything was very old-fashioned, as if the town had been left behind by the world – certainly a far cry from Belgrade or even Valjevo. Up a narrow side street a café served cakes and pastries and I sat outside to watch the world go by, but not much was going by off the main street. Two women came in and ordered coffee to accompany their stream of cigarettes and non-stop chatter. I paid and went back to the hotel to put on something warmer. Perhaps the cooler weather was affecting everyone's humour.

The sound of British voices at reception came as a shock. My world of lone-traveller in the Balkans had been invaded. They were a retired couple on a walking holiday and based in Bajina Bašta for a few nights.

"A strange place," the man confided quietly into my ear.

He was right. It did feel strange, uncomfortable; I could not quite understand why. I gladly exchanged my shorts for a pair of jeans too warm to wear until now and set out once again around the town. Wood lay stacked high against the walls of houses in readiness for the winter. It would soon be an isolated, cold place, I thought. A pizza takeaway shop had a couple of tables for customers. The two female cooks chatted and laughed together, creating a bubble of positive atmosphere in a town of otherwise distant – unapproachable – inhabitants. I ate my doughy pizza slice and ventured out once more. The evening ritual walk had not missed Bajina Bašta but it was dark with no streetlights. I felt distinctly uneasy as though I should not be here, that I was intruding. I retreated back to the hotel and opened the guidebook's section on history. Perhaps the answers lay there.

- Bajina Bašta/Mokra Gora(47km) -

Unusually, I was awake early. I stared up at the grey sky from my bedroom window. A white dot on the distant mountains continued to puzzle me. What was it? I pulled out my binoculars and scanned the landscape – it looked like a mosque. Reaching for my compass, the arrow swung round. I looked again at the map. West. Then the penny dropped. Less than 30km away, over the mountains, lay Srebrenica in eastern Bosnia. Was that the reason everything felt so closed here? Dragomir had said many Serbs had been killed in the region. War. From the little I had read last night, there had been a horrific loss of Muslim life – civilian life – just over the border. I knew about Srebrenica. It had happened in Višegrad also. But this was the Serbian side and no doubt the civilians had been affected too, although my guidebook said nothing.

There was a border crossing here at Bajina Bašta. I contemplated whether to take this route into Bosnia instead of the one further south through the Tara Mountains to Višegrad. Either direction looked fairly isolated territory. What if Tito broke down? I felt nervous suddenly – unprepared to enter a region which I knew had been rocked with grief and ethnic sensitivities. But how do you prepare? The lives of ordinary Bosniaks, Croats and Serbs had all been deeply affected. Would it be provocative to be driving a Zastava through Srebenica? How would I be received? Was I over-reacting? Was it wise to be travelling alone? Bajina Bašta had sucked the courage and positivity out of me and I was no longer sure what to do.

Instinct prevailed. I would leave Srebrenica for another time, in a more reliable car and with a better understanding of what to expect. I certainly did not wish to provoke anyone or unwittingly put myself in danger. The decision made, I left Bajina Bašta and followed the Drina River, eyeing the Bosnian landscape across the river with interest – just a river separating countries. It had become a familiar scene and yet still surprised me coming from Britain; invasion is a real threat, and unsurprisingly boundary lines have changed many times in the course of southeast European history.

———

The Drina River road led upstream to a dam. Beyond lay Lake Perućac. The local tourist map illustrated it as a place with water sports and sunbathing areas but the path was barred. I was reluctant to explore. A police car crawled past. I pretended not to notice, acting the tourist taking photos. I drove back and forth along the narrow river road, passing clusters of roadside graves, trying to work out which of these minor roads leading off would take us across the mountains to Mokra Gora. Some villagers watched with interest our to-ings and fro-ings. The police turned up again but no one attempted to question my indecisive behaviour. It was a guess but eventually I took the plunge and we headed upwards. A heavily loaded log truck slogged its way past. Then we were left to ourselves. The view down into the valley was spectacular; the River Drina stretching back and forth, a natural delineation between Serbia and Bosnia and Herzegovina. The immediate territory on the Bosnian side, close to the River Drina, was now referred to as Republika Srpska. Although a part of Bosnia and Herzegovina, it was largely inhabited by Bosnian Serbs – a result of the war and mass ethnic cleansing of Muslims (Bosniaks) from the region. Until now, thoughts of war and politics had been far from my mind but as Tito spluttered and puffed his way up the steep hairpin bends, I realised how little I knew about this region.

The road weaved onwards and upwards. Tunnels cut through the mountainside and led us into the Tara National Park, an area of protected natural beauty. Mitrovac village lay ahead. A cluster of buildings – all shut. With no road signs, I drove on, hoping I was going in the right direction. The minor tarmac road led to a crossroads. Two men had stopped and got out to have a chat, their vehicles straddling the road in both directions. I pulled over. They looked at me and then at Tito and smiled at one another.

"*Dobar dan*," greeted one of them. "*Makedonski*, eh?" he said in an enquiring tone, "Skopje?"

"*Dobar dan*," I responded. "*Da, da*. But me, *Engleski*."

"*Engleski*?" They looked at me doubtfully.

I pointed to Mokra Gora and raised my shoulders as if to ask which way. One of them took the map from me and put on his glasses. Conferring with his friend, they both decided I had to turn left and then head straight – or so I gathered from their frantic arm movements. I hesitated. My map illustrated a minor road all the way to Mokra Gora. This road to the left was anything but tarmac. But they were adamant. Straight on would take me to the lake, they said, stabbing at the map's blue blob.

"Ok, ok. *Hvala*."

The road surface was well-compacted and easy to drive on but before long all that changed. A vertical slope of thick loose gravel and numerous potholes confronted us. We surged forward but second gear was not powerful enough to get Tito up such a steep and unstable surface and he stalled. I needed a 4-wheel drive for this! I pushed firmly down on the brake, flung the gear stick into neutral and pulled heavily upwards on the handbrake. Now what to do? Switching feet on the brake pedal, my right foot was now free for the accelerator. With my left foot pushing firmly down on the brake pedal, I let go of the handbrake, turned the ignition key and swiftly transferred my right hand back to the handbrake. So far so good. It was just a question of sequence and coordination, I kept telling myself. If I did not get it right, we would hurtle backwards with uncertain speed down the steep track. I did not dare to think about the consequences. If only I had a proper functioning handbrake! Transferring my left foot from the brake to the clutch, and with my left hand across my body, I could put Tito into first gear. *Ok, here goes!* With a deep breath, I lowered the handbrake and put just enough balanced pressure on the accelerator and clutch to hold him. How impressed my driving instructor would have been! Gently adding more pressure to the accelerator and releasing the clutch, Tito charged upwards with a spray of gravel. 'These cars are great for off roading,' John had said excitedly when I had taken on the earthen bank in Skopje all those weeks ago. Little had I known I would be putting Tito's abilities to this kind of test.

Revving hard on the accelerator while levering up and down on the clutch, we made it halfway up the slope before stalling again. I went through the same start-up procedure and off we set with a lurch. The accelerator pedal was hard to the floor and first gear was engaged. Tito tore assuredly up the hill with amazing tenacity, an inner strength exuding from within him. I laughed out loud in surprise. With dust clouds billowing behind us, he made it to the top. Momentarily, I felt we were indomitable.

Apart from a grazing cow and some sheep it was a barren pastoral landscape. The higher we climbed, the more isolated it became and the lower the cloud level fell. Soon we were in thick fog and my exhilaration was quickly tempered by the realisation that I actually had no idea where I was. Had the men sent me off on a wild goose chase? Narrow tracks appeared out of the gloom but there were no road markers to suggest where they led.

'Do you not ever feel scared that something might go wrong?' Nada had asked me in Belgrade. Fear crept in. No one had any idea where I was – least of all me. I could hardly see two feet in front of me; I had a couple of peaches, a bottle of water, and half a packet of peppermints as food rations, a dwindling tank of petrol with the needle creeping ever closer to the 12 o'clock empty point, and a tourist map that made no sense at all. I just had to keep driving and hope. Surprisingly, Tito was not overheating despite his uphill exertions but he was burning fuel fast. Over the next hill the fog lifted to a thin haze. We were driving along a plateau. Green fields surrounded us on both sides and within this landscape emerged old traditional shepherds' houses. Buildings with white-washed stone foundations, timber clad walls and long elegantly sloped shingled roofs crafted from close-fitting strips of wood, each overlapping the other to provide a weathertight covering to the shepherd's home. We had stumbled across an area remote and seemingly lost in time. My reverie was interrupted by the presence of a roadside grave. The face of a young man in uniform was etched on the headstone. I stopped momentarily. The dates implied he had been killed during the recent war, which had reached these isolated parts too although today, apart from Tito and myself, there was stillness and silence in a world of pine forests and mountain homes in which no life was willing to expose itself.

The road descended sharply, requiring my full concentration. With a firm and continuous pressure on the brake pedal, we crawled slowly downwards. My right foot ached but I dared not lessen the pressure for fear of losing control. The road was littered with felled pine trees. It was indiscriminate logging – possibly illegal – haphazardly abandoned. Most lay on the hillside perpendicular to the road, threatening to slide full tilt across our path at the slightest provocation. We would not stand a chance against the momentum of these huge masses but we made it past without incident.

The road levelled out to a T-junction. A hand-painted advertising board might have told me which way to turn, if only I could read Cyrillic. I sat there in despair. Nothing on my tourist map seemed to reflect the journey we had just undertaken across the National Park. A truck appeared from nowhere and tore past us, kicking up clouds of dust in its path. Then silence. I took a chance and followed. A series of hairpin bends began weaving us further down. I braked hard, hoping our destiny was not to end life jack-knifing into the valley below. With every extra push of pressure on the brake, a sound uttered from somewhere near the front wheels. "Please don't fail me Tito, not now!" I muttered desperately. I took it more slowly, every nerve in my body straining. We rounded a bend and I involuntarily braked to a standstill.

There, by the side of the road, was a wooden bench on which an old lady sat carding wool. I leaned over and wound down the passenger window, trying to stifle a laugh at this wholly unexpected scene.

"*Dobar dan*. Mokra Gora?"

She smiled, nodding her head in confirmation. I gave her a grateful wave to which she did not respond but continued to card her wool with a far-off look in her eyes. Perhaps she had been a mirage; still, as we crawled around the next few hairpin bends, I thanked fate for putting her there. Tito was objecting strongly to my heavy use of the brake but soon we were back in civilisation.

I parked and stiffly climbed out of the car, flexing my aching right foot. My relief at having made it across the Tara mountain ranges without disaster was huge and although the petrol indicator cast a deep shadow across the empty marker, it was not quite empty. We had passed the purpose-made rural village film set created by the internationally famous film director Emir Kusturica and entered the village of Mokra Gora. I booked into the railway station hotel and sat down to a large bowl of ćorba soup (a traditional dish popular across the whole Balkan region, made with chunks of veal, beef or lamb, stock and vegetables and considered a hearty meal served with homemade flat bread), cup cake moulds of corn bread and a generous heap of shopska salad. Although late, it was lunchtime for everyone, including the steam train mechanics.

"*Bon appétit!*" one of them ventured.

"*Merci*," I responded and he raised his glass of *rakija* with a wink and a satisfied look of delight at having successfully communicated with me, while his colleagues laughed and nudged him in the ribs.

———

The Mokra Gora railway line is famous for its figure-of-eight switchbacks, which allow the trains to successfully climb the mountainside and access the otherwise isolated villages located there. Today, it was just a tourist attraction rather than a fully operational line, with the next round trip scheduled for the morning. Conserving what remained of Tito's petrol reserves, I hiked up the hill to Emir Kusturica's film village, where apparently I would find internet access. The fake village recreated a scene of traditional houses, outside which vintage cars sat. It was strange to encounter this artificial world, which had been walled off from a countryside filled with villages and old houses representing the real article. But who was I to judge, when I was ready to make full use of the modern facilities that had been installed and which allowed me to contact the outside world? Kusturica himself seemed a controversial character, revoking his native land of Bosnia and Herzegovina and his Muslim roots for Serbia and the Orthodox religion. He claimed his family only converted to the Muslim faith 200 years ago during the Ottoman period.

———

The railway hotel streamed live footage of the evening's football match for its small array of hotel guests and Mokra Gora locals. We sat magnetically glued to the screen while eating *domaći ćevapi* (homemade sausages), accompanied by clay dishes of butter beans oven baked in a spicy tomato sauce, enjoyed with hunks of homemade breads and washed down with beer or *rakija*. As the evening advanced, so did the drinking. I beat a subtle retreat to my room and left the middle-aged football fanatics to their game and to the drink.

I awoke with a start. It was the middle of the night. A woman screamed. I sat up in bed, instantly awake. There was loud talking and then another frightened scream. It came from the reception area below. I opened my bedroom door a crack to hear men's voices. *What should I do?* I listened nervously. A door opened and closed. Voices continued in hushed tones. Then quiet. I gently pushed a chair up against my bedroom door, wishing I was not alone or such a coward. My ears strained for sounds of danger. Nothing. I lay awake fearing what I did not know. The staircase creaked as someone made their slow ascent. A door clicked shut and – silence.

- Mokra Gora/Kotroman Border Control (6km) -

The pale-faced receptionist paused and smiled weakly at my concern. There had been a little problem with some of the guests, she said diplomatically. Her colleague shot her an alarmed look. I paid, glad I would not be here for a second night.

The steam train took us on an exhilarating ride up the mountainside. For the first time I was in the company of other travellers; two American women who had hired a Serbian guide for the day. With open arms they encouraged me to join their afternoon sightseeing. Milan's black 4-wheel drive vehicle had smoked glass windows and air-conditioning. He picked us up from a station stop on the mountainside and drove us in style from one sightseeing place of interest to the next. I revelled in the vehicle's comfort from its well-upholstered body-hugging seats to its individually controlled temperature settings – a pleasant change from sitting on broken springs and breathing in copious amounts of dust while the hot air tore through my hair and made my eyes water.

A substantial lunch and an exchange of travelling tales did much to refuel my confidence for adventure. It was mid-afternoon and my aim was to cross the border into Bosnia and

Herzegovina before evening. I had practically no fuel, about three Euros' worth of Serbian dinars, no phone connection and no clean clothes. The nearest town was Višegrad, where I hoped I would be able to address all my current concerns and deficiencies. I waved farewell to the American travellers and their guide and headed optimistically towards the border, just 6km away, chewing distractedly on a peppermint and hoping the petrol dial was inaccurately in our favour.

The Serbian customs officer at Kotroman border control point exclaimed, "Fića! *Dobro, dobro*," then nodded reassuringly.

"*Da, da*," I agreed confidently. He checked my passport and waved me through.

We drove along the valley road which separated Serbia from Bosnia and Herzegovina. The mountain ranges towered above Tito's petite form, heightening the sense of drama and excitement I felt at leaving our sixth country but not knowing what to expect of our seventh – a land of many mountains and reputedly great beauty, yet severely damaged by war and fragmented by ethnic division.

BOSNIA AND HERZEGOVINA

OF MOUNTAINS, CHEESE AND RED SHOES

- Donje Vardište Border Control/Višegrad (16km) -

We arrived at Donje Vardište, dwarfed on all sides by mountains – a most magnificent setting for a border crossing. I cobbled together the last of my Euros to pay an unexpected environmental tax.

"British?" the passport officer enquired, "In a Fića?"

I passed over my car documents with a smile. He idly glanced at them but was more interested to know where I had been. His dark eyes widened and his tall body rocked backwards and forwards with hearty laughter as I recounted my route.

"Good luck!" he said, with more than a hint of doubt in his voice as he cast a critical eye over Tito and returned my documentation.

It was a spectacular journey to Višegrad but one that had me wondering how on earth so many centuries of bloodshed had been possible – the terrain seemed impenetrable the moment you left the road.

I booked into the vibrantly yellow-painted Višegrad Hotel, which stood next to the Mehmed-Pasha Sokolović Bridge: a structure immortalised in Ivo Andrić's book *The Bridge on the Drina* and constructed to symbolise inter-ethnic unity within the region, which ironically became the frontline stronghold between advancing and retreating forces, including the Austrian and Turkish armies respectively. It was damaged during both World Wars I and II and most recently became a gruesome centrepiece for the Višegrad massacres of Muslims in 1992 by Serb police and militia. Despite the atrocities that have been committed here throughout history, it is hard not to admire this 16th century stone bridge – undeniably beautiful, sweeping in grand Ottoman style across the river, its eleven stone-pointed arches supported by elegantly shaped buttresses. At the centre of the bridge is a niche with a stone seat recessed into its thick walls. Opposite, a stone panel rises upwards, elaborate Arabic text inscribed upon it.

I sat down and a sense of calm washed over me, which was quickly replaced by a sense of guilt, knowing as I did that this spot had been a public stage from where many had gone to their deaths less than 20 years ago, shot and pushed into the river. The mountains and sky were perfectly reflected in the almost still waters of the river below and I stared into its depths. A slight breeze picked up. The river's surface began to ripple and a shiver ran through my body.

In 2007 the Mehmet Pasha Sokolovič Bridge was added to the UNESCO world heritage list for its architectural merit. I wondered how the families whose relatives were killed here must feel. Today the bridge receives much attention from tourists travelling through Višegrad. They admire its architectural significance, but are they aware of the awful truth it hides from a cursory glance or a walk across its majestic length? A twisted irony, one might say, but time marches on, pulling us into the present without, one hopes, being disrespectful to the past. For some this iconic structure must always conjure up many emotions; the least, I would imagine, being admiration.

E vening set in. I wandered back to the hotel and pulled out my jacket from the bottom of the rucksack – autumn was most definitely on its way. I headed to a nearby internet café made incongruous by its modern smoked glass appearance in a streetscape of cracked concrete and shell-pitted façades. I was instantly engulfed in a pungent haze of smoke. Teenagers dragged heavily on cigarettes and larked around good-naturedly in the subdued lighting. The atmosphere was upbeat and friendly. They all spoke some English, although sniggered at one another's attempts to communicate with me. Although I was clearly an oddity, they accepted my presence as I charged up one of the café's dinosauric computers to Skype with a friend on the other side of the world – a situation I found more than unusually surreal, yet I accepted it in the need for a momentary escape from my own travelling reality.

On my way to the café I noticed Višegrad had both a mosque and an Orthodox church but one thing was missing: there had been no call to prayer. Were there any Bosniaks (Muslims), as they are officially referred to, in Višegrad? I was not sure. White gravestones dotted the hillside intensely above, while in the town the Orthodox cemetery was filled with row upon row of headstones, each one depicting the face of a proud young man in army uniform holding a rifle or machine gun. I found this all rather disturbing. These were very young Serbian men. It all seemed such a waste, with no winners. Many had lost one way or another, most of all the ordinary civilians of Višegrad – a once mixed ethnic community. Had Muslim and Serb neighbours been forced to turn against one another? I observed the teenagers in the café with renewed interest; the next young generation of Višegrad, but all, I imagined, were Serb.

Višegrad lies within the territory of Republika Srpska. This, along with the Federation, comprises the two official territories of Bosnia and Herzegovina, which is further complicated by the fact that the country is geographically and historically split between two regions; that of Bosnia, and that of Herzegovina. Republika Srpska has a majority Serb population who follow the Orthodox faith. An invisible line wanders confusingly across the terrains of Bosnia and Herzegovina, separating Republika Srpska from the Federation of Bosnia and Herzegovina territory. The Federation has a majority Bosniak and Croat population of Muslim and Catholic faith respectively; in many parts of the country they are separate communities.

Although the Federation of Bosnia and Herzegovina and Republika Srpska are to the outsider one country (Bosnia and Herzegovina), in practice they are diametrically different in every way possible. Republika Srpska is no more a part of Bosnia and Herzegovina, to which it officially belongs, than a part of Serbia, to which it would like to belong. As a result of the war, Serbia is obliged, although with increasing reluctance, to support Republika Srpska, whose institutional systems and politics it purports to follow. The currency is Dinars, not the Bosnian Mark (KM); the education and health systems are separate; even the mobile network system is different. Thus, the territory tries to maintain as distant a stance from being a part of Bosnia and Herzegovina as it possibly can and to the uninformed tourist this can be somewhat perplexing.

I could only speculate at the polarised politics of Višegrad and imagined it was much the same in other areas of Republika Srpska. It was a larger-than-life reality and ironically seemed to have created a living prison for all its inhabitants. It was destructive and controlling, isolating the population of Republika Srpska so that they could not integrate with the one and were shunned by the other and young Bosnian Serbs were trapped by this; victims of a war in which they had played no part, born into a no-man's land of political manipulation with no future in sight.

I had only just arrived in Bosnia and Herzegovina and already found myself plunged into an environment I did not really understand, hoping somehow to be able to see beyond the politics and the war and meet with the ordinary person. I said farewell to the teenagers of the internet café and emerged into the evening air, gulping in its freshness in an attempt to rinse my lungs of nicotine.

I felt like an object of speculation in Višegrad. Although children smiled and some ventured a "hello" when I passed them on the street, the older generation would look quickly and then look away, not wishing to engage with me at all, just as in Bajina Bašta. I passed the Ivo Andrić museum. It had closed for the day but from one of the windows above, my every move was being observed by a shadowy figure. If only I had been able to speak the language, I would have been able to make contact with their world, even in some small way, but I could not. I could only observe and be observed in return.

- Višegrad/Sarajevo (96km) -

The change in the weather came as a shock. A thick layer of mist hung over the mountains, obscuring any hope of sunshine or blue skies. Even the trees seemed to be turning an autumnal colour. Leaving town, we passed a newly built mosque with its shiny copper-topped minaret and I glimpsed the Orthodox church on the hill above. Can people really return after a war and believe in a new beginning? I found myself being engulfed by a complexity of questions with no answers.

We crossed the vehicular bridge to the opposite bank. The

Drina resembled a millpond rather than a river this morning – no doubt the controlling effect of hydroelectric dams both up and downstream. I glanced back at the Mehmet Pasha Sokolović Bridge one last time. It was as majestic looking as it had been yesterday, holding centuries of never-to-be-told secrets within its walls.

The road weaved and turned, following the river's course. The scenery was dramatic; a contrast of calm waters and karst rock formations rising up on either side of the water. Tunnels have been blasted through large sections of the rock to create the only vehicular route westwards. We entered the first tunnel, dark and strangely claustrophobic. Tito's headlights created dim pools of light through which we picked our way. Returning out into the light, I felt as though I was coming up for air before we dived once more into the gloom of the next tunnel. Signs warned drivers not to use their horns but as a car came the other way through the tunnel, the driver blasted his horn defiantly. I panicked, furious with him and fearful of an imminent tunnel collapse in this dimly lit space. With my eyes fixed firmly on the speck of daylight ahead, I pushed down harder on the accelerator, willing Tito to go faster and get us out of there. I steered through an endless series of long, dark tunnels. It was a rollercoaster ride but eventually we headed northwards, away from the River Drina and its tunnels, and towards Sarajevo.

A steady ascent into the Romanije mountain range took us past the small town of Rogatica and up into a dense range of hills. I was no longer sure whether I was in Republika Srpska or had crossed the invisible line into the Federation but our 20km/h speed was met with haughty amusement from a group of stray dogs straddled along the empty roadside in the sun. They were snoozing and startled by the sound of Tito's engine; they lifted their heads in wonder as we slowly cruised past, never feeling the need to get to their feet and bark as they would at any faster moving vehicle. Reaching the

ultimate peak of Romanije, we began a free-wheeling descent
into Sarajevo, well ahead of my three-hour journey estimation
– not bad for a Fića!

––––––

Tito's presence in the street was met with huge surprise
and delight. The hotel owner allocated him a special
parking spot right outside his double garage doors and
assured me that he would be safe. Gratefully, I piled into my
bright and airy room, dumped my luggage and went out
immediately, longing to meet up with friends as soon as
possible, while indulging in the happy thought I had three
whole days in one place. And where better a place to be than
in Sarajevo?

- Sarajevo -

Sarajevo was alive. Exciting. Invigorating. Sounds, smells and
music filled the air, from traditional lilting melodies to the
pounding throb of turbo-folk. Trams clattered by and traffic
belched forth its carbon monoxide fumes. It was a colourful
city with its decorated buildings, woven cloths and modern
textiles. Locals mingled with tourists, babies cried, and
pigeons flew low in a frenzy at being fed endless bags of
seeds. Bells rang out from the Orthodox church, a muezzin's
voice called his followers to prayer and the hour chimes from
the Catholic church's clock tower close to the synagogue
welcomed all who wished to enter. Everywhere people were
talking, drinking coffee, smoking and watching the world go
by. Some read a newspaper, sitting on low wooden stools in
the many traditional cafés or on higher perches in the modern
looking establishments strewn across the squares and
pavements of the city, enjoying their *merak* moment – a ritual
which was explained to me as being 'impossible to translate,

yet easy to enjoy'. Loosely speaking, it represents the first coffee of the day shared with friends or alone, the first of anything of that day being considered "special" or "sacred" – the *merak* moment.

To the traveller Sarajevo is a gem, a pearl, a unique Balkan experience with food to match. Making a Bosnian coffee (also known as a Turkish coffee) is a skill and seems mainly to be entrusted to the gentlemen in cafés. They whisked gracefully between tables and chairs or through the cobbled lanes of the old city's bazaar carrying round copper trays above their shoulders laden with miniature porcelain cups which sat snugly in copper bases. A tantalising aroma of sugar and coffee emanated from small copper jugs, each filled to the brim with dark liquid topped with froth. It was a pleasure to drink, accompanied by a rose-coloured cube of *rahat lokum* – a taste of the Orient which is sweet yet not synthetic and which melts in your mouth like no other Turkish delight I had ever tried – complementing the richness of the coffee to perfection.

For the more hungry, the *ćevapčići* (pronounced something like che-VAP-chee-chi) is famous in Sarajevo and popular with everyone. Delicious small minced meat sausages are grilled and served in multiples of five, ten or fifteen, and inserted into round parcels of freshly baked traditional bread with thin slices of onion and topped with a large dollop of thick buttery *kajmak* (pronounced kye-mak), which slowly melts over everything. There is an art to eating this meal and I, for one, had trouble mastering it. The local clientele watched with some amusement as the juices from ćevapčići, onions and cream streamed down between my fingers and I reached for yet another napkin to stem the flow. Although the meal could be cooked quickly and therefore termed as fast food, it was, in my opinion, impossible to consume fast. But as I sat on the open terrace of *Hodzic 'A'* in the old district of Bašćaršija (pronounced Bash-char-sheeja), mopping up melting *kajmak*, I found myself being drawn into Sarajevo life.

———

A queue of people grew outside a bakery. The doors to the cooking area had been flung open and I could see flying saucer shapes of bread being pulled at an amazing speed from the oven on long wooden-handled boards shaped like paddles. A woman arranged the newly baked breads in batches to cool in front of the growing crowd of anticipatory faces.

The atmosphere in town was positive and vibrant, a far cry from Višegrad; but on lifting one's eyes above the buildings and to the surrounding hills, row upon row of white headstones come into focus. It was a sobering sight and yet the stark reality of a war fought less than twenty years ago, the trauma of which must still affect so many families privately behind closed doors.

———

My friends were not from Bosnia; they came from Spain and Belarus and have lived in Sarajevo for some time. They had become familiar with where to walk in the region and were keen to show me the beauty of the countryside. Despite being a damp, cold Sunday afternoon, we ascended into the hills towards Barice mountain. The higher we climbed, the more hair-raising the taxi journey became. As the driver cornered tight hairpin bends at sick-making speed, how I wished for Tito's sedate 20km/h pace, but eventually the road petered out by a thick clump of fir trees and we all piled out gratefully. From here it was a steady climb on foot, up through the forest tracks and out into a world of wild flowers and meadows. Purple thistles grew abundantly and wild autumnal crocuses nestled in amongst the tall green grass. Old stone houses lay sparingly across the landscape; their shingled roofs, like those I had seen in the

Tara mountains in Serbia, had been repaired with sheets of rusting corrugated iron. As the sun began to sink, a pink glow lit the sky and the dusky outlines of undulating mountains merged into one continuous line as far as the eye could see.

The magic was quickly shattered as I noticed a sign pinned to a tree just metres away. The area had been cordoned off with string so old it was fraying but it would be foolhardy to venture any further – the area was peppered with land mines. Captivated by the natural beauty of the surroundings, I had now been caught out – I almost felt cheated. The landmine sign had brought with it a sense of sadness replacing my initial elation at the view. Then guilt crept in. Should I be admiring the beauty of this place when only fifteen years ago it had witnessed war, the consequences of which were still very much a part of people's daily life? Conflicting emotions whirled around in my head as they had done while I had stood on the bridge in Višegrad. What had happened here? Perhaps nothing atrocious, but I had no idea. Maybe it was a good thing not to know, but I had had a powerful reality check.

———

I t was that moment between dusk and nightfall when Sarajevo's streetlights had not fully illuminated. Suddenly I was running. A pregnant woman had rushed towards me and adeptly grappled inside my handbag, a cloth laid across her arm to hide her rummaging as her young accomplice cornered me from the other side. I found myself doing a sort of Irish jig down the street with these two women latched on to me. From their faces and dress they were undoubtedly Roma. I managed to break free, sprinting away as fast as I could, infuriated at being caught out. My handbag was a complicated mass of pockets and zips which not even I had mastered, so nothing had been taken, but it had been a wake-up call. War or no war, the good, the bad, the desperate and the hopeful opportunists were around at all times, although I was not sure into which category these two fell. Life as a Roma in the Balkans did not appear to be an easy one for most. Generally considered third-class citizens, they are a much-maligned ethnic minority group, many of whom live in abject poverty. Perhaps cornering tourists was a short-term solution which eased their daily poverty, while they continued to be everyone's problem but no one's priority to support.

- Sarajevo/Vareš (52km) -

"Of course I must help, you are one of my guests!" The cheerful, plump hotel owner took complete control of my routine pre-journey Tito checks. "Oil, please," he said, relishing the moment. I gave in and handed him the bottle. He checked the level on the dipstick and flicked up the plastic top to check the water. "Ok, now you are ready!"

I smiled in appreciation and thanked him for his assistance. Today I was off to Vareš, a town just 50km north of Sarajevo and by all accounts a place not to be missed (according to my friend with whom I had been Skyping in Višegrad). Rather than disappoint him, and indeed rather intrigued, I set off with strict instructions to meet a man named Bojan outside the *'Turist Office'* at noon. Already I was late.

After a brief stop for petrol we headed northwards out through the city's district of Ciglane, with its concrete jungle of apartments resembling a modern take on the jumble of a Brazilian favela – each level interlinked diagonally and vertically by steep stairways. The upper levels had the added luxury of a funicular that trundled down to the shopping area below. It seemed to be inhabited by a mix of illustrious bohemians and successful professionals equally entranced by the architecture and fascinating blend of rundown and glamourous apartments of all sizes and values alike. A thriving organic market with stalls piled high with fruit and vegetables lay opposite, beyond which huge cemeteries stretched across the surrounding landscape of Sarajevo, a constant and sobering reminder of all those who had perished in the recent conflict. The road wove through satellite villages and out into the countryside until it split. One direction headed to Visoko; the other to Tuzla, both still firmly within the Federation of Bosnia and Herzegovina and the region of Bosnia. We took the former. A toll booth loomed.

"Ah! *Makedonski*?" came the usual question.

"No, *Engleski.*"

The young man peered at me enquiringly and then smiled, as if he should have known. "Ha! And where are you going in a Fića?"

"To Vareš, I hope!" I responded.

He nodded reassuringly. "Take the next junction off the highway and the road will lead you to Vareš. Good luck!"

It all seemed perfectly simple and we might even make up some lost time.

We peeled off right as advised, passing through the Roman town of Breza, from where I began to count. There were 105 bends to Vareš and, as we looped our way following the path of the River Strica, the old railway line built during the Austro-Hungarian Empire appeared and disappeared from view. It had once supported the export of vast quantities of steel from the region and we were heading to the very source from where this industry had originally flourished back in Roman times – although it was hard to believe that an industry had thrived so successfully up here in the mountains.

Today it was a different scene. The industrial smoke had long dissipated and the sky was clear. Big columns of white cloud hung in the sky between large patches of blue. The sun shone and the mountains came ever closer with every passing bend. They rose in front of us, covered in a thick blanket of dark green forest. My expectations grew but nothing could have prepared me for the industrial assault that met my eyes. Two brick chimneys towered upwards like beacons but the factory gates were padlocked shut and the buildings lay redundant, some representing the splendid era of Austro-Hungarian industry. On the left side of the road, old 19th century houses huddled together, their delicate façades battered, their windows smashed and yet a fragile reminder of an elegant past over-shadowed by a second phase of industrialisation – the more functional communist style. These housing blocks also had a distinctive style, all too readily dismissed by historians and conservationists alike. They showed equal signs of decay and their shabby appearance dampened my expectations further. The road bent again, revealing a landscape viciously scarred by an open cast mine. Another bend and its ugliness was hidden from sight, but more industrial buildings dating to the communist Yugoslav times came into view – a third phase of the town's development perhaps? Bend 104. As I rounded the corner, a signpost read *Majdan*, a word that I learned later means a mill. We were almost there. Another bend: 105. The road continued to follow the river, more communist-style apartment blocks lined the main street but these had a certain refinement with balconies and vertical timber cladding to the walls. They were angled in an almost welcoming manner to the arriving visitor. This was Vareš.

I pulled up outside the '*Turist Office*', so the piece of paper stuck to the window assured me. It was 12.30. I was late but as I had phoned ahead, with any luck, Bojan would still be there. A man approached diffidently.

"Hello. Emma? It must be you. No one else drives Fiĉa!" he said shyly, revealing a mouth full of metal braces. "Welcome to Vareš!"

This was Bojan. He had arranged some accommodation for me just outside the town.

"It is all I could find," he said apologetically.

I suspected the demand was not high and I wondered briefly whether my friend had sent me on a fool's errand – surely not; he had worked here after the war and had wanted to know whether I thought this place should be UNESCO-listed. There must be more to uncover. Bojan led the way in his aging VW Golf out of Vareš and onto a narrow country road. We turned right and immediately plunged into pitch black. Bojan's headlights lit the way through the immense darkness – a cave that had been carved out through the base of an otherwise impregnable rock. Large drops of water fell out of the darkness above and landed heavily on the windscreen. I flicked on the wipers with a rising sense of adventure. We crawled cautiously through the tunnel, lunging in and out of water-filled potholes, and emerged the other end into the brightness of daylight. We had driven through the famous cave road popular with film directors – Angelina Jolie allegedly being one such director currently scouting it out for a scene in her forthcoming film.

The bed & breakfast was identifiable by a large black pock-marked stone ball – a meteorite which had quite literally dropped out of the sky some years ago. As I looked up nervously, hoping no others would decide to fall in the next couple of days, Bojan excused himself. He was on the afternoon shift in Sarajevo and would see me in the morning.

"7 o'clock, so we have time to see many things."

I stared after his departing car and wondered how I would manage so early a start but that was tomorrow; for now, the afternoon was mine.

———

Perhaps it was the unexpectedness of it all, but Vareš was hypnotising me, from the depth of its sky, accentuating the majesty of the steep green pastoral hillsides rising above the town, to the Kosovar bakery serving freshly made *burek* and *pita* (a filo pastry stuffed with meat and cheese, spinach or potato) rolled into long sausage lengths – though sometimes wound into a large round pan – and cooked until the insides are piping hot and the pastry is crisp, all helped down with a pot of *kefir*, a yoghurt so runny, its refreshingly tart milkiness is easy to drink. Then there were the five ladies in the local craft shop who had looked tentatively at me, but once realising I did not understand a word of Bosnian, they had put their heads back together and continued to hotly debate their differences. The architecture was a clear indication of the development of the town and as I followed the river upstream along an array of footpaths, I seemed to be going back in time until I was standing outside a 17th century Ottoman house surrounded by others of a similar style.

A voice made me jump.

"*Dobar dan*," he said, followed by a flow of Bosnian. I turned to look at him. His tall, lean body was bent over as he tied up a shoelace.

I looked at the shoe and said, "Sorry. *Engleski*."

"Ah, that's ok," he said, "Where are you from and what are you doing in Vareš? Why are you looking at this house? There are others just as interesting. My house is just here, would you like to see it? Would you like some coffee?"

His English grew with confidence and he spoke more quickly and loudly until I was sure the whole of Vareš must know he was talking to a foreigner. A couple walked by, acknowledging him cheerily and looking at me with interest. That was a good sign, I thought. Not some nutter out to rob me.

"Come on. I will make you coffee. There is no need to worry. What is your name? I am Marijan."

The front door opened into a minute cottage with two rooms. The first was his living room and kitchen; the second his bedroom. The furniture was quaintly dated rather than historic and to most of the vertical surfaces were taped newspaper cuttings and notes. He must have been in his fifties, but it was difficult to tell; everyone looked much older than they were.

"Sit down, Emma; no need to be scared," Marijan said, shutting the door and turning the key in the lock.

With one eye on the key, I watched him calmly prepare coffee in the traditional Bosnian way – clearly, Marijan just wanted to talk. And talk he did, about music, his band, his work at the Vareš factory identifying stones, his religion – Catholic. "And that means I am a Croat," he said, almost defensively.

Marijan talked of his mother who had died recently – in the room next door – and of Vareš and its people, but as he spoke his voice grew in volume. He swung from jokes to serious thought and all the while I sat quietly as he patiently boiled the coffee, let it settle and boiled it again. Marijan opened the door and went out into the garden, leaving me to take in this claustrophobic but wildly fascinating scene. He returned moments later with a bowl full of freshly picked plums and three red roses. He presented them to me with a smile. I was touched and yet unsure how to react. The key turned in the lock once again and we drank our coffee in the small confines of his home. Marijan's mood became negative: he did not play music now; he did not have a job; the factory had closed; his friends had died; he had had to fight in the war; Vareš was no longer the same; everything was a mess; it had been a different, a happier life before the "bloody f****** war" changed everything. I nodded gently and drank in the scent from the roses while I thought carefully what to say, battling down a rising sense of panic. Had the war unhinged him or was he just letting off steam because he could, to a stranger? I did not know, but thought being outside would be better for us both.

"It is such a sunny day outside and you say there are other houses that you think I should see?"

There was a pause. Marijan looked at me and seemed to shake himself out of his melancholic anger. "I will be your guide," he announced cheerfully.

The key turned and the door was opened with a flourish. I stepped outside and breathed deeply.

————

I said my farewells to Marijan, thanking him for his hospitality, a generosity which many have been enthusiastic to offer me on my journey across the Balkan peninsula. Sometimes I step cautiously into the lives of these ordinary men and women and I am aware of the privilege it is to witness their world: their laughter, humour, struggles and fears. It regularly humbles me, for in most cases they do not have much but they wish to share what they have generously, and with a stranger with whom often they cannot communicate easily – it does not matter to them because I, for some surprising reason, have come to *their* town or village and am travelling in a Zastava, a car from *their* past.

————

A woman sat in the empty gloom of a café. She hiked up the volume on the music system as the church bells rang from the Catholic church. Outside, children played in the street. They stopped to smile and say "hello," shyly turning away, only to turn back again with a grin when I said "hello" back. Life may be politically complicated but for now these children remained unaware. A monument stood in the schoolyard. It was in stone, formed in the shape of a hammer and anvil linked together like pieces in a jigsaw. A five-pointed red star was chiselled into a separate block of stone, underneath which nine lines of text were inscribed. The star, I assumed, represented communism – brotherhood and unity. Josip Broz was the leader then – President Tito. His landmark monuments dating back to the 1940s were scattered across the former Yugoslav territories, of which Bosnia and Herzegovina was one. Some monuments were large, some small; some remembered but most forgotten or abandoned. Many had the names of Partisans who had fought and died for Tito's ideal, now also forgotten by some, maligned by others and revered publicly by very few. Some romanticised or were nostalgic about the Yugoslav period but many questioned and openly criticised the efficacy of Tito's leadership. It was now 2009, over twenty years since his death and fourteen years since the war, yet the monument survived here. There was a slight crack in the hammer's head but that was all. There were two verses of text.

Rade Slobode (For freedom,)
Smo krvljli (We have blood,)
Zemlju kupali (Forming pools,)
I ona je (Which have)
Procvala (Blossomed)
Kad krvena ruža (Like red roses)
Al nismo pali (But we have not fallen,)
Već ustali (But have risen,)
Silom (Power,)
I prkosom (And defiance,)
Snagom (Strength)
I srcem (And heart.)

Poignant words inspired by events fifty years ago, yet which could just as easily fit today's post-conflict situation, although I wondered whether, like many monuments, its presence was so familiar, it had become invisible.

The Vareš tourist office was run by Jadranko. He folded his gangly figure down onto a chair behind the desk and gave me a youthful grin. Next to him, his equally fresh-faced assistant and recent bride was eagerly putting together gift bags for a party of visitors due to arrive shortly. She looked up at me and smiled warmly. They were a dynamic team driven by Jadranko's ideas for promoting tourism in Vareš and the surrounding countryside. Their enthusiasm was infectious and I could not help but hope that they would be successful.

The industrial boom had ended some thirty years ago and with it the employment of thousands. Gone were the days when at the end of their working shift 3000 employees would march up the hill from the factory into the town and home for dinner. The thundering sound of boots on tarmac was now no more than a nostalgic memory but the eclectic mix of socialist-style apartment blocks, which housed the workers' families, still survived, although many lay empty. A plaque inscribed a surname on each door and reflected the owner's ethnic origins. Bosniak, Croat and Serb and in some cases families of mixed ethnicity – the true Yugoslav, we might say, who now found himself torn between deciding to which group he belonged, yet a product of mixed origins. Jadranko assured me that it was not like this in Vareš.

"We do not care whether someone is Croat, Bosniak, Serb. I am Bosnian. That is what is important to me. That is what is important to us, for our future."

His answer surprised me, for I was sure that most Croats and Serbs believed that to be Bosnian denoted being Muslim and therefore a Bosniak, which is why most were particular to qualify that they were 'Bosnian Serb' or 'Bosnian Croat'. I wondered if the country changed its name, whether that might help to unite everyone?

"What would we call ourselves?" Jadranko answered, amused by the suggestion.

Of course, he was right; what would they call themselves? Bound so tightly by history, religion and politics, there seemed no room for lateral thinking. Would European membership really be a solution, as Europe seemed to think? Would it be the answer for the ordinary person living in Bosnia and Herzegovina or merely a temporary diversion?

- Budozelje/Karići (46km) -

6.30am. I crawled out from beneath a pile of duvets into the damp cold air. Condensation ran down the bedroom windows and outside a low fog surrounded the bed & breakfast. I made a dash for the shower room, banged my head on the unusually low doorframe, ricocheted backwards then dived forwards into the shower, grasping my throbbing head with one hand while turning on the hot water tap with the other. Half an hour later, I greeted Bojan in the breakfast room downstairs and cradled a cup of hot steaming coffee between my hands, gazing sleepily into its rich velvety darkness through a cloud of Bojan's cigarette smoke.

It was an early start for a tour of the countryside but Bojan's time was limited. His shift began at 3 o'clock in Sarajevo so we had six hours. We set off in his car along a winding forest road. The fog lingered in patches, mystical and ethereal, and as Bojan recounted a local tale, I felt myself transported back into medieval times to a world of Bosnian Kings, battles against advancing Turks and legends of heroes and villains. The final stage of our journey was on foot down a path and into a clearing from where the ruins of Bobovac Castle sat comfortably, almost untouched by the world. On the opposite slope there were signs of a village; it sat in an area of high pasture lands bespeckled with haystacks shaped like wigwams, a vertical pole emerging from the top of each, which acted as an anchor to prevent them from slipping down the hillside. The fog lifted and an early morning sun illuminated a scene of peaceful serenity. Bojan stood quietly smoking a cigarette. He felt a natural affinity with this land, his country, and although he worked in the city, he had no wish to live there.

Like Vareš, Bobovac was once a thriving community. It too was waiting to be rediscovered, its paths and connections with the valley obscured and overgrown, their history protected, but not lost, ready for those curious enough to want to discover it again. A faded newspaper cutting with a photograph of Bojan's grandmother in traditional dress was pinned to the noticeboard of another village nearby. The cutting had been there many years and was a reminder to all that Strica village was the first to be classified by the government as a tourist village. The war prevented tourism of any kind developing in the countryside. The village had remained a quiet place, and selfishly I felt glad to have seen it like this. On the other hand, if Jadranko's *Turist Office* initiatives were to be successful, it would be something positive for those living in these small communities.

A dog lay like a sentry across the middle of the village track defending his territory. Bojan parked in front of him and a man dressed in baggy old trousers and rolled-up shirt sleeves rushed out from his home to greet us. They shook hands and hugged while the dog, maintaining his position, wagged his tail in sweeping motions across the dirt track. The man acknowledged me with a polite "*Dobar dan*," and a handshake and disappeared back into the house. He reappeared moments later carrying in his strong, weather-beaten hands a litre bottle of clear liquid. Bojan announced that this was the best *rakija* in the region.

"A present," he added proudly.

I accepted graciously, wondering how I would be able to drink 40 percent proof "nectar" – it could take years!

A rusting old orange Zastava with no registration plates drove past. The driver grinned from beneath his wildly thick moustache, revealing a mouth largely lacking in teeth. He waved to Bojan and peered curiously at me. The sight of his Fića brought an involuntary smile to my face and I realised it just could not be helped. To see a Fića was a smiling matter.

———

The houses in Strica were a mixture of new and old, some in dire need of immediate attention. Their steep shingled roofs, timber walls plastered in white mortar accompanied by a balcony at first floor level, and three-paned windows were becoming a familiar sight on this leg of my journey. I continued to marvel at how many different styles of homes had managed to survive in the Balkans, despite much neglect and the desire for modern homes. If they could be saved, they would be a unique, living reminder of the region, but from what I had seen, old homes were sadly undervalued; they were not being adapted to suit modern living but rather demolished in favour of completely new concrete houses. A reality facing many old vernacular buildings in the world today.

Serena was one such rebuilt place but it had a very specific function. It was the trout restaurant, popular with everyone and considered legendary among some of the expatriate community in Sarajevo. There was no menu – there was no need. Freshly grilled trout and homemade potato salad were all one would want here. Bojan snapped off a well-grilled trout tail.

"This is the best bit!" he said, putting it into his mouth with a final crunch.

I eyed the discarded trout tails on my plate with renewed interest, took a bite and nodded in approval. I had been instantly converted to that fine delicacy, the trout tail.

———

Bojan headed off to work and I prepared for an afternoon's exploration with Tito who, having sat in the sunshine all morning, burst into life with a pull on the choke and a swift turn of the ignition key.

Budoželje did not resemble the remote mountain village I was expecting, despite the admirably-sized haystack marking its farthest boundary. Green fields and summer grazing lay beyond this marker, and in the distance a minaret and the roofs of a surprising number of houses lined the horizon. As we drove along the plateau road, we were overtaken by a clapped-out old bus. The occupants studied us solemnly as they passed and we followed at a distance in their dusty wake until the road ended abruptly. A square stretch of baked earth acted as bus station, basketball court, kiosk and general play area. I pulled up behind the bus as the last passenger was making his way gingerly down a well-trodden footpath, his bandied legs supported by a stout cane, his back stooped. He turned to look momentarily as I got out of the car and then carried on his way. The bus driver was busily brushing out the inside of his now empty bus and I ventured a "*Dobar dan*," through the open door. He stopped and looked down from the top step.

"*Dobar dan*," I said more quietly. "*Café*?"

This I asked with a sweep of my arms in the hope he would understand I was looking for a coffee shop in the village. He shrugged his shoulders, shook his head and without uttering a word, went back to sweeping out his bus. Undeterred, I walked up the lane to admire the never-ending line of mountains which lay beyond a flimsy picket fence separating the village and relatively firm ground from a sheer drop. Irregular lengths of weathered stone lay like discarded farm objects across Budoželje's common village land, and as I traced my fingers over the top of one, I noticed the wind-eroded surface had the outlines of writing on it, a motif so faint it was impossible to make out the shape. I peered wide-eyed at the object and then across at the next one and realised that these were not discarded objects at all. I had stumbled across a group of mediaeval tombstones known as *Stećci*. My excitement rose as I walked to the next one, a similarly abandoned sarcophagus, tightly sealed by the weight and size of its stone top, but the markings were indecipherable.

Close by, a cluster of rectangular tombs lay in a stone-walled graveyard in which more recent tombstones, with the familiar sultan-style turban top, were also placed. These significantly older medieval tombstones symbolised the presence of independent groups who had lived up here in the mountains, perhaps following their own laws and answerable to no one but themselves. Little is known of these people who had sought mountain isolation, and who had settled in a number of Balkan countries. They have bequeathed a host of cultural relics to the peninsular region, some of which are still being uncovered in woods and forests today. I wanted to climb over the graveyard wall for a closer look but, although no one was around, I felt sure the inhabitants were there watching from behind half-closed curtains.

Was I intruding? It felt so. Cut off from everything and most certainly isolated throughout the winter, Budoželje was a village on top of the world. I was sure there was more to discover down the dirt track; the mosque, traditional houses and a lifestyle time had forgotten, but I felt too conspicuous to investigate. This was definitely a conservative Muslim village and I doubted anyone spoke English. I needed Bojan here if I was to even scrape beneath the surface of this tightly knit, private world. I climbed back into Tito, disappointed that nobody had been curious, or indeed outraged, enough to come out to say hello or to confront me. I drove back through the village past the only obvious-looking shop. Two middle-aged men sat drinking coffee outside while another stood talking to them. A young boy on a bicycle was idly turning tight circles on the road in front of them, listening distractedly to their conversation. I slowed Tito to a stop and ventured a "*Dobar dan.*"

They nodded politely and mumbled, "*Dobar dan.*"

"*Café?*" I asked hopefully, and they shook their heads despite the cups in front of them. I looked longingly at their half-empty cups and pulled an "*Oh well, never mind,*" sort of a face and with an apologetic wave for disturbing them, I drove on. The young boy who had been observing all of this seized an opportunity for some excitement and began to follow on his bicycle. As I picked up the pace, he raced past, peddling with determination, taking full advantage of the downward slope, the wind tearing through his hair as he went. At the end of the village he came to a standstill. The fun was over. We passed and with a gleeful look he turned his bicycle around before beginning the slow peddle up the hill and back to the older men's conversation, and his incessant wheel turns.

K arići mosque is considered the oldest Muslim site in Bosnia. The densely gravelled track was to prove a serious challenge for Tito's wheels. The only signpost read '*Kadarici*' – it looked an easier road and I wondered if my guidebook had misspelt the name. It was a possibility, but the campervan couple who had burst out onto the track in front of us as I sat pondering the slight differentiations between the two names, assured me Karići was the "mosquee" so we ploughed on until the thick porridge-like surface proved too much for Tito's wheels and he ground to a halt. I reversed cautiously down the slope onto a more stable surface, put him into first gear, turned off the engine and quickly rammed a brick behind each back wheel. I then walked up the slope to see how bad it was going to get. The silence was broken by the sound of the fir trees swaying gently in the light breeze and here I was, only halfway up a mountain track, in the middle of the forest with no mobile signal even though John had assured me, all those weeks ago in Skopje, that 'Zastava wheels are made for mountains.' With renewed determination I pulled the driver's door shut and pushed the gear stick into first. I drove at it like a possessed rally car driver and before long we were through the worst of it as a car of similar vintage came over the crest of the hill and down towards us. A round-faced man sat behind the wheel with three young Muslim women, discernible only by their headscarves, wedged into the back seat. We stared in surprise at one another, each cautiously aware of not skidding into the other, the women gently smiling to each other at the sight of Tito. The dust settled and the road was once again deserted but I was heartened by the fact that I was not totally alone in this wilderness.

———

'*Dobro došli*' read the vast banner pinned to the house next to the Karići Mosque '*Welcome*'. We had arrived. The mosque itself was an unassuming building of timber with a slim turret-shaped minaret. It was newly constructed, the original having been destroyed by fire during the war, but the graveyard behind it bore the much older hallmarks of turban-style tombstones, many painted pale green. A number of footpaths disappeared into the forest – the haunting sign of a skull and cross bones set in a red triangle once again brought me up sharp. Mines. The remains of a tombstone barely held together with rusted reinforcement wires lay alone, separate from the mosque. Fragments of Cyrillic wording clung to one edge of the headstone. A Partisan memorial, perhaps, or did it belong to someone more recent? A Serb or Montenegrin soldier would have Cyrillic text on his or her gravestone. After my time in Kosovo, where I had seen the consequences of the mindless destruction of gravestones, it was hard not to make the same assumption here. But, by all accounts, Vareš was a unique place. The communities had tried to support and protect each other against the militia forces that strove to attack their region. It was true that unity had broken down, as it had in many other parts of the country, but the difference here appeared to be that it was being rebuilt again. Vareš still maintained an ethnic mix although the ratio was largely altered; the challenge now is how to keep its younger generation. Opportunities beckon abroad, bringing with them the hope of a future, whereas at home politics and corruption limit the chance of stability except perhaps for a lucky few.

———

Tonight my host was cooking pasta. His daughter had invited two of her friends over and they giggled self-consciously as they joined me at the table. She placed bowls of steaming hot spaghetti in front of them and after a few solemnly whispered words of prayer the girl opposite me crossed herself and carefully swirled up a forkful of sauce-covered strands. They eagerly spoke to me in English, poking one another and correcting each other's sentences while my host quietly looked on, watching the playful antics of the girls and smiling to himself. With their stomachs soon full, they bounded off to watch a DVD and the room lapsed into a companionable silence. My host placed a large mug of fresh mint tea in front of me and sat down diffidently. He could not speak English but the girls' enthusiasm had sparked an urge in him to talk. Using German words, Bosnian words from my guidebook and my road map as an illustrative tool, we passed a sociable hour attempting to communicate with one another. Whether we succeeded, neither of us will ever know, but the moment did much to strengthen my respect for people who appear to have few choices yet continue to be hospitable, generous and prepared to share with pride what they do have, however little that may be.

- Vareš/Travnik (102km) -

Smoke furled upwards from black mounds by the side of the road. Around us the fog lay like a thick blanket but above it a glimmer of sunlight hit the top of the forest. It was early morning as Bojan parked. We walked towards a picket fence and through a narrow gate. A path wove through the trees and into a clearing where a regular banging rhythm of metal on metal reached my ears. The sound grew louder the closer we got to the building lying in a hollow of the densely wooded valley. It looked like a home for a hobbit. The timber door creaked as we pushed it open and entered into the unexpected world which lay within. A man crouched beside a large wooden hammer, its head clamped in metal. It beat up and down with a continuous thud and piercing clang. The man moved a hot glowing disc of metal beneath it, held between large metal pincers. Each strike of the hammer dented the flat disc into the shape of a bowl. He had to work quickly. There was no room for error if he wanted to keep his fingers intact. A timber pole rose up through the roof and with one hand he grasped it. The regular beating of the hammer came to an eventual stop. He removed the beaten piece of metal just as the hammer thudded down to a standstill. Immediately, he was on his feet and over to the fire. Another piece of metal was being heated within the coals. He removed the red, hot disk dexterously with long tongs and with his thickly gloved hand he shuffled the newly beaten dish into the coals to heat once more. Moving swiftly back to the hammer, he pushed the pole upwards, activating it once more. The noise was deafening. Iron tools hung from the walls of the workshop and newly crafted pots were stacked, awaiting sale on market day. Outside, a river rushed by between banks of thick green foliage. This natural resource generated enough energy to turn the water mill, which subsequently powered the hammer inside. It was a mesmerising spectacle – a small-scale industry dating back to Roman times. The spirit of tradition lived on, except that the demand for weapons and armour had now been replaced by the demand for domestic and agricultural products – and although the craftsmanship was appreciated locally, it had remained hidden from the rest of the world for decades.

———

Bojan ended his tour of Vareš's wonders by the edge of an enormous pool of water: the "accidental" lake. Accidental, because one of the open cast mine's employees forgot to turn on the water pump one evening over twenty years ago. The result – a lake appeared in the hollowed-out landscape, above which the natural habitat, now devoid of vegetation, was a stark reminder of how mining can destroy the environment. The water seemed almost inviting but the high-sided banks of brittle stone and earth which surrounded it seemed fragile, as if at any moment they would break apart and slip at speed into the lake, bringing everything in their wake. Two trucks hurtled by on the road behind us, kicking up clouds of dust from the dirt surface. We covered our eyes and headed back into the car, leaving this bleak scene, also popular with film crews, to its own devices. I wondered fleetingly what secrets the lake held and shuddered. Better not to think about that. Time for some Vareš *ćevapčići*.

My skill at eating this national dish had not improved since my first attempt in Sarajevo but everyone's attention was on four suited men at the next table. They talked loudly and I watched as Bojan and most of the other restaurant clientele became nervously distracted by their presence. Apparently, one was known to be a corrupt regional administrative official.

"He is powerful," Bojan acknowledged warily, adding, "And he is not liked."

He did not elaborate further and I did not enquire further.

Although Vareš had captivated me, the consistently damp misty mornings had not. The expectation of the dry heat on the Croatian coast beckoned instead. It was time to leave and, with a rueful farewell, Bojan headed off to Sarajevo to his afternoon shift and I packed my bags. My B&B hosts hovered, looking for a way in which to help. My driver's seat was in need of serious repair. A number of springs had 'pinged' out of position, making it almost impossible to sit comfortably. I pulled at them feebly, trying to hook them back into position. Some tough blue plastic strapping was offered and my host took charge, weaving it through the seat frame, catching each spring in turn and pulling them taut. The seat was level once more and I congratulated him on his success. He beamed and rushed off once more, to return moments later with a cushion, which he plumped up and placed on the driver's seat. I protested but he insisted I should have it. Meanwhile, a picnic was being prepared in the kitchen. A large brown paper bag, neatly folded over at the top, was presented to me with a "*sretan put*" (have a good journey). I waved and shouted "*hvala*" as I turned out of the driveway and headed back through the cave road into Vareš, past the old houses and Marijan's cottage, the Kosovar bakery, the redundant iron factory, to join the road to Visoko in search of a pyramid.

A right-hand turn took us off the main road and up a lane lined with newly built houses. A local food store sat at the end of the lane and provided me with a convenient asking point. The group of people inside appeared to be gossiping rather than buying. They all turned to look at me as I walked in.

"Visoko pyramid?" I asked, rather self-consciously, and the shopkeeper pointed up the road, shaking his head as though to indicate his doubts about the object's authenticity. Nevertheless, I bought a bottle of water from him in thanks and set off up the road. A hill looking more like a grassed-over spoil heap than a pyramid came into view. I abandoned Tito and his orchestra of cooling noises while I headed for the well-trodden track up the side of the hill. Rows of young trees and wild flowers teemed down the slopes and an information board told me that this indeed was no ordinary historic site, but a pyramid considered to have similarities to those in Mexico. I was currently looking at the *'Bosnian Pyramid of the Sun'* discovered by archaeologist Semir Osmanagic.

There was not a soul in sight and I could not resist clambering up the path to the top. Localised excavations into the hillside revealed stone plinths, a doorway and what looked like a tunnel entrance, although too small to enter and disappointingly too dark to reveal anything more than impenetrable blackness. Was I standing on the first known pyramid in Europe? How exciting to think so. However, a castle had existed here many centuries previously. It had been a curious diversion but I remained unconvinced that it was authentic.

———

Kraljeva Sutjeska is a quiet, picturesque village in the valley below Bobovac Castle. A river tumbles through it and stone bridges span its banks. Historically, these two places were linked. A Franciscan monastery had been established here in the 16th century and now houses relics from Vareš as well as an enviable collection of mediaeval manuscripts from across Europe. In times of invasion or threat, the village inhabitants had fled up to Bobovac but today the foot route was heavily overgrown in both directions and the only way to reach the monastery was via the road system.

"Ask for Father Bozić. Just say 'Kićo'," Bojan had said, "He will know who I am. He will give you a tour of the library. It is very impressive."

I was not so sure this kind of familiarity from a female tourist would open doors, but I would give it a try. We stopped in front of the monastery's majestic sweeping stone-stepped entrance. I opened Tito's engine door. The familiar scene of spurting oil and bubbling water was in full swing. Leaving him in the sultry, humid heat of late afternoon, I walked hesitantly towards the entrance, conscious of the calm aura surrounding the building, as though it were sleeping.

It did not seem quite right to walk up the steps and bang on the huge wooden doors and I was relieved to spot a sign leading me around the side of the monastery and into a walled courtyard laid out in the form of a mediaeval herb garden. As I ventured towards the building, a monk dressed in a long dark brown gown emerged through a side door. He looked surprised.

"*Dobar dan…* um… *Padre Bozić? Kićo?*"

He looked at me with complete incomprehension and, with rising embarrassment, I repeated my request a little louder as he strained to understand me. He pointed to an entry phone to the side of the door and walked slowly down the path without a word. Tentatively, I pushed the button and waited while the old monk tottered back and forth along the boxed hedged paths speaking softly to himself – perhaps praying for me to leave. There was no answer from the entry phone system but pinned to the door was a notice. I tried the number. The phone answered within moments, but it was hopeless; the man did not understand my English and I did not understand his Bosnian and I hung up with an apologetic "hvala". I walked back to Tito, who was still bubbling though less furiously, and jumped as my mobile rang out into the peaceful air, breaking the spell of calm.

"Hello?"

A woman answered. "Hello! I am niece of my uncle of tourist agency Katarina. You spoke with him. But he do not understand English! Where are you? We coming to find you."

Within five minutes a white mini-bus pulled up and out jumped the tourist officer and his niece. They negotiated enthusiastically with the monastery by phone and before I knew it a monk was shaking my hand and regarding me unappreciatively. Somehow they had convinced him to take me on a tour. I was ceremoniously ushered inside and whisked upstairs into the library while they departed with a wave, leaving me to my fate. Whatever inconvenience my appearance had caused, the monk remained impassive but on hearing how I had travelled here, he softened somewhat and soon seemed to have forgiven me for my sudden intrusion outside visiting hours. I marvelled at the collection of first edition medieval books and the many valuable artefacts which had been entrusted into the monastery's care, and although I had not found Father Bozić, and no one seemed to know to whom I was referring, I once again found myself grateful to be on the receiving end of gracious Balkan hospitality.

———

It was a 46km drive to Travnik – my night's proposed stopover. The road weaved alongside the River Lasva, while heavy clouds hung low in the sky and rain began to fall. Tito's wipers screeched across the windscreen, the rubber blades leaving a smeary film of dirt through which I peered optimistically. We drove slowly, the rain powering down in short bursts. The rubber blades softened and their grease trail eased to a fine film. Finally, I could see and we ate up the kilometres, arriving at the town of Travnik, the amazing array of minarets reminding me of my entrance into Edirne all those weeks ago.

I circled around the old part of town, staring at the stone terraced dwellings and timber framed houses languishing dangerously close to the river. Motel Aba was the rather uninspiring, but seemingly only choice of accommodation. I bundled into a room, tired and hungry, and reached gratefully for the picnic bag filled with two enormous steak sandwiches, which I munched heartily while slumped on the bed, wishing I was back in the comfortable surroundings of Vareš.

———

Travnik, with its coffee and baklava, and people-gazing opportunities from a glass-fronted corner café positioned directly opposite the Šarena Džamija mosque, was the evening highlight of my stay. Although Travnik had once been a vibrant Ottoman town known as the Istanbul of Europe, today little of the grandeur remained because of a fire which had swept through the city in the early 20th century. However, the mosque had survived. It stood on stout carved stone columns which formed an arcade for small shops in its basement. In the evening, a warm yellow glow permeated through the latticed wooden shutters and softly coloured designs could be picked out around each window opening. The call to prayer brought with it a sudden rush of activity as men gathered to take part while others wandered idly past on their habitual evening stroll, all to be casually observed by those like myself in the café opposite.

- Travnik/Livno (105km) -

Travnik was not inundated with tourists clamouring to walk the walls of its ancient fortress and as there was very little to learn about its history, I walked back into the town in search of the locally famous Travnik cheese. This salty, savoury delicacy came in a number of guises, from creamy to vintage. The shop assistant eagerly cut me slivers of cheese to taste from the huge selection bundled closely together in the refrigerated cabinet in front of him. He shrink-wrapped a large white wedge from the block I had chosen and handed it to me with pride. Armed with some freshly baked Bosnian bread from the bakery next to Motel Aba, it was time to set off again. A mountain crossing lay between here and Livno, my final destination in Bosnia.

I had toyed with the idea of venturing northwest to take in Bosanski Petrovac and Bihać, entering Croatia at a more northerly point. However, the route from there southwards through Croatia looked so alarmingly mountainous on the map that I had decided to head directly west through what looked like a gap between mountain ranges. The idea was to get back to Macedonia in one piece and not to conquer all the mountains between here and Skopje. It was mid-September and we had been on the road for six weeks. With only four weeks left until Tito's car registration documents expired, there were still three countries to cover and for the first time I began to wonder if we had enough time. Certainly, I was ready to see the sea again and the thought of island-hopping Tito southwards on ferries was very appealing and would possibly spare our strength for the final legs through Montenegro, Albania and the Greek Peleponnese. But I dared not get too far ahead of myself; today was going to be a challenge.

————

A medley of grey and white clouds drifted across a blue sky, leaving white horsetails in their wake. The road looped between the hills passing through villages, interspersed with large sections of lush pastoral land. The signs of war appeared and disappeared from view. A shelled building, bullet holes on houses, an abandoned church, then moments of deeply forested hillsides on the brink of an autumnal colour change. The town of Donji Vakuf seemed out of place with its newly constructed shops painted in vibrant colours: green, yellow, red. We drove under a banner strung high across the street, '*Bajram Serif Mubarek Olsun*', the words heralding a "Happy Bajram" to its Muslim community, no doubt glad to be feasting after the month's fasting. At the far end of the main street, a large mosque dominated the landscape – its brightly coloured blue-domed roof matched an equally blue-topped minaret – and then we were back into the countryside once more.

The road veered south through the valley then turned sharply again, traversing the edges of a Muslim cemetery with a stone *turbe*, an enclosed family tomb, at its centre. It was an unusual sight and I involuntarily braked, peering through the passenger window. With no traffic ahead or behind, the temptation to investigate was too great, and I veered across the road onto a short track and came to a halt beside a low stone wall. Houses lay to the side of it. I felt I was being watched as I walked through the long grass hiding the now familiar turban-topped tombstones towards the *turbe*. As I peered through an opening into the round stone building at the two tombs lying lengthways across the whole diameter of the structure, and then looked up at the rounded stone ceiling, which arched to a soft point above them, a man parked and hurriedly walked towards me.

"*Dobar dan*," he beckoned questioningly.

I pointed to the building and smiled admiringly. He nodded and I attempted to explain in a kind of international language my interest in old buildings. He spoke a smattering of German and as we talked, his initial suspicion of me ebbed and was replaced with a sense of growing pride that I was taking an interest. He reset his glasses on his nose and informed me that this 100-year-old *turbe* contained the tombs of his family, while the cemetery itself also belonged to his family and went back 500 years. I gathered these facts from him by counting the fingers he raised. The conversation dried up and I wondered whether I had understood anything correctly, but I waved and thanked him, my curiosity satisfied. He watched me leave and I marvelled at the speed with which the neighbourhood network had leapt into action. Eyes were everywhere in this land – I was not sure if that comforted me or not, but I hoped for the best.

———

We had passed through Kopćić and Bugojno and now began the ascent – the challenge of the day. I changed down into second gear and settled back for a long climb. The road was quiet with few cars passing in either direction. Air flowed freely through the windows and I tore off a piece of today's baked bread from Travnik, idly eying the approaching articulated lorry through the rear-view mirror, its bulky body gradually gaining on us. After several bends and short climbs, it caught up. With not enough power to overtake on the short stretches between sweeping upward bends, the lorry plunged up and down gears, struggling to maintain the consistent cruise of Tito's 20km/h. The noise of its brakes, pistons, gear changes and creaking body mass was impossible to ignore. Would the elephant finally crush the ant? I hoped not. In vain, I searched for a place to pull over but there was none. The minutes ticked by and the tailback of vehicles grew. We entered a bend wide enough for me to indicate I was stopping. A long appreciative honk on the horn filled the air, enthusiastically re-echoed by the stream of cars behind him. Finally, the cacophony of toots died away as the last car disappeared around the bend ahead of us and we set off once again into the silence and solitude of the mountain road.

The ascent was so gradual it felt like torture. There was no knowing how close we were to the top, as the thickly forested landscape obscured all but the short stretches of road in front, and to drive Tito any faster would most likely end in a breakdown. There was nothing to do but try to relax and believe we would get there eventually. I had until this moment never considered using the cassette radio, which had been dubiously wired into the dashboard. I turned a button. Click. A low thunderous rumbling filled the air. I hastily turned the button back but the sound only increased in volume. I nervously prodded the machine, hoping it was not about to blow up. I negotiated the bend and stared ahead in disbelief. Another uphill stretch, and coming down in a dense green line towards us were army patrol vehicles, tanks, Land Rovers and lorries: the Bosnian Army on manoeuvres. A hefty force of metal, wheels and weapon power thundered past, their downward travelling pace being only fractionally faster than our upward one, but as they did, soldiers' heads appeared from every available opening to whoop and whistle encouragement. The pleasure at seeing a Zastava on the upward climb had brought about a spontaneous show of support which did much to spur Tito and me up the 1384 metres to the top.

———

There was no time to revel in our success as we hurtled downwards through a long, brightly lit tunnel, leaving the forests and greenery behind to emerge into a grey, open landscape which looked distinctly threatening and unfriendly.

The town of Kupres lay ahead, ghostlike and, to all appearances, uninhabited. Rows of empty new houses lay in the shadow of a church still under construction. It was on a colossal scale, way beyond the size of its surroundings, and I drove past it feeling small and vaguely intimidated. It was startling but there was no doubt as to the meaning – this was Catholic-dominated land. The tunnel had been the geographical dividing point. Beyond the reconstructed town, the landscape was a bleak wilderness. Whatever dwellings had existed in this region now lay bombed out and abandoned, their walls peppered with bullet holes. It was a shock to see such clear evidence of the war and for the first time I sensed how fierce the fighting must have been. Whoever had owned the land here previously, it was now a Croat-dominated area, and although a part of the Federation, there was no obvious sign of a mixed community living here. If they were, they were doing so quietly with no mosque or Orthodox church to mark their possible existence.

The road stretched endlessly across a sombre, desolate plain. It was entrancing and scary in equal measure; I had no choice but to drive across its immensity if I wanted to reach the coast and Croatia. I set my sights on the hills beyond the plain and drove.

———

B lack clouds were gathering into mammoth clumps and the curtain of heavy rain, although still some way away, appeared to be heading straight for us. The visual drama was spellbinding. We were only halfway across the plain but I felt compelled to stop the car. I had to photograph the scene, capture the essence of the moment, the colours and the vividly strange, overwhelming power this landscape was having on my emotions as I drove across it in a miniature car. It was the quiet before the storm – the road, the landscape and the sky, devoid of life. It was just Tito and me. Click. I took a stream of photographs and as the wind whipped up I quickly dived back into the car. In that split second, a red souped-up sports car raced towards us from across the other side of the plain. I fumbled with the ignition key, visions of murder or worse fuelling my imagination in this bleak wilderness. The car passed but in a sudden screech of brakes and a grinding gear change, I watched in horrified disbelief through the rear-view mirror as the car reversed at speed, and was paralysed into inaction. The car drew parallel with Tito and two young men with slicked-back dark hair and deep brown eyes stared out at me.

"*Dobar dan. Makedonski*?" This was followed by a string of Bosnian words.

I raised my shoulders, feeling a sense of calm wash over me, and said, "*Engleski*?"

"Is everything ok with the car? Have you broken down?" one of them asked earnestly. The murder scene evaporated as I absorbed their polite enquiry in perfect English.

"No, no; everything is fine, thank you."

"Ok, but we will wait until you start the engine," the other insisted.

I obliged, and Tito thankfully sprang into life at my first turn of the ignition key.

"Oh, it's fine, see? Thank you very much."

With that they drove off at high speed, leaving me feeling slightly taken aback by this unexpected encounter in the middle of nowhere.

———

Although the first band of rain missed us, we were not so lucky with the second. A momentary glimpse of a Byzantine – or perhaps Ottoman – bridge in the middle of the open plains was consumed by the rainstorm, obscuring it from sight. We had reached the hills on the far side of the plain where a wilder and more unforgiving landscape awaited us, as did a set of temporary road lights. A queue of traffic waited patiently ahead. From where they had come, I had no idea. Nothing had overtaken me since I had emerged from the tunnel and crossed the plain. The lights turned to green and we set off gingerly across a deeply raked tarmac surface. The rain came down in torrents and Tito's windscreen wipers flicked slowly backwards and forwards, unable to clear the quantity of water hitting the windscreen. I gripped the steering wheel tightly as his wheels were pulled this way and that, totally at the mercy of the drunkenly raked lines. The windscreen steamed up, further obscuring my vision and I frantically unwound the window. The rain drove in through the opening and battered against the roof but the blast of cool air cleared a patch of screen through which I peered as we began our descent into Livno, glad to be back in civilisation.

My relief was to be short-lived. As I circled through the residential streets looking for accommodation, our way was suddenly barred by a combi van screeching to a halt in front. A man got out and walked purposefully towards me. My heart jumped into my mouth. I felt I had had enough drama for one day. For a fleeting moment my imagination resurfaced. Had I been misidentified and was about to be mistakenly gunned down? His face scrutinised mine closely.

"*Makedonski*?" he enquired. "Skopje?"

I shook my head and squeaked, "*Engleski*."

His disappointment was evident. He turned on his heels and drove off without a further word, leaving me feeling drained, baffled but excessively relieved to be alive!

———

L ivno gleamed wet and green in a sudden burst of evening sunshine. A colourful mix of wild and domestically grown flowers in soft hues of pink, red and white grew in abundance along the banks of the river dividing the historic part of town in two. Former mill houses straddled a stream running parallel to the river, behind which lay a dramatic backdrop of steeply rising rock. Traditional stone and timber houses lined the street up to an elegantly arched stone bridge, which gracefully linked the two sides of the town for pedestrians. A man on the opposite bank was reading a newspaper, his back propped up against the wall of a destroyed masonry house, while his goats grazed quietly beside him. As I absorbed the scene, a man walked by.

He turned and said, *"Dobar dan."*

I was taken by surprise. Not many people had initiated a conversation with me in the street. This time I was sure I had been mistaken for someone else, but I answered anyway, and he walked on muttering to himself.

Ahead, and at the foot of the rockface, lay the source of the Bistrica River. A footpath encouraged walkers to follow its trail into a cave to view the river's source or to take another track up the hill to a lookout point. It was tempting, but after the events of today, instinct made me hesitate. A couple of metres up the track an interpretation panel quoting a poet's masterpiece briefly held my attention while I debated whether to risk the walk alone. The man who had greeted me moments before reappeared. He was a short, balding character wearing an oversized jacket of no particular colour but in which he seemed comically dwarfed, and on his feet were a pair of bright red trainers, possibly brand new and completely out of context with the rest of his rather sober appearance.

He smiled and said "Dobar dan," walking determinedly towards me as he spoke. He wanted me to follow him up the hill. "Viewpoint... photo... photo," he said disjointedly.

"No, no," I shook my head politely.

A figure came out and stood watching us from his garden below. I was not sure whether he had something to do with this red-shoed man or not.

Undeterred by my reticence, the red-shoed man said encouragingly, "Bistrica, Bistrica!" He tried to take my arm.

I backed away calmly, saying, "*Hvala, hvala,*" and shaking my head determinedly.

"Ok," he said, "Bye."

He put his hand out to shake mine. Caught unawares by his sudden acceptance of my unwillingness to follow, I offered him my right hand. He caught it quickly, deftly feeling my fingers while with his left hand he pushed up my jacket sleeve. Where my watch would normally be strapped, he looked in disgust at a woven pink friendship bracelet. I pulled my hand from his and backed off down the slope, glad that my handbag and camera were both firmly slung across my body. He did not follow and the figure in the garden retreated into his house as I walked onto the finely arched pedestrian bridge. I looked down into the river and then back up to where the red-shoed man stood watching me. It was an illogical reaction but I waved goodbye and then carried on across the bridge and down the road on the opposite bank, my adrenalin racing. I scoured the opposite slope and up to the lookout point. A younger man stood observing me. Maybe I was getting tired, exposing a sense of vulnerability I had not felt until today. Were the wheels of fortune turning with the season? I had to keep my imagination in check but certainly I would never again trust a Livno man wearing red shoes.

- Livno/Kamensko Border Control (31km) -

The day dawned bright, clear and sunny. I stashed a large chunk of Livno cheese, wrapped in multiple layers of plastic, on the backseat, another 'must eat' delicacy which vies with Travnik cheese as the best in Bosnia – I would leave that decision until I could picnic on the Croatian coast. The thought of crossing another border and entering my eighth Balkan country filled me with excitement, but first we had another plain to cross as well as an ominously high wall of grey mountains.

Much rain had fallen over night and Tito took some serious coaxing to start. We lunged haphazardly forward like a bucking bronco out of town with the choke at full throttle and into a garage for a much needed petrol stop. I joined a happy union of drivers on the forecourt making a similar stop. Tito's Macedonian number plate was drawing the usual amount of attention but by this time I had become so used to it, I was less conscious of the stares and more embarrassed by the disorganised mass of shoes, clothes and general paraphernalia which I had got into the habit of flinging onto the backseat rather than packing. Tito was turning into a walk-in wardrobe. I endeavoured to sort it out while I had the opportunity. Gathering a pile of empty water bottles and rubbish in the process, I reversed my body out from the backseat and straightened up. Seven pairs of eyes and seven amused faces stared at me, all of whom had been watching my moment of domesticity with interest. One by one, they smiled.

"Dobar dan," I said rather sheepishly, which was enough to trigger a barrage of questions.

They all began talking at once with the familiar words "Fića", *"Zastava"*, *"Makedonski'* and "Skopje" popping up.

"Engleski?" I interjected hopefully. They stopped and all shook their heads. I tried French and German but still there was no common language. Resignedly, we shrugged our shoulders, and with a polite, internationally recognisable "ciao" and a wave, Tito and I set off. Perhaps Livno was not

such a bad place after all – of course, none of them had been wearing red shoes.

———

A long, grey wall of mountain loomed large and impenetrable ahead of us. I braced myself for the climb of all climbs but as we came closer to its mass the road veered unexpectedly 90 degrees to the left and we were all of a sudden running parallel to it. It was an easy climb horizontally around a tapering end, past Lake Buško and to the border crossing. I had become accustomed to crossing traffic-free borders and this was no exception. Within minutes I had an exit stamp in my passport. We left the beauty and complexities of Bosnia and Herzegovina behind us and as we approached the Croatian border, I could almost smell the sea air 60 kilometres away.

CROATIA

SUNSHINE AND SHADOWS

- Kamensko Border Control/Split (61km) -

"You are doing journey in Fića?" he asked incredulously. "*Sretan put!*"

It had become the usual sceptical reaction to my presence behind the wheel of a vintage Yugoslav car, particularly at border crossings, but I took it as a positive endorsement of my journey and this meant more to me than a stamp in my passport.

I felt a rush of excitement at having reached another country, a further milestone in our journey. I could even begin to imagine that we might make it full circle, with just three countries left to negotiate before we crossed the border back into Macedonia. As we drove through a landscape dominated by grey-white stone, the houses and buildings constructed of the same material, I sensed a different Balkan environment; one that felt strangely appealing, or perhaps I was being wooed by the rising temperature akin to a glorious Mediterranean autumn day – hot, but not scorching.

The final 13km stretch to the coastal town of Split fanned out into a three-lane highway. Flashy cars sped past as Tito laboured up the hill. Roadworks ahead reduced the lanes from three to one and soon we became the lead car, with all the vehicles in front disappearing from view while everyone else, unlucky enough not to have passed us in time, crawled bumper to bumper behind us. As the tailback lengthened, an atmosphere of pent-up engine power followed us but there was nothing I could do; there was only one lane and we headed it. We advanced slowly to the summit. The van behind kept a respectful distance. Like a protective elder brother, the driver held back the super-charged tiger of power from overwhelming us. We picked up speed over the crest and down through a series of tunnels, the traffic snaking elegantly behind us like a royal motorcade following in the wake of Tito their king! Finally, the road widened into three lanes and cars sailed past in their droves, many giving us a friendly toot as we forked off onto a slip road and into the 'Centar'.

The absurd feeling of euphoria I had felt from our grand progression down into Split was short-lived as I struggled to negotiate the underpasses and one-way system which swung us around the city. It was more than I had bargained for – I needed two of me. One to drive, and the other to navigate, spot the accommodation, ensure I took the right turning, remain calm and not get despondent when every hotel I tried was fully booked and every apartment accommodation was unresponsive to my incessant bell ringing. I was not used to the heat after a week of cool Bosnian weather. The sheer number of people, cars and tourists, and English being spoken with such relative ease was a shock. It was a far cry from the unassuming interior Balkan world through which I had been travelling for the last six weeks, and I realised life was going to be considerably more expensive as a result.

The hotel staff referred to me as Madam and my swish bedroom, for which I had to pay a princely sum, was so European I had difficulty believing I was still in the Balkans;

but Tito was safely stowed in the hotel underground car park away from the frenetic life at street level and I could relax. I too was relieved to be in a cool, safe haven while I tried to adapt to this more popular, hedonistic Balkan world, and what better way to do it than to sleep a while?

- Split -

Large slabs of smooth white marble formed the pedestrian harbour front – the hub of a fascinating city oozing history, architecture, leisure and pleasure from every pore. Children raced their bicycles along it and glamorous bronzed women walked arm in arm with their handsome boyfriends, lovers or husbands while café terraces clamoured with customers. The old Roman palace of Diocletian dominated one end while the harbour itself encircled cruise boats and sailing vessels waiting to take young adventurous travellers out to sea or to the islands. The buzz and sophistication of it all was distinctly overwhelming after six weeks discovering an inland peninsular life of tradition, moderate means and self-sufficiency. Here, life appeared very modern and wealthy but I wondered whether it was just a façade fabricated for tourism.

Armed with a map, the Jadrolinija ferry timetable and a blank sheet of paper, I settled myself at a café table in one of the many squares in the old town and drafted an itinerary of island-hopping which would take us onto the Adriatic Sea and southwards to Dubrovnik.

Pleased with my two-week master plan, I prepared for the island adventure with a trip to Split's lively fruit and vegetable market, where I caught my first glimpse of a Croatian world beyond the tourists. Old women dressed in black shirts, ankle-length skirts and matching black headscarves sold their fresh produce from long rickety tables. I loaded up with bags of ripe plums, tomatoes, dried fruits and nuts and dragged myself away quickly; the impulse to buy more was difficult to ignore.

Evening came all too soon and in the warm night air people sat at intimate candlelit tables drinking wine, or wandered the vaulted depths of Diocletian's palace basements packed with local crafts for sale. They walked idly and browsed through the narrow lanes, Balkan tourists eyeing up their European counterparts while on their evening ritual stroll. A walk-in gallery was exhibiting photographs from the past; President Tito swimming underwater was one image that caught most people's eyes for its comical appeal. A middle-aged local man staggered drunkenly in through the door and roared with laughter at President Tito's compromising pose, cheeks puffed out as he held his breath and eyes narrowed within the confines of his goggles, his rather portly body on show beyond a pair of black swimming trunks. The man stared at him more soberly and then promptly began a conversation with the image. The words were lost on me, but people turned to smile at what he was saying and it struck me that no one really talked about President Tito; it was the recent war that preoccupied most who ventured an opinion. Was he liked or disliked? I did not know, and it was for this reason alone I was keeping the name of my four-wheeled companion to myself, not wishing to cause offence.

- Split/Vis (10km of driving) -

This would be my first journey out onto the Adriatic; I wondered whether Tito had ever been to sea in a previous life. Like everyone else, I parked illegally in front of the ticket office and joined the pushing and shoving for ferry tickets. An essential ingredient was to glare indignantly at everyone who jostled you, to talk loudly at them, and certainly to forget any British queuing etiquette. By some small miracle I eventually found myself at the front of the line handing over vast numbers of Croatian Kuna notes. In return I received a ticket to Vis – the most western and smallest of the southern Dalmatian group of islands – and the advice to hurry, as the boat would be leaving within the hour.

For such a small island destination, we mounted the ramp of an enormous ferry. I slid a cautionary brick behind the front and back wheels as compensation for Tito's lack of handbrake hold and headed up to the top deck. My expectations of quiet isolation disappeared; I was an English-speaking tourist among many and conversations flowed between an unlikely array of European and Canadian travellers as we left Split through a cloud of racing yachts heading towards the outer reaches of Croatian island life.

Two hours later, Vis appeared like a quaint rocky speck, gaining in clarity as we approached. Stone houses huddled together along the clear waters of the bay; the odd church spire broke the line of low-level roof tops above which rose the island heights, layers of rock and a mounded green covering of trees against a cloudless blue sky. In the harbour, boats moored at a respectable distance from one another, their sleek lines creating the perfect picture-postcard shot against the backdrop of the island. The dockside tourist agency endeavoured to meet my specific accommodation request and I was not disappointed. Tucked away at the far end of Vis town in the outer curve of the bay was Kut. Here, I had my own modest retreat, an attic room in an old stone house away from the port and general noise of town life. As I peered from my rooftop location I could hear the sea lapping against the pebbled shore below. Peace was restored once more and I tucked heartily into a picnic of fresh bread and tomatoes, accompanied by a hunk of Livno cheese, glad to have a blissful solitary moment while I savoured a final taste of Bosnia.

- Around the island of Vis (30km) -

Last night's dinner had consisted of king-sized prawns drowning in a *buzara* sauce – a Croatian delicacy which mingles the rich flavours of garlic, onion and tomato – accompanied by a glass or two of the local wine. I was glad to be by the sea once more, dining in the warmth of a September evening while still basking in a daytime heat. The climate does much to encourage wine-growing in the region and my first encounter with the island's wine had whetted my appetite for more – an expedition to the island's inland vineyards was essential.

We climbed steadily, high above sea level, where the sun blazed hot across a beautiful, yet unforgiving terrain. The colours reminded me of a Tuscan, Greek, Turkish and Provence environment all combined; a wide sloping plateau of olive trees, wild thyme and lavender, interspersed with manicured rows of vines on hillsides, above which low stone walls divided sections of the arid scrubland into patchwork quilt patterns and scattered piles of shale. Stone houses mingled together in pairs or lay in isolation, accessible only by an intricate network of spidery tracks.

I followed one. It led to a vineyard, rather unwelcoming in appearance with no sign of life. I backtracked in search of a friendlier establishment, and an old wooden sign caught my attention. I steered Tito up an adjoining track. Washing had been hung out to dry and as we approached the rustic stone house, the front door burst open and a middle-aged lady came out to greet me, beaming from ear to ear.

"*Dobar dan!*" she said in a cheerful booming voice, "Ah – Fića! *Makedonski!*"

I laughed and shook my head apologetically, pointing to the car and then to myself, uttering the words, "*Da! Auto Makedonski*, me *Engleski.*"

I had spontaneously created my own dialect,

incorporating German, English and Croatian words, in the hope that she might understand one of them. She nodded wisely and beckoned me into her front garden while at the same moment calling up to an upstairs window. The window shot open and a bearded head peered out at us. He looked at me and disappeared quickly back in through the window. In two seconds flat he was down with us, laughing jovially with his wife about some private joke. This slim, curious looking man in a freshly ironed white t-shirt, grey shorts and black clogs had a strange makeshift bandage wound around his head. It covered both his ears but whatever ailed him, it did not seem to be lowering his spirits in any way. The three of us proceeded down a path through the garden and into a stone vaulted cellar with white-washed walls. It was blissfully cool and a welcome relief from the searing midday heat.

In one half of the room sat enormous brown plastic vats of wine covered with white cloths. In the other half of the room, tables topped with an array of bottles and glasses had been assembled, constituting the tasting area. The owner enthusiastically joined me in sampling red and white wines and port. He talked and laughed constantly and although it was clear that neither of us had a clue what the other was saying, it did not seem to matter. I decided on a bottle of his fruity full-bodied *domaći* red wine, which he handed to me with great ceremony, self-consciously removing the bandages from his head in one sweep before he did so.

———

W ho would have believed that Britain had once possessed Vis, this beautifully remote island? But it had been many years ago, when Napoleon was on the attack and the British Empire seemed to be everywhere.

It was late afternoon as I forged along an overgrown path down to a sheltered cove for a quick dip in the ocean, and

stumbled across a small graveyard discreetly set between four
stone walls. The iron gates were rusting but one side opened
smoothly on its hinges and I entered. Within this secluded
space lay the graves of several British soldiers. I wondered
whether anyone remembered they were here. It all looked a
little unkempt and, as I closed the gate, I hoped someone,
somewhere did pay his or her respects to them from time to
time.

———

The long steep downward spiral into the fishing port of
Komiža had Tito's brakes squeaking in the dry heat of
the day. We had made it to the other end of the island
successfully and freewheeled the last stretch to the harbour
front and parked opposite a line of fishing boats bobbing up
and down in the marina. Tito was an instant attraction and I
left him to the scrutiny of others while I went to explore the
centuries-old fishermen's houses which lay appealingly at the
far end of the bay – a glimpse into life from the past, but
clearly under pressure to embrace the present with the
island's rise in popularity as a tourist destination.

The harbourside was lined with cafés bursting with
European tourists and I found myself in amongst them,
tempted by the smell of coffee. Tables were crammed together
tightly and I found myself sitting next to an English couple,
Sandra and Doug, both keen to engage me in conversation,
and I found myself enjoying a dose of British rhetoric. Not
since Edirne had I met any Britons or ones who possessed the
dry wit and banter I so much enjoyed. Before long, they had
enthusiastically accepted my casual invitation of a ride back
to Vis in an old Yugoslav car. It was the first time I had
travelled any real distance with passengers but, unconcerned
by the extra weight, Tito charged steadily up the mountain
road of Hum. The roadside acknowledgements, which I had

become so used to accepting as part of life with a Fića, became all the more enjoyable with Sandra's loud exclamations of, "Did you see that, Doug? They're waving at us! That's hysterical!" And Doug's snorts of amusement, "Is this as fast as you can go?" and, "Where's the wing mirrors? Did they drop off?" He pulled up the seat belt end and declared dismissively, "Who needs it! Ha, luckily not me!" While Sandra in the backseat warned, "Well, there isn't even a belt in the back so I'm gonna end up crushing you if we crash."

"Please don't crash, Emma!" Doug whispered.

"Don't worry, I won't," I said, giggling like a teenager and feeling like I was enacting a *Famous Five* adventure.

We were the noisiest and jolliest car on the road and as we reached the narrow residential streets of Kut, but one car's width, I regained my sobriety as I felt the brakes straining to hold the weight of all three of us. We were cautiously creaking down the hill when a man rushed out in front of us. I flung up the handbrake, giving extra support to Tito's already straining brake mechanism, and came to a halt. The man's rapturous cries of "Fića!" and "*Dobra, dobra!*" flowed through the window. Doug and Sandra stared in disbelief at this spontaneous outburst of lively communication from a local Croatian. When he realised we were all "*Engleski*" he backed off with a disappointed sigh, while Sandra, unable to restrain her laughter for a moment longer, burst out: "That's amazing! People talk to you because of the car! That's fantastic! What a... oh that's so funny!"

She continued to enthuse all the way down the hill until we were parked. Doug insisted I show him the engine and took a step back in alarm as the fireworks of bubbling oil and gurgling water emerged from behind the engine door. Sandra's face said it all.

"Oooh, aren't you afraid you're gonna break down?"

"Well, yes, sometimes," I admitted. "But I've got this far

with only two major catastrophes, so that's not bad going really. And if I'm going to break down, I'm in the best place; everyone knows about Fićas in former Yugoslavia and apparently," I said conspiratorially, "All they need is a spoon to be able to fix it – so someone told me in Belgrade – so what could go wrong?" I laughed at Sandra's apparent belief in this but quietly hoped I had not jinxed my long run of mechanical-free mishaps since Bulgaria.

- Vis/Brač (34km) -

The Jadrolinija ferry left promptly at 1.30pm as I peeled back the wrapping to my picnic of bread and cheese, courtesy of Livno, accompanied by the remaining tomato and plums which I had bought from the Split market – a perfect "*al fresco*" meal. Doug and Sandra bowled over with cries of surprise that we were on the same ferry. We passed a pleasant few hours on the calm seas of the Adriatic, discussing our next destinations, but before too long the boat docked into Split and we said our final farewells as they headed back to the town centre to prepare for their flight home and I went in search of the boat to Supetar and the Island of Brač.

The ferry looked more like a large raft, and much smaller than everyone had expected. Earnest-faced drivers vied for pole queuing position, blocking other cars to ensure their chances of getting on board. No one wanted to be left behind and chaos ensued until a Jadrolinija official called a halt to the pushing and shoving. He organised us into an orderly line, making no concession to those who thought they should be nearer the front and, with calm restored, obediently we filed up the ferry ramp for the short 45-minute crossing and no one was left behind.

Supetar harbour was crowded with people; some laden with suitcases and sun hats waiting to board, while others looked eagerly for friends or relatives leaving the boat. As

Tito and I disembarked, I could hear the word "Fića!" ripple through the crowd. We edged our way slowly through the port towards the road signposted to Bol. A flurry of ferry traffic tore past us, some with a backward glance and a smile. Soon we were the only car left to conquer the 800-metre climb ahead. On recommendation, I had booked my accommodation in advance and for once I had no need to worry, nor any reason to hurry; a bed was waiting.

The island of Brač is famed for its white marble. It forms the walls of Diocletian's Palace in Split and the White House in Washington DC. Interesting as this may be to some, the island's real tourist attraction is a pebbly peninsula known as Zlatni Rat. This UNESCO-listed wonder was in darkness by the time Tito and I descended the rocky marble laden heights of Brač into the town of Bol.

A sliver of moon cast a delicate stream of light across the night sky. The streets were eerily silent as I walked up from the town square in search of dinner. A restaurant had been recommended to me by my hostess.

"The best seafood in Bol," she had said with conviction, and I had headed up the hilly residential quarter in search of it. A yellow pool of electric light shone out in the darkness and as I pulled open the door I was hit by the sound of rhythmic traditional music. The waiters sang gustily in between taking orders and serving food. Diners talked at full volume, their faces glowing from a day in the sun and I, tucked into my corner table, was happy to be a part of such a joyful crowd.

Filled with fresh seafood delicacies, I left the boisterous atmosphere of the restaurant for the cool and quiet of a warm evening. My footsteps broke the silence as they made contact with the tarmac surface and I passed a number of stairways leading back down into the gloom. It was darker than when I had walked up. I could not remember which stairway I had taken; they all looked the same. A biker in black leathers and helmet drove past. He turned to look as I hesitated at the top of a long flight of steps. *Was it this one?* He manoeuvred his motorbike round and parked metres away. His helmet was still on as he strode towards me, perhaps unaware of his intimidating appearance. I heard voices below and hurtled down the steps towards them, calling out, "*Dobro veče*. Hello?"

Four tanned, wrinkled faces looked up at me. Thankfully, they spoke English. I cast a glance upwards. The biker's strides had shortened.

"Come with us," one of the elderly women said, while her male companion nodded in agreement, "We will show you the way down. It is easy to get lost here." Perhaps it was my encounter in Livno that had made me so nervous, but I was grateful for the unexpected arrival and generosity of these two elderly Croatian couples, as we sauntered down the badly lit passageways into the town square.

- Bol, Brač Island -

I relished a momentary sense of being on holiday from travelling. Breakfast on the terrace, reading a book in the garden, and drinking coffee by the sea. In this window of relaxation, it was fascinating to observe the world of packaged holidays going on around me.

Zlatni Rat was the focus of most people's attention. Day-trippers poured off excursion boats, blasting out music as their anchors clattered and mooring ropes were thrown to shore in a wild frenzy. For two hours each morning the silence of Bol was broken as more and more people arrived on the island. They disembarked from their boats. Some broke into a run towards the famous pebbled peninsula, seemingly fearful of missing something if they did not hurry, while others looked sternly at their maps and argued about what they should do first.

Earlier I had walked along the cool, shadowy avenue of trees to Zlatni Rat – a natural wonder of the world, yet an ever-shifting one as the bank of stones, half-submerged in the sea, move. This is probably insignificant to most except to the environmentalists and geographers who must constantly have to re-map its location. I walked with difficulty across the large pebbles to the point at which they disappeared into the shallow waters and paddled awkwardly in the clear blue sea, searching for a flat stone on which to place my feet. A sleek private motorboat edged cautiously into shallow water and dropped anchor. It was the first of the day. A bronzed, overweight couple were helped into the water by their skipper. They swam around, staring upwards at Vidova Gora, a stark but striking mountain which loomed above us all. The walk to the top was for those with more energy than those who preferred to lie on towels in uncomfortable huddles, soaking in the full intensity of the sun. Personally, I could not see the attraction of either option. It was too hot for hiking and the alternative of draping myself uncomfortably across a pile of stones all day with no hope of shade, certainly did not appeal. I walked back along the avenue of trees, passing the large faceless hotels, and headed to the other side of the harbour. Here, a small beach nestled within the rocks, a haven for those who, like me, had decided Zlatni Rat was not for them.

An evening festival – celebrating what, I never did find out – brought stalls selling locally produced crafts, food and music to the streets. Children danced and adults clasped a bottle of beer or glass of island wine, enjoying the last of what September brings.

"How much Brač has changed with tourism!" A local photographer expressed to me ruefully, "But if you go deeper into the island's centre, you will see a more remote side to island life – and these," he said, pointing to the photograph I had just bought from him. Conical-shaped stone shelters dotted the island landscape. Shepherds' huts – a necessary shelter for them and their flock during the sudden weather changes which occur frequently and without warning in winter. Such was life after the summer tourism season was over.

- Bol/Makarska (22km) -

A fresh wind blew as I sat down to breakfast on the terrace. A single red leaf fluttered through the air and pirouetted onto the tablecloth. I picked up its delicate form by the stem and regarded it thoughtfully. There was no denying that autumn was on its way; we could not escape it by heading any further west. October was less than a week away. However, despite the wind, the day was going to be warm and I felt confident I still had a couple of weeks of good weather ahead of me.

Tito started effortlessly; it would be he who would tell me when it was time to hurry back to Skopje but for now all was well. The road wound inland and along the island's central spine. On either side the landscape rolled out bleak and harsh. It was not long before I spotted a shepherd's shelter, almost invisible within the rocky landscape, but my interest in it was short-lived as the geological mass ahead became more apparent. A grey wall of mountain gripped the side of Croatia's coastline. Its immensity horrified me, perhaps more because I viewed it through the confines of Tito's matchbox-sized windscreen. This was the way we had to travel; the mainland route southwards, which would link us with our next island destination. There was no direct island hop. It filled me with trepidation. Could Tito really survive a journey through these, the Dinaric Alps?

———

The road dipped down into Selca, to a scene of islanders going about their daily lives. School children played basketball, while adults drank coffee and dogs lazed in the early afternoon sunshine. Some of the stone-tiled roofs were blanketed in a protective layer of white mortar, giving the effect of sugar-frosting to these 17th century houses. Old battered Renaults lay parked in the tree-lined square. All in all, life seemed quiet, civilised and even a touch old-fashioned – a refreshing change to witness a moment of ordinary Croatian island life.

Sumartin lay but a short distance from Selca. I parked behind a queue of two locked vehicles and waited for the Jadrolinija ferry to arrive. Boats bobbed gently on their moorings in the marina, the doors and window shutters around the bay remained firmly closed, including those of the ticket office. A fisherman soundlessly organised his boat, inspecting the lantern which hung gracefully over the bow, while across the bay a larger bellied fishing vessel was under construction, the timber still clean and pure. It was comforting to see that small-scale industry did exist, albeit discreetly behind the veil of tourism.

The diminutive ferry slid gently into Sumartin, hardly disturbing the afternoon peace. The two drivers ahead of us in the queue strolled back to their locked vehicles as the ferry ropes were coiled around the harbour moorings. A sizeable line of cars had formed behind us but every waiting vehicle was squeezed onto the deck with military precision and we headed across the sea towards the coastal town of Makarska, behind which the Dinaric Alps rose incongruously. The proximity of Brač to the mainland was such that only a narrow band of water separated us, and although this was still the Adriatic Sea, it was like glass; so clear that one could easily see down through its depths to the seabed.

The ramp was lowered onto a grassy kerb and we disembarked into a world buzzing with street cafés, cruising cars, ice cream stalls, and a market teeming with holidaymakers. The choice of immediate accommodation was limited and I was keen to get somewhere without too much cruising around.

The Balkan ritual of evening strolling got underway as I settled onto a wooden bench overlooking the harbour to devour, as elegantly as I could in fast tongue-sweeping movements, two fast melting scoops of Makarska's finest chocolate and raspberry ice cream, propped precariously together on top of a wafer cone. As the sky turned pink, a high-masted boat resembling something out of *Pirates of the Caribbean* nosed its way towards Makarska. Music reverberated from the deck, instantaneously engaging my attention. Strollers turned in mid-stride. We were all stunned by the unexpected sight that had exploded into the bay. The sun set, but we all missed it, transfixed by the deck load of dancing passengers, totally oblivious to the impact they were having upon Makarska's inhabitants. The boat anchored and a stream of sun-scorched, adrenalin-racing passengers disembarked. To where they disappeared I could not tell, but where they ended up later that night could not have been any other place than the nightclub opposite my hotel bedroom window, where they partied until dawn while I tried ineffectually to block out the sounds under a towering pile of pillows.

- Makarska/Hvar (104km) -

The standard Balkan hotel breakfast of omelette, featherlight bread, orange juice and coffee did little to re-energise me and any thoughts I had had of exploring the national parklands of the Dinaric mountains paled to nothing. Instead, we headed directly south along the coast, running parallel to the ominous heights of the Dinaric range which, thankfully, did not need to be scaled to reach the village port of Drvenik.

———

There is a natural fault line running down Croatia's coastline and into the neighbouring country of Montenegro. A number of devastating earthquakes have been recorded along its length, the last being experienced as recently as the 1990s. On the slopes of this grey indomitable mass there were signs of abandoned houses. Graceful stone structures with the most astounding views of the coast and islands beyond; today, they were roofless empty shells. Life would be harsh and isolated in this rough, unforgiving terrain and not at all for the faint-hearted. Of course, I did not know whether these houses had been abandoned because of earthquakes, or as a result of the recent war. Either way, it seemed tragic that communities had abandoned their courageous way of life, which must have been built up over generations, and for their homes to be left to face the elements, unprotected and at the mercy of nature. Perhaps, even more tragically, it might be that these homes belonged to those who felt they could not return for fear of retribution or ostracism.

———

Drvenik's port was small and unassuming. Cars had gathered in line although the next ferry was not due for another hour.

"Ah! Fića!" someone shouted out in recognition, but at that moment I had already locked up Tito and was strolling towards the ticket office. Drivers turned to look at him and I found myself compelled to look too, happy to be admiring him in the knowledge that he was mine.

The crossing to the Island of Hvar, the next island south of Brač in the Dalmatian chain of islands, was not the millpond experience of yesterday, although the sun continued to shine and the sea remained clear and inviting. As the ferry docked, I removed the bricks from behind Tito's wheels and climbed in ready to disembark.

Within minutes everyone had overtaken us and I was left to admire the island's wild beauty at my leisure, as we journeyed westwards from the port of Sucaraj across the backbone of Hvar Island to the former Venetian capital port of Stari Grad. Although forest fires had swept across the island years previously, destroying much of its flora and fauna, nature was fighting back. Where forests had once dominated the landscape, swathes of wild lavender and thyme, olive and fig trees now took their place. A handful of villages lined the route and as Tito and I travelled through these tranquil places with their elegant stone houses, a curious inhabitant occasionally lifted his or her head from their gardening endeavours and gave us a spontaneous friendly wave as we passed by.

Between villages, the road was narrow, steep and extremely frightening – one error of judgement and we would be over the side with no road barriers to prevent almost certain death. I took things even more slowly than usual, wary of Tito's basic braking system and the acute bends which must be navigated, and equally fearful of meeting a vehicle travelling in the opposite direction. I spotted a stone shelter largely hidden beneath the low branches of a stout fir tree bent over by strong winds. Curious, I pulled over and got out to investigate. The undergrowth was thick with wild thyme, unleashing a heady scent with my every step. I was wearing the wrong footwear for such a venture but I managed to reach this low-built igloo-shaped structure and poke my head in through the sturdy doorway. It was pitch dark inside. I could see nothing and retreated quickly, not wishing to disturb anything that may be lurking in its cool depths. It did not look as though it was used much these days. As we continued along the route, I scoured the landscape for more such shelters, but taking take my eyes from the road was becoming more hazardous as it became increasingly filled with twists and turns and I gave up my quest; reaching Stari Grad in one piece was more important.

Once the capital of Hvar, today Stari Grad, which directly translated means "Old Town", is just that and, disappointingly, very quiet. Given my expectations of finding a bustling historic fishing town filled with atmosphere and Venetian history, the town was almost without life. Fishermen quietly mended their nets strung out between trees down the street but the quaint, narrow alleyways revealed shuttered windows and doorways, the squares filled with terracotta pots of flowers and no one to appreciate them. I decided to head further south to the current capital of the island, also called Hvar, in search of life.

The tunnel was long but lit and its downhill slope gave the impression of freefalling into another place. This was indeed the case as we emerged into daylight and continued down into a walled city, sophisticated and filled with elite tourism. On the town's outer edge sat the bus station, car parking and anything else that might spoil the beautiful face of Hvar. In a moment of indecision, I parked in one of the four empty parking bays of the bus station, outside of which the tourist office had been conveniently located. It was closed despite the fact it should have been open, according to the hours posted in the window. Glancing back at Tito to check he was ok, I risked a quick sprint down into the main square in the hope of spotting anything that might resemble a place to stay. The smell of wealth hit me full in the face: affluent people enjoying the afternoon sun, eating a late lunch, some on board their yacht. The level of luxury was immeasurable, whether compact or deluxe; sophistication spilled out of every boat.

A loud honk, closely followed by another more prolonged blast, heralded the arrival of a bus and brought me out of my reverie and hurtling back across the square to Tito. The driver regarded me with bored tolerance, chin in hand, elbow on steering wheel. It was clearly not the first time that his parking bay had been obstructed. The passengers appeared less tolerant of my blatant parking violation and glared disapprovingly at me. With an apologetic smile, I hurriedly reversed Tito out and took to the road above the town, hoping it might lead me to some accommodation and easy parking. We gained height, passing through another tunnel and out into an area high above a second bay, where there was a hotel and a couple of pensions. Neither of these responded to my doorbell ringing so I braced myself for the hotel, which looked rather chic with a terrace bar and plush seating from where one could admire the sea view. It had to be tried.

"Yes madam, we have a room. How many are you?"

"Oh, just myself," I responded.

"Ah, you are alone, madam?"

I nodded.

"In which case we do not have a room. You must be two persons."

"I must be two persons to have a room?" I repeated incredulously.

"Yes madam, if you can be two persons, we have a room for you."

I looked at him in amazement and wondered for a moment whether he was joking but his face was a picture of seriousness. It was the end of the holiday season yet because I was one and not two persons, he was turning me away.

"This is ridiculous. You have a room. I need a room. But because I am on my own, I am not able to stay?"

"That is quite right, madam. Hotel policy," he stated, and was clearly not going to make an exception.

Mildly fuming at the hotel's policy but convinced that there would be something better closer to the harbour, I threw Tito around the bends like a rally driver, becoming more carefree with our speed than perhaps I should, but we arrived safely back at the bus station and a public car park. I had rarely left him so publicly exposed and out of observational distance when packed to the gills with my luggage, but on this occasion I had no choice.

Passport, money, camera, sunglasses – nothing else really matters anyway, except Tito; but even he has done me proud, so if this is the moment for him or my possessions to be stolen, I thought dramatically, *so be it.* I walked away from him in the direction of the harbour for a coffee, and to think what to do next.

Hvar seemed to be in a different league to everywhere else I had been. It evoked a sense of unruffled grace and polite behaviour. Cradled in charm and wealth, even the coffee looked chic, although thankfully the price was still affordable. I admired the cobblestoned square, smoothed over the decades by the passage of countless feet. Along its lengths, shops were set discreetly into the old stone walls. A number of restaurants had prime terrace space allocated to them, from which one could either look out to sea or inwards towards the hallowed lines of the cathedral and its bell tower, the town rising up on all but one side of the square, that one being open to the sea. Suitably re-energised by a luxurious coffee or two, I headed up one side of the town, taking the steps two at a time, following a number of signs leading to pension accommodation. However, no one seemed to be home and I wondered if, for the first time, I would be sleeping across Tito's backseat – homeless in Hvar.

One possibility remained. I had been eyeing it from afar, nestled above the bay. I wandered thoughtfully up the stone steps towards the white-washed building, my instinct telling me this was the place. Croatia had become the most expensive part of my journey and I continued to swallow hard at the prices I had had to pay anywhere as a single guest. The entrance door slid open automatically and as I walked into the reception area, good fortune followed me. A room overlooking the harbour was free and at a generous last-week-of-the-season rate which I could not only afford, but could not possibly refuse. The curly red-headed hotel porter stepped forward magnanimously.

"I am Leopoldo. I will help you with your luggage." He extended his tanned and freckled hand in welcome and we set off in search of Tito.

The narrow lanes of Hvar connected together like an intricate game of snakes and ladders but Leopoldo knew exactly how to get us to the public car park with the minimum of fuss.

"I will drive," Leopoldo said with complete Balkan male confidence.

I hesitated. "Well actually, I think I should drive if you don't mind; it would be easier and I think I would prefer it."

He looked a little taken aback but as I walked towards Tito his expression changed. "You have Fića!" he exclaimed, and enthusiastically smacked his hand on the roof.

I carefully removed the red roses given to me by Marijan in Vares, which had now dried to a deep red colour, and untwisted the coat hanger locking device to open the passenger door. Leopoldo climbed in, talking nineteen to the dozen about the wonders of Fićas, unconcerned that his kneecaps were firmly squashed up against the dashboard or that he had to hold his head at an awkward angle under the low roof. He wound down the window and I was instructed to slow down or stop while he greeted his many acquaintances *en route* to the hotel parking. His delight at travelling in a Fića that had come all the way from Macedonia was all too obvious.

"Your car is safe here," he said with grave authority, unwinding himself out of the passenger seat as we arrived at the out-of-town hotel parking. I secured the passenger door once more and with Leopoldo beguiling me with tales of

Fićas, I locked the driver's door and turned my back on Tito for a few days by the sea.

- Hvar -

Expensive boats glided in and out of the harbour, diners ate in the glow of the cathedral by night and by day drank coffee and explored the rocky shoreline, finding their own private space among the rocks to sunbathe, picnic, and launch themselves into the sea, aided by conveniently placed metal ladders fixed to the rocks courtesy of Hvar's conscientious service towards its visitors.

My favourite spot was further along the shore than most wished to walk, and as I perched on the rocks to dry off after a long swim, swathed in a beach towel against the wind, a man I had seen taking over "my place" as I had left the day before, arrived. He swam out further than I had dared and then ascended one of the metal ladders nearby. It moved unsteadily and he commented in Croatian.

I shrugged. "Sorry, *Engleski*."

"You tourists are all the same; break everything and then leave." He winked flirtatiously.

"Actually, it was probably the Italians. They come here. Many, many!"

It transpired that he was the owner of a luxury villa on the hillside. Tourists from all over Europe stayed. The problem was finding staff who would work hard.

"In Croatia, no one wants to work – we are all too lazy," he said, almost to himself.

"If I can have free accommodation and a chance to stay here longer, I'll come and work for you," I said cheekily.

"Why don't you?" he encouraged.

It was tempting but I had a journey to finish. I shook my head.

"Well, it was worth a try. Maybe next time…?" he said

playfully and dived into the sea again as I gathered my things and headed back to the hotel to pack.

- Hvar/Korcula (18km) -

Leopoldo was waiting. He handed me a strong hot coffee on the breakfast terrace. The day had dawned clear and bright but an autumnal cool hovered over us. Hvar was still asleep, the luxury boats, hotels and homes barely breathing.

"OK, let's go." Leopoldo picked up my rucksack and strode off. I quickly downed the last drops of coffee and hurried after him. It was the end of the working season and in two days he would be travelling to Bosnia with his wife and son to visit family. Although summer work was all they could rely on, their life was in Hvar, he as the hotel porter and general maintenance man, and she cleaning the rooms. Here he said they could earn a good living if the tourist season was kind to them – and it was currently the best income opportunity open to them.

A heavy blanket of condensation lay over Tito. I braced myself for a tricky start-up. While Leopoldo dried the windows, I gently tried to coax the engine into life. The choke was angled at full lift, my foot pushed firmly down on the accelerator pedal and the gears in neutral. I turned on the ignition. Nothing. My heart sank. I went through the motions again. Leopoldo was desperate to take over but I knew Tito and the tricks required to spark him into action. It was just going to take a bit longer than usual this morning.

"Come on, Tito, don't make us miss the ferry," I said between gritted teeth, turning the ignition key with determination. He wheezed faintly to show me he was alive. Leopoldo stood with his arms on his hips; he was all for pushing the car into a jump start. "Just a bit longer; he'll be ok," I said with a confident smile.

The engine roared into life and then died. But with the

next try he held out, backfiring with the effort, the exhaust shattering the early morning peace. I sat with my foot pressed firmly on the accelerator pedal while he warmed up. Leopoldo rolled his eyes heavenwards in relief. I reversed out of the parking space and we lurched our way towards the exit and out onto the road, not daring to stop. "*Hvala, ciao!*" I shouted out of the window and Leopoldo waved farewell. I shifted into second, then third gear, then back into second as we advanced up the hill and out of Hvar.

The ferry terminal signage loomed larger than life above an equally vast dockside area totally out of proportion to the few cars waiting there. The numerous queuing lanes, for Italy as well as Croatia, were indicative of how busy Hvar must get at the height of the holiday season. A Jadrolinija official directed me into one lane then changed his mind, twice. We zigzagged across the empty queuing markers while he decided where to place us. He peered at me through the open window.

"Italy?" he said hopefully.

"No, Korčula."

"Ah, must go over there."

I once again crossed the many empty lanes for a final time.

The ferry arrived and departed, filling only one-quarter of its interior. It was 9.00am as we cruised out of Hvar's western bay and followed the island's coastline southwards to Korčula. The remnants of old abandoned stone houses and villages could be clearly seen, their life long over, perhaps waiting for a new one with the financial help of a wealthy owner. I was sure there would be many willing to take on the dream in time.

As the defensive walls of Korčula's old town came into view, a few of us prepared to disembark. The majority, it seemed, had no time to stop; they were heading to the mainland, but Tito and I descended the ramp, passing a small crowd who had gathered to welcome friends or family, and while Tito received his usual attention from passersby, I kept my focus on the road signs and headed around the old town to the other side of the bay, once again in search of somewhere to stay.

———

K orčula is proud of its Marco Polo connections, although the one remaining tower of his alleged birthplace did little to increase my paltry knowledge of the man, his life on the island or his purported capture by the Venetians in the 13th century. It did, however, provide a superb view over the old terracotta roofs of Korčula and back towards the mainland of Croatia, where I would be returning once again, although a fair few kilometres south of my previous stop in Makarska and subsequent departure point from Drvenik.

Disappointed to have missed the season of Moreška sword dancing and fighting which, by all accounts, embodied all one could hope for in a live performance, I drifted through the town's centuries-old lanes and alleyways, across which rows of washing hung out to dry. A cruise ship anchored, and large groups of tourists descended onto the streets, filling the cafés, shops and pavements with wealthy individuals ready to consume Korčula's history, architecture, churches, seafood, pizza, coffee and ice cream in equal measures. I found myself retreating up onto the town's defensive walls and into a rooftop bar accessible only by a dubious looking stepladder. The view from the top was both dizzy and exhilarating but a strong wind made it difficult to enjoy the moment for long.

I descended back to ground level with a sigh and indulged in a double-tiered cone of vanilla and chocolate ice cream for comfort. Travelling in a Zastava had drawn unexpected moments of spontaneous generosity and hospitality from many along the way but the novelty of going it alone was definitely wearing off. The frustration of not being able to communicate with people, beyond the niceties, had at times been isolating and for the first time, I was starting to tire of my own company and to relish the thought of being back in Skopje, the journey over.

- Korcula/Viganj (10km) -

Large noses, crooked noses, long faces, bony faces, fat cheeks and furrowed brows. The row of comic faces and ogling eyes etched in the cornice above was hard to ignore as they stared down on me from the building opposite. I ate my breakfast in amused contemplation, gazing up at these curious faces – former Korčula inhabitants, perhaps? They were not a particularly handsome bunch but their mere existence had been company enough.

It was the last day of September; the sun shone and I wondered how long our luck would hold as we joined the waiting line of vehicles for the ferry to the mainland. As the boat arrived, the queue slowly edged forward until we were on board for the short crossing to Orebić on the Pelješac peninsula.

The road took us high above the coast before dropping down onto a narrow tarmac lane precariously close to the sea, from where it wound its way along a kind of high tide mark. It provided the only link to the string of private homes, holiday apartments and village clusters on the landward side. Two women were busily hanging out white linen bed sheets. I called up to them but they shook their heads. Closed. It was the end of the season now. No, they did not know of any place in Viganj still open.

As I climbed back into the car, smoke gently rose up from the steering column and a burning smell filled the air. I hurriedly wound down the window and peered more closely at the smoking cables bulging from the side of the steering casing. Was it just the sun pouring through the windscreen and heating up the plastic sheathing, or was this more serious? It certainly had not happened before. I reversed back into the lane. The steering wheel still moved, so surely nothing was about to blow up? As I contemplated whether to ignore it or not, a man and woman meandered past hand in hand. They looked inquisitively at me and I at them. I hazarded a "*Dobar dan, Engleski*?"

They stopped.

"Yes, yes we speak English," the elegant looking white-haired lady responded with a thick German accent.

"Do you know if there is any accommodation? An apartment free or something?"

"There are many here; you will have no problem," she said reassuringly. "Is this your car? Where are you coming from?"

As I began to explain, she stopped me in mid-sentence and, turning to include her husband who had stood patiently by while we ladies talked, announced, "We were just going for something to eat; why don't you join us?"

It seemed as though providence had just hit me smack between the eyes.

"Actually, that would be great! Should I park here or would you like a ride?"

They looked at each other and then at me. "We would love to go in your car!"

"Of course! Climb in."

Oda and Klaus clambered in tentatively, and we set off down the road, their enjoyment at being in a Fića being more than evident while I kept a quietly concerned eye on the smoking steering column, hoping I was not about to blow us all up. We arrived at a bar on the water's edge which looked more like something you would see in Hawaii, with its timber platform, tables and benches and thatched roof. This was Bistro Montun and for the following three hours we dined on fish, meat and vegetables, grilled traditionally on an open fire and under a terracotta bell-shaped hood. To eat, drink and revel in the company of strangers whom I felt I had known all my life was an unexpected pleasure and did much to bolster my spirits once more. Although Oda and Klaus were not from Croatia, it did not matter; it was our human connection which mattered and the ease of communication which did much to renew my zest for the journey and appreciation for the encounters one can be fortunate enough to have, however short, while on the road as a single traveller.

———

Tomorrow Oda and Klaus were heading north. I, in the meantime, was heading south but first I had to find some accommodation for the night. Within a couple of hundred yards down from the bistro, a sign signalling *'Apartmani'* caught my attention. I pulled over. "*Dobar dan. Apartmani*?" I enquired hopefully.

The man and woman looked at each other, hesitated momentarily, then the woman smiled and said, "*Da, da*, why not. It's ok. Are you by yourself?"

I nodded. They directed me to park on the right of the driveway under a fig tree laden with plump, ripe fruit. I unloaded my luggage and the man helped me to my room, excusing himself quickly.

"There is much to do. I am leaving in two days." He had received a phone call. The boat would be sailing earlier than expected. Six months at sea and as usual not much notice had been given. He must organise things for his family before he left. This was the reality of life for many living on the coast of Croatia. The men could earn a living during the tourist season. Afterwards they left for six months or longer. Going to sea ensured enough income for the family to survive the rest of the year.

My offer to help, although warmly received, was politely turned down. I went for a swim. Although it was the end of September, the sea was still warm and as I swam up and down, I watched the preparations going on, on land. It was a well-rehearsed drill and everyone knew what to do. The fishing boat was unloaded onto the marina, the motor removed and then rowed up to the shore. The neighbours appeared and together they helped pull the boat ashore, up to dry land to where it would lie upside down until the spring. A community spirit filled the air, helpful, positive yet mindful of the family's sadness at the forthcoming departure. I watched with curiosity the dynamics, the support, and the unity of families whatever their age; this was one side of Croatian life which faces many households once the short tourism season is over.

The sun set over the Pelješac peninsula. It was a peaceful evening intermittently broken by the slap of small waves hitting the harbour wall and the distant hum of an outboard motor as a fisherman checked his lobster pots. The apartment owner's wife waved to me from the house and held up a bowl of food. I got up from my perch on the marina wall and climbed the steps up to her.

"You must be hungry. Come and eat." She handed me an enormous bowl of spaghetti bolognese and a glass of their homemade *'domaći'* wine.

"*Hvala,*" I said, overcome by her hospitality at a time when so much else was going on. "Yes, it is never easy," she admitted, "But we are used to it. It is my son who is the most upset; he misses his father and it is harder for him to accept that he must leave for such a long time. Six months is a long time for a boy to be without his father. Because my husband never gets much notice, it is always a shock and then a rush to prepare him for his departure. This year it seems the boat is leaving earlier than usual but he is a ship's engineer and cannot refuse the work. We need the money. The tourist season is only six weeks. It is good, but it is not enough to survive. But I talk too much! There are things to be done and your food is getting cold! *Dobar tek*!" She left my apartment terrace and I ate the homemade pasta gratefully, sipping my wine, glad to have witnessed a glimpse into real life in Croatia. It helped to balance the perspective, and to recognise that for many life on the tourist coast is not as idyllic as it may appear to the tourist passing through.

- Viganj/Mali Ston (54km) -

It was as though someone, somewhere, had flicked a switch. Suddenly, the temperature dropped, the sun disappeared and in its place the sky looked grey and the wind speed increased. It was the first day of October. Journey day fifty-seven; my eighth week on the road. I walked along the shore and into the village. A bar was serving coffee but there were no other customers. Fishing boats were firmly tied into the harbour in a huddle. My hosts at the '*Apartmani*' had been up early. They had already been into and back from Orebić and as they headed off again they said a final farewell. I packed up Tito. The neighbour I had spotted sitting silently on his timber balcony last night was nowhere in sight. I peered over the fence. His garden was a curious mix of organised chaos, an uncut lawn and untended flowerbeds. A high chain-linked fence clearly delineated his territory. Fishing nets had been hung out to dry above a scattered pile of fish crates and other fishing accoutrements. He and his house seemed out of place in this very neat shoreline community; almost as if he was the last in a line of true rustic fishermen whose lives had been unexpectedly and regretfully interrupted by the onslaught of tourism along this coastal stretch. His house looked an interesting glory hole, filled with a cache from the past. I could only speculate what relics lay inside. I pulled a fig from the tree and others followed, thumping freely down onto

Tito's roof as I bit into the rich, sweet flavour of the ripened fruit.

The smoking steering column was no more as we headed out of the drive and along the shoreline road eastwards and back into Orebić. I put it down to a temporary glitch which had sorted itself, helped by my few pokes at the bunched-up wiring. Windsurfers scudded out to sea, blown by the strong wind, hurdling the choppy waves with enthusiasm. Soon we left the coast and headed inland, while keeping a wary eye on the massing grey clouds above.

The petrol attendant came out onto the garage forecourt and gave the expected exclamation of "Fića!"

To which I gave my standard response of "*Da*," with a smile. I was his only customer. "*Makedonski*?" he enquired sceptically.

"*Engleski*."

He appeared almost relieved and broke into perfect English. He had much to say and as I followed him into the shop to pay, he covered topics such as the rise and fall in popularity of the Fića, European politics, Croatia's eventual integration into Europe, the recent war, European funding, my journey, his family and most of all his concerns at my travelling alone.

"You are a woman!" he admonished me. The arrival and departure of other customers did not seem to stop his flow of conversation and, try as I might, it was hard to get away without appearing rude. He clearly felt the need to impart two of his major concerns. "The European Union will not last long." he announced dramatically. "How can it be, with all of us in it? We are not united. In twenty years everyone will be fighting each other and it will fall apart."

His second worry was more specific, relating to Croatia joining the European Union. "Look at us now! Funding is not going towards what we need," he said emphatically. "For example, we need proper water systems but the projects and the money is not going towards that, or to improving the life of Croatians. No one is listening," he said mournfully. I listened, although perhaps for too long. I needed to get away. The arrival of another customer was my moment and I backed towards the door.

"Sorry, I really must get going. It's been lovely talking to you."

He had begun to rant in Croatian to his latest customer, but he nodded and with a casual wave said, "*Sretan put!*"

———

The Pelješac peninsular road was a pretty bleak experience, perhaps influenced by the weather and time of year. For some reason I felt threatened. There was no traffic on the road, and the sun was not shining. If Tito decided to break down, I would be nervous. I pushed the thought to the back of my mind and concentrated on getting us across the desolate stretch of land which would eventually connect us with the mainland proper.

A colossal concrete monument emulating two planks of wood standing on end rose up from the side of the road and, intrigued, I stopped to take a look. At its base, a curved structure depicted scenes of the Partisans' struggle against the Nazis during World War II – the list of those who had died stretched the full length of the outer curve. The monument was peppered with bullet holes; graffiti had been roughly cleaned off the communist 5-pointed star, but the words beneath it remained clear:

'Iz vatre i pepela, Iz krvi i suza, Radala i nova, Jugoslavija.'
'From the fire and ash, From the blood and tears, A new work, Yugoslavia.'

This memorial, and the many others like it which I had

stumbled across during my journey through the Balkan peninsula, had been abandoned, neither cared for nor removed; President Tito's legacy and Yugoslavia a mere moment in time for historians to contemplate and those nostalgic for the past to reflect upon. Had Josip Broz ever really managed to make it work, to hold everyone together? He had died in 1980 and in a decade Yugoslavia had collapsed into fractured pieces. Was this an inevitability that President Tito would have had to deal with, had he been alive? I wondered. Instead, he remained an enigma to the West. And here in the former countries of Yugoslavia it was difficult to tell whether they loved him or hated him; many, both young and old, held him in high nostalgic affection but could this be escapism from a confused present? The bullet holes were real and certainly appeared to reflect a less affectionate sentiment towards the expressed ideals of their former leader.

———

We took the road down into the valley and began the climb towards the earthquake-devastated town of Veliki Ston. I changed down into second gear as an open-backed truck overtook us. It was heavily loaded with building materials and a concrete mixer. It lurched unsteadily from side to side as it struggled up the hill in front of us. I laughed at the driver's optimism in carrying such a large load and expecting his vehicle to go fast. I leaned across the passenger seat to grab my camera to capture this comical scene but then thought better of it. It might provoke an unwanted reaction from the driver.

The truck gradually pulled ahead and was gone, leaving Tito and me to our own slow crawl up the hill. At the top, a striped landscape of vineyards on the one side and emptiness on the other opened up in front, while at the bottom of the hill the truck had pulled over and off the road. As we began to descend, the driver got out. He appeared to be checking his back tyres. I sensed trouble but, short of stopping halfway down the hill, there was nothing to do but to keep going. Sure enough, as we came closer the man turned towards us. He signalled for me to pull over. *No way!* I thought. If he had broken down, there was nothing I could do and I was sure he was local. Why did he need me to stop? As we passed, I raised my hands in a polite expression of *"Sorry, I can't help,"* and kept going. He came out into the road behind us and pointed frantically at Tito, as if to say there was something wrong with his back wheels. But he must have known as well as I did that Zastava wheels angle inwards at their base. My heart sank but I was not stopping here to let him look.

Another hill loomed ahead. Nervously, I checked the rear-view mirror and once again changed down into second gear. With a great deal more power than Tito could muster, the truck was gaining on us again. The driver began to hoot. Quick, insistent blasts, while almost driving into us to try to get me to stop. I kept going. Every nerve in my body strained in a bid to make Tito go faster, while a rising sense of panic washed over me at this forceful intimidation. The truck pulled out into the opposite lane. It came level with us and the driver hooted more persistently, swerving his truck to within inches of us in a bid to get my attention. I was frozen to my seat, not daring to look at him. *What did he want? Go away!* He continued to mirror our 20km/h pace while pulling in closer. I defiantly held my course, hoping he would not ram us, and eyed one of the bricks which lay on the passenger side floor. Thankfully, I had not got around to putting it back under the bonnet, and as a result this brick was my only means of defence – not that I was particularly adept at throwing bricks about, or at people for that matter.

We continued in this almost comic fashion up the hill until the truck was forced to overtake when a car came over the crest of the hill and down towards him. I slowed Tito to 15km/h, creating further distance between us and to allow the car coming up behind to easily overtake. The truck and the car neared the top of the hill and then disappeared up, over and out of sight.

The outskirts of a village lined each side of the road as I pulled over, willing myself not to burst into tears. Taking in deep breaths of air, I turned off the engine and sat shaking from intimidation. Had he also pulled over on the other side of the hill? Was he waiting for me? I wondered what to do next, my confidence fading by the second. Until now, Tito had felt like my castle. I had been untouchable. But I had had to face a stark reality. A Zastava was no longer a sporting hero on the road. Almost any vehicle could outrun us. A blanket of fear folded itself around me as I imagined the truck driver waiting patiently. Perhaps he was not there at all, but I could not know for sure.

Don't cry, don't cry! Look at the map! Where can I go? There was a ferry crossing to Miljet Island. Perhaps I should go there? But what if the truck was also doing that? What if there was no ferry and no cars? I could be trapped. The road was a dead end. Too risky. I did not want to go back to Orebić so it seemed the only option was to continue towards Veliki Ston. It was not far. I continued to sit. Afraid of the road ahead. Too scared to drive on.

After half an hour of hesitation, I started the engine. As we reached the crest of the hill, my heart began to thump. We were in the village now. I travelled slowly down the main street on full alert. Still no sign of the truck. It was 7km to Veliki Ston. I had to keep going. Tears flowed unchecked down my cheeks and for the first time I drove Tito in fear.

———

Above, Veliki Ston defence walls scaled the hillsides like another Great Wall of China. Stone houses lay empty, wide cracks grinned through to the interior – signs of the 1996 earthquake still in evidence. I parked in trepidation. Was the truck here? I was struggling to remember exactly how it looked and wished I had taken that photograph of his overladen load after all. Was the driver watching me? I had no idea. I locked Tito and wandered into the town square. Its beauty and architecture were lost on me. I crept around the narrow alleyways nervously, looking back to check if I was being followed. I could not focus and I felt claustrophobic. I had to get out of there.

————

One kilometre on, a lane brought us around the perimeter wall of a stone tower and into a secluded bay – a place of sanctuary. A haven. Somewhere to forget today's drama.

Mali Ston sat in a bay connecting many smaller inlets where oysters and mussels were farmed. Walls rose up above the settlement and linked with those of Veliki Ston. They were built in the 13th century to defend the salt lakes which straddle the two bays from potential raiders. Today it was mussels and oysters for which the area was now popular and the scene was one of sleepy tranquillity with a collection of stone houses and a family run hotel huddled together in contented harmony. Two restaurants sat side by side vying for custom, their terraces filled with relaxed lunchtime diners. I found a table and gladly cocooned myself in this oasis of calm. The October afternoon was cool but each customer was given a blanket to keep any chill at bay and I wrapped myself in it, rediscovering the balance I feared I had lost completely.

————

T he food and wine had worked their magic and I walked along the shoreline to digest my meal. Although Mali Ston was affected by the 1996 earthquake, it seemed to have recovered well from the damage. Most houses had been rebuilt and the defence walls shored up for restoration. I sat on a wooden bench and breathed in the salty air, trying to put what had happened earlier into a sensible perspective. Although nothing had physically happened to me, mentally I was still shaken.

I watched as three young boys took their newly constructed go-kart on its maiden voyage around the village. The tallest and oldest of the three sat like a king on the makeshift seat while ordering the two younger and skinnier boys to push, seemingly oblivious of the fact that one boy already had his arm in plaster up to his armpit. I watched as they struggled to push the older, heavier boy down the dirt track, their efforts being so great that the young boy with the broken arm fell over on countless occasions. The older boy would give him a withering look over the top of his glasses and the young boy would pick himself up and start pushing again. I laughed to myself at the spectacle. I watched their slow progression through the village; the older boy refusing to get off and the younger ones protesting yet continuing to push their 'king' around the village as if their lives depended upon it. This seemed a fitting metaphor for today. I just needed to find the same tenacity of spirit that the boy with the broken arm was displaying and reclaim my belief in Tito and in the journey.

- Mali Ston/Dubrovnik (38km) -

An old man with bowed shoulders stood tall in his fishing boat and rowed himself across the bay of Mali Ston. Having successfully made the crossing and moored, he picked up a long black umbrella and strode toward the village carrying a small white plastic bucket and an empty fishing cage. With ease he had deftly switched between an oarsman and an elegant gentleman, striding confidently along the shore, his grey shorts, light blue collared shirt and grey ribbed cardigan belying his age – all that seemed to be missing was a bowler hat.

The rain began to fall, albeit not heavily. I shook off the dread and climbed in behind the wheel. "Come on, Tito, we can do this!" We set off tentatively out of Mali Ston and joined the main No. 8 road. The Pelješac peninsula was behind us. My feet were being pleasantly warmed by the hole under the gearbox cover – the same hole which only a week ago had been mercilessly burning my toes with its constant blast of hot air – tempered only by the strategic rearrangement of the rubber foot mats. A trickle of water seeped through a minute hole in the windscreen rubber seal and a droplet of water fell lightly onto my left foot. Although I was still on red alert for the truck, my fears were diminishing and Tito was once again reasserting himself as my four-wheeled castle of indomitable strength.

Oda and Klaus had recommended I visit the Arboretum at Trsteno on my way to Dubrovnik, and here it was! Applying the brakes with sudden force at the emergence of a sign to the entrance, Tito came to a shuddering stop. Thankfully, there was no one behind us. I turned off down a track to an empty parking area. The café was in semi-darkness but I poked my head through the door. A man sat at a table surrounded by piles of paper. He looked up.

"*Dobar dan.* Are you open?"

"Yes, would you like a coffee?"

I needed no further encouragement and stepped inside. He chatted enthusiastically in a stilted English and asked how I had got here. He waxed lyrical about Zastavas and the unexpected snow of last spring, then paused momentarily to ask where I was going and how I had found his place.

"But your friends, Oda and Klaus, they are here on my campsite!"

"Really? But they were heading north; are you sure it is them?"

"Yes, yes – go and look for yourself."

I could feel my eyes filling with tears as I walked through the drizzly rain and over to the only vehicle parked in the campsite. The door was wide open and inside my German friends were sitting writing postcards and drinking tea, a scene of absolute campsite domesticity. They took a moment to register that it was me and I was quickly hustled into their four-wheeled home to dry. A steaming cup of tea was thrust into my hands as I described the absurd events of yesterday and I began to suspect they had been assigned to me as guardian angels.

They took me under their wings as we walked the lengths and breadths of Trsteno's arboretum, which Oda referred to as "her garden" as she had been holidaying here with her family, and now with Klaus, for over thirty years. She adored the place and I was swept along by her enthusiasm for the cultivated beauty which had been nurtured within the rugged coastline – a combination of formal gardens and forest with a terrace perched high on the cliff edge overlooking a stormy sea. We descended adventurously down roughly hewn windswept stone steps onto balconies of stone until we reached sea level. The wind was strong and the sea's swell high – it was exhilarating. I felt all my fears and insecurities being sucked out of me while I focused on remaining upright against the powerful force of the wind. The sea rose and troughed beneath us as we stood on the walls of an empty marina, mesmerised by its energy, but as the rain began to fall more heavily, we headed up a footpath under a canopy of pine and then fig trees, whose fruit was so ripe, it was falling to the ground, the skins splitting open to reveal the sweet tender flesh. We plucked some from the trees and ate in noisy delight but our invigorating walk had made us hungry for something more substantial.

Steaming portions of homemade goulash, fried potatoes in their skins and a mountain of salad were placed before us. The Konoba Hill restaurant was the only place open in Trsteno. As the rainfall increased with no sign of letting up, we had piled in through its doors in the hope of shelter and food and were not disappointed on either account. By four o'clock I knew I must leave. The rain had not eased and it was almost dark. Oda and Klaus escorted me back to Tito. Klaus checked him over but could find nothing wrong. I firmly pushed any further thoughts of the truck driver's antics to the back of my mind and coaxed Tito into life. With a final and grateful wave to my new friends, we headed back up the track and out onto the main road towards Dubrovnik.

I flicked on the windscreen wipers and they swept into squeaky motion. Headlights were on, and a quick test of the brakes convinced me all was in order. The road was filled with traffic and even for Tito it was slow going. The rain clattered deafeningly down on the roof. The wipers valiantly swung back and forth but they were unable to deal with the deluge of rain and spray being thrown up by the oncoming traffic as it forged through vast puddles. Visibility was getting worse and as the road ascended, we lost sight of the cars in front while a stream of cars crept bumper to bumper behind us. Once again, Tito had become the involuntary leader of a travelcade of vehicles and at this seemingly unhurried pace we entered Dubrovnik.

The windscreen was so steamed up I had to pull over. The rain continued to hammer down on the roof, drowning out all other sounds. I cleared the window as best I could. Volumes of water flowed down the road as we forged uphill against its force, looking for somewhere to stay. *'Apartmani'* the sign read, fixed prominently to a gate. A man huddled under the arc of a golf umbrella at the front door. I swung Tito over and ran across the road and up the steps as fast as I could. The man did his best to convince me to stay but there was nowhere to park Tito. I had to find him somewhere undercover. I continued my search along the one-way streets but I could find nothing. The road curved up and bent back on itself down towards the old city and we rafted towards it on a tide of water.

A sign emerged out of the gloom. *'Parking. Clients only.'* I took a chance and parked haphazardly beyond the entrance. I grabbed my rain jacket and sprinted wildly through the pelting rain, leaping across the torrent of water as it swept in waves down the street, and into the hotel foyer opposite. I had travelled all of ten metres but I was drenched. Inside, an atmosphere of professional conference sophistication surrounded me. I battled my way towards the reception desk, trying to look as though I belonged, despite my rain-soaked appearance.

"Good evening, Madam; how can I help you?" said the tall dark-eyed man behind the counter, giving me the standard 5-star non-committal hotel welcome.

"I was wondering if you might have a room for tonight and garage parking for my car?" He raised his eyebrows and cast me a disparaging glance.

"I'm afraid we are completely booked."

"Oh, really?" I said in complete dismay.

His expression softened slightly and he added in a conspiratorial way, "But we do keep a spare room available for emergencies – or unexpected arrivals."

I smiled and asked apprehensively, "And how much would that cost?"

His answer brought further despondency but I could not help but play the game.

"And you have underground parking available? You see, I have a Zastava and I really need to get it out of this rain."

There was a pause while he wondered if he had heard me

correctly. "You are driving a Fića?" he asked in surprise, the polite mask of propriety slipping from his face.

"Yes," I answered enthusiastically, milking the moment of his sudden interest, "I have been all across the Balkans. And now I am heading back towards Macedonia."

"In a Fića?" he repeated, laughing unreservedly.

"That's right, and I desperately need to get the car under cover. Is it possible you could do me a discounted rate – for a late arrival?" I asked with a desperate look of hope.

He thought for a moment. "Let us see."

He made a phone call and consulted with one of his colleagues while I hung on, looking as destitute as I could. It seemed to work. Yes, a discount was possible as long as I paid immediately. I smiled gratefully at him.

"Thank you."

It was still grossly expensive but, if Tito was dry, it would be worth it.

The hotel porter followed me out to the garage entrance. I hopped back in behind the wheel and reversed haphazardly up the road against the tide of water flowing down the street and swept up the garage ramp.

"Ah, you do not have a Jaguar! You have a "Figuar"!" he said with a flourish of 5-star charm, as I slotted Tito into the only remaining parking space, dwarfed between a BMW and a 4-wheel drive Porsche Cayenne. My love for Tito re-emerged; a "Figuar" certainly added a sense of vintage chic to the garage parking, or so I thought.

———

The rain continued to cascade down unrelentingly. The wind whirled fiercely, bringing with it a thunderstorm so powerful all the lights in my bedroom fused. I blundered around in the pitch dark, found my torch and mobile phone and called reception.

"The maintenance man will arrive soon, Madam," I was informed.

I watched as lightning tore across the sky in brilliant flickers. The thunder claps vibrated through the building, while the wind trebled in strength in response. There seemed to be no end to the storm's ferocity but Tito was safe, and he was dry, and that was the only thing that mattered.

- Dubrovnik/Cavtat (19km) -

Breakfast was a huge affair, a banquet of so much choice, I found myself staring at it, unsure where to start. The storm had raged on for hours into the night, and through the expansive dining room windows we eyed the havoc that it had wreaked on everything which had not been tied down on the beach below. A watery sun shimmered weakly through the grey sky, offering the hope that things were going to get better as the day progressed. I checked out of my 5-star luxury room and walked down towards the old city of Dubrovnik, which lay hidden behind steep defensive walls.

I climbed the stone steps up onto the 8th century wall walk, ticket in hand, ready to traverse the 2km perimeter. A song blasted out from the ticket collector's radio.

"Tina Turner!" I pointed out nostalgically.

"Yes," he said with a twinkle in his eye, "She is Queen of the wall!"

The walk dipped and rose between defence towers; below, 15th, 16th and 17th century architecture filled the city; tall stone buildings squeezed together, connected by thin stone passageways which linked a square at each end of a pedestrian boulevard. Churches, an avenue of shops, an ice cream parlour, cafés, and a drinking fountain, which famously had kept Dubrovnik's citizens alive by providing fresh water to those trapped during the siege of their city. Each nook and cranny – another surprise.

Despite their height, the walls had not been able to protect Dubrovnik's citizens against a sustained assault from above. Bombarded by grenades, bombs and sniper shots from the hills, it was a miracle that so many had survived and the buildings had been reclaimed for use. A map of the damage caused by the Yugoslav Army, the Serbs and Montenegrins during 1991-1992 shows that 85 per cent of roofs had been destroyed. Remarkably, this UNESCO-listed city had been saved and restored, and tourists were once more flocking in by land, sea and air.

A cruise liner anchored out in the bay and, like an invading army, the first tranche of passengers were deployed into a posse of launches. Horrified by the sight of hundreds heading for shore, I hurried around the rest of the wall walk and down into one of the squares in search of a café – a strategic place from which to watch the world go by. I had been lucky enough to experience the city with a modicum of peace but now a tidal wave of ocean liner daytrippers quickly filled the narrow streets.

A bride raced through the crowd, white satin streaming behind her. She took the steep steps at a run as the church bells rang. Costumed singers, musicians and dancers entertained the pedestrians while market vendors merrily sold their locally produced crafts. Tourists continued to arrive in ever-increasing numbers, all eager to experience Dubrovnik – a heroic city recovering from war, now looking positively towards the future, its popularity dispelling all thoughts of an ordinary daily life, although I imagined it must exist somewhere in the backstreets, behind closed doors.

―――――

P alm trees lined the promenade of Cavtat, a small fishing town only 16km away from Dubrovnik. This had once been the pleasure ground of the Austro-Hungarian rich, elite classes, and the architecture, although crumbling, reflected their Renaissance style. Today the town attracts a more down-to-earth clientele to its now quiet harbourfront, where children skip by and men play chess for hours on end.

I parked outside the old communist-style Hotel Supetar. The receptionist shook her head – they were full.

"Is that your car?" she asked, pointing to Tito. I nodded.

"You need to move it." She looked again. "Is it a Fića?"

I nodded again and she smiled widely.

"Oh, but my friends, we all had Fićas, when we were seventeen or eighteen. The boys, they added things to make them go fast then they would race each other. It was fun in those days!" She laughed nostalgically and looked at me again. "Perhaps my friend has a free apartment. I will call him for you. Then I will tell you a story. Please, you must move your Fića."

I moved Tito out of the way and returned. She was on the telephone and pointed for me to sit down. Moments later, her friend arrived. Yes, he had an apartment to rent, if I would follow him. I mouthed "*Hvala*" to the receptionist and she waved in response, still talking loudly down the phone – her Fića story still hers for the telling.

———

For 20 euros, I had an apartment with a view over Cavtat, the bay and Dubrovnik in the distance. It was more than I could have hoped, and it more than compensated for my 5-star expensive stay the night before. Tito had a place under the family's car porch and I walked the 15 minutes back down the hill into Cavtat for a coffee in the early evening sunshine. It was a calm, relaxed place after the buzz of Dubrovnik and I found myself hearing a familiar language – a sound which brought with it a sense that I was getting closer to my final destination. I turned to see if I knew the people but I did not. The word "Kosova" came up in their conversation and with a strange jolt I realised that, despite only a few months having passed, I felt as far removed from work, and the world that is Kosovo, as I had done in a very long time.

As the Albanian words flowed over me, still incomprehensible despite the time I had spent in Kosovo, I realised I could not miss travelling to Albania. Kosovars spoke highly of this country; some considered it their fatherland but, whatever their interpretation, I realised I needed to see it for myself. My main concern was that Tito would break down. The Zastava was not known in Albania; perhaps no one would speak English. Who could I turn to if I needed help? I had heard that driving conditions were difficult. I was apprehensive but I was also very curious. I knew I had to see Albania. I had to somehow overcome my doubts and take the risk, even if it was only for a few days – but I was thinking too far ahead. First, we had to negotiate our way through Montenegro.

- Cavtat/Karasovići Border Control(24km) -

It was Sunday. The roads were almost deserted as we moved along at a steady 60km/h. The sun disappeared behind an ominous mass of dark cloud and the landscape seemed to close in. The mountains were dark and numerous; it would not be long before we reached Montenegro, a land of "black mountains".

MONTENEGRO

AS WEARINESS CREEPS IN

- Debeli Brijeg Border Control/Perast (51km) -

Our passage across the border into Montenegro, our ninth country, was so swift and uneventful I hardly believed we had made it.

"A Fića?" the customs officer remarked drolly. He was interested neither in me, nor Tito's documentation. It was raining and he was getting wet. I paid 10 Euros road tax and pressed the sticker neatly to the right-hand side of the windscreen. It entitled us to 60 days' travel – a rather abundant number for a country smaller than Wales and a mere freckle on the face of America – yet the mountains looked as though they would pose a challenge. We would be sticking to the flat where possible. *Five days*, I thought – fewer if the rain continued.

The road descended through forest and mountain pass towards Herceg Novi and the sea, leaving the grey mass of Croatia's alpine range behind us. Ahead, the Montenegrin variety stretched outwards. I had two options: the high road or the low road into town. Through habit and Scottish origins, I took the high road. A line of traffic slowed our progress to a crawl and eventually to a halt as the car in front stopped. The sound of trumpets, tuba, French horn and drums filled the air and suddenly we were surrounded by Roma musicians. A car door opened and a bride dressed in bountiful quantities of white fabric slid out from the backseat. She was closely followed by the groom in a shiny silver grey suit, a contrast to the dishevelled attire of the Roma men. The brass band circled the bride and then the groom, while the drummer banged out a hearty beat from a distance. The music was loud and tuneful and its spontaneous folk rhythms brought a smile to everyone's faces. The band followed the delighted couple across the road towards a hotel entrance, where the groom paid them off. He and his bride disappeared inside and the music trickled out. The show was over and the traffic moved on.

It all seemed rather quiet in Herceg Novi after the musical interlude. The rain had eased but the town's inhabitants remained firmly indoors. I headed for the shoreline and the Bay of Tivat, shaped like a badly constructed bow tie, with uneven-sized loops that did not quite meet in the middle. Here the connection between mountain and sea appeared seamless. We travelled along a man-made division between these two elements. Visitor parking allowed me to pull over to admire the view; two vehicles did likewise and we acknowledged each other with a polite nod.

Perast lay at the base of a conical-shaped mountain across a narrow stretch of water. We were at the heart of the bow and to reach Perast we had one complete bow loop to cover as the bay widened into a basin between the mountains. I had been to Perast on business a few years previously and had been enchanted by the old stone houses rising majestically up the hillside with grace and old-fashioned dignity. They had been grand palatial homes in the 16th century but now many of them lay in a bad state of disrepair.

———

I carefully negotiated the narrow coastal street of Perast, while cameras clicked and lenses zoomed in and out. Tito was creating a small sensation amongst the locals and tourists. One of the couples I had acknowledged at the visitor parking across the bay when we had all stopped to admire the scenery was amongst them. They smiled and waved in recognition as I drove my celebrity car through the crowd, faintly embarrassed by all the adulation but mightily proud that Tito had got me this far.

On the spur of the moment I booked into the Admiral Hotel, the balcony room overlooking the bay being too tempting to pass by. It was perfect apart from the eight mosquitoes lingering on the bedroom walls, hungrily awaiting my blood. I stealthily leapt up and down off the furniture on a mosquito eradication mission, and then plugged my insect deterrent into the mains socket in the hope that any I had missed would soon be no more.

I wiped down my bloodied guidebook and hastily escaped the murder scene to the peaceful sounds of the bay. The early evening sky began to reveal a hypnotic light show. Sunbeams bounced between the rain clouds and filtered through a narrow opening in an otherwise soft blanket of low cloud. The streams of light fanned out across the still water of the bay, lighting up the mountains in hues of red, orange and yellow while other parts were thrown into deep black shadow. I stood motionless as the spectacle unfolded in front of my eyes. A fish leapt out of the calm waters, interrupting the stillness. As it dived out of sight, its body slapped against the surface. The moment had passed and the light faded into darkness.

Perast/Sveti Stefan (44km)

A morning mist lingered like a feathery layer across the bay. The sky was blue and as the sun rose, the wisps of white mist evaporated. Breakfast was served on the terrace overlooking the bay. The other guests were retired Germans, two of whom had just come from Albania. Their enthusiasm was infectious. They insisted I go; I would be a fool to miss it, it seemed, and they donated their remaining Albanian coinage to me as an incentive. The number of Germans travelling independently through the Balkans had surprised me. Were British retirees this adventurous? I did not think so, but I had also been impressed by how many locals spoke German. A throwback to Germany's relative closeness to Yugoslavia as a holiday destination perhaps, or the influx of Balkan refugees to Germany during war or maybe, like Russian, it had been another language to learn at school. Whatever the reasons, it did make life easier for the German travelling across the Balkan peninsula and I envied their advantage.

———

The boat motored across the glassy water of the bay away from the numerous stone churches, 15th century Venetian-style villas and faded grandeur of Perast, towards two islands, one of which was the Monastery of St George and the resting place of many a famous seaman, but it was the second island, The Lady of the Rocks, towards which I was heading.

I was met by a tour guide who, but for his blue cardigan, was dressed entirely in white. His tight jeans, fitted shirt, polished white shoes and clutch bag added an unexpected drama to the moment as I was swept up ashore to join a cluster of people already awaiting the tour.

The Lady of the Rocks is a man-made island. An island for the people, built by the people. Legend has it that in the 15th century, the discovery of an icon of the Virgin Mary had been enough to encourage those who could to contribute to the construction of an island using the current-scattered rocks on which the icon had been found as its core. In time, seamen and fishermen contributed enough rocks to form a solid island base. Eventually, a chapel was built and its interiors painted by Tripo Kokolja, a self-taught artist from Perast.

Historically, the island became a place for the reconciliation of disputes. Here seemed more appealing to most than the Venetian Courts in Italy. Our white-clad guide led us into the chapel and regaled us with stories, myths and legends, all so elaborately embellished with wit and detail it was impossible to remember any of them. And while one should have been admiring the artwork, I found myself engrossed by the rows of silver votive plates, which were displayed in their hundreds below and above the biblical scenes. Each plate was a different size; embossed, engraved and meticulously detailed, they illustrated the ships of the time, and depicted tales of voyage and hardship which the seamen had endured but ultimately survived. Each had brought a silver votive, an offering of their gratitude, to the chapel as thanks. "*Votum Feci Gratiam Accepi*". They were fixed side by side to the church walls with barely a hair's width between them, their legacy an unknown quantity, but for me they represented a story just as alluring as that of the local artist Kokolja or his contemporary Dobričević, who had painted the much-revered Madonna and Child icon positioned above the altar.

Our guide swung us through into the adjoining museum rooms, a collection of pieces from across the world, including English Victoriana in the forms of hot irons, umbrellas and sewing machines, to name but a few; each donation also a gesture of thanks. With theatrical indulgence, the guide held our attention with the story of Jacinta Kunić who, in the early 19th century, had created a finely embroidered icon sewn in gold, silver and silk threads. It had taken her 25 years to complete. She had even gone so far as to use her own hair for that of the Virgin mother and child.

"After which she turned grey!" the guide added for effect.

———

After laidback Perast, Kotor was somewhat chaotic. The recent arrival of an ocean liner in the bay had policemen on full alert. They blew whistles, arbitrarily halting the reluctant traffic to allow swathes of dazed passengers to cross the street from their ship into the pedestrianised old town enclosed by huge defending walls of stone. The air was buzzing with excitement. I parked Tito in the shadow of the boat's sleek, floating mass and was pulled along by the tidal wave of passengers and in through one of Kotor's historic gateways. Miraculously, Kotor and its fortress perched high above the town had survived numerous earthquakes and countless reconstructions.

I wandered along ancient marbled alleyways into courtyards large and small. Accommodation seemed terribly expensive and, while I considered what to do next, I retreated to a café and under a large sun umbrella to observe from a distance the noise of tourists exclaiming at the marvellous sights of Kotor. It was midday yet large mosquitoes were out, hovering and biting. The couple whom I had seen yesterday in Perast, and formerly at the visitor parking *en route*, appeared again and came up to me. As I had guessed from their dress, they were English – and the mosquitoes were also biting them. Kotor was proving a bit of shock, they admitted after several days down the coast in Sveti Stefan.

"You should go. It's very friendly, much quieter than here, and the sea is still warm enough for swimming."

They were leaving tomorrow. Back to England and back to work – a notion that seemed almost alien to me after all these weeks on the road, but momentarily I yearned to go home, back to the UK where I had not lived for several years. My desire for the road was beginning to wane, though their enthusiasm for what I was doing countered these negative thoughts.

"Don't stop; you must make it to Skopje!"

Their words had me taking to the road once more, leaving the clamour of Kotor behind for those with greater fortitude than I, and instead heading for Sveti Stefan for a final rest-up before making the push back to Skopje.

Negotiating my way out of Kotor was a more complicated procedure than I had imagined, or perhaps I was just not on the ball. Somehow, I missed the tunnel road – the shortcut across the other loop of the bow – and then equally I missed the alternative, which would have taken me around the bow of Kotor Bay. Instead I found myself heading up into the mountains on a minor road. I checked the map. Although it was not clear, it seemed the road would take us southwards via an old inland route. As we climbed, we passed a number of Roma settlements, their distinctive ramshackle fragility a clear sign of poverty and isolation from any form of supportive social structure. A truck overtook us and its young Roma passengers gazed at me in amazement. No other vehicles appeared and as the road continued to head deeper into the mountains and off the beaten track, I wondered if my map was right. I caught a glimpse of the sea. The road climbed then dropped and, after what seemed hours, we emerged suddenly into civilisation, unwittingly having *'cut the corner'* to such an extent that we were practically in Budva and thus only a short distance from Sveti Stefan.

L arge trucks dwarfed Tito and I veered into a petrol station for fuel and to catch my breath. The sudden increase and speed of the traffic was overwhelming. Montenegro appeared to be a country of two halves; a quieter north and a crazy south. It was not far to our destination but we had a steep incline to negotiate and two lanes of fast-moving traffic.

I had last been here in 2005 and the change was astonishing. Huge vulgar-looking hotel complexes now lined this part of the coast, buoyed by the influx of Russian money. For such a small country it seemed all out of proportion and I felt denied the beautiful coastline I had once known, destroyed forever by tourism, too much uncontrolled investment and a flagrantly poor planning strategy to cope with the demand. As a result, development projects had sprouted up with such ferocity they had destroyed everything in their path. Ironically, the result was a Budva Riviera that everyone eagerly embraced, and as some would say to me, 'This is progress!' and I would swallow a retort, knowing it was futile to disagree.

- Sveti Stefan -

Tito wheezed and gasped his way upwards; the deceptively gradual gradient of modern roads always tired him out, but he made it and we were soon signalling right and into the village of Sveti Stefan.

A large cluster of houses hung perilously on the edge of the cliff looking down on the once glamorous, highly exclusive island peninsula of Sveti Stefan, made famous as the not-so-secret hideaway of Greta Garbo. Today the causeway was closed. A major refurbishment and more investment. A high-class resort was its current destiny, with considerable financial support from Asia, or so I was told. I booked into Villa Drago high up on the hill – a recommendation from the British couple I had spoken with in Kotor.

From my one-chair-wide apartment balcony I heard the sounds of revving dumper trucks swerving back and forth, falling debris, and shouts from the construction site echoing across the bay. A delegation of smartly dressed officials marched in single file along the causeway and in through the island gates. Some were armed with briefcases and rolls of architects' drawings, while others staggered in, shoulder high with documents and lever-arched files.

"The financier is here," so went the whisperings at Villa Drago, "from Singapore!"

It was difficult to distinguish him from the others. If I could, I would have liked to ask him if he knew how much the construction workers were being paid and whether he could investigate their living conditions. One of the German guests had been horrified to learn that most of them were earning very little and therefore had to sleep rough in a deserted building so they could save enough to send to their families in Albania. This was not an uncommon story but was this true here or just hearsay? A security guard stood formidably at the entrance to the causeway, daring anyone to get too close. All contact was impossible and thus my sympathies remained with the workers.

———

The sunset was swift yet memorable. An orange fireball of sun dramatically plunged into the ocean, momentarily lighting up the horizon. The surface of the sea glittered like a sequinned dress caught in disco lights, but as the final sliver of fireball slipped from sight there was instant darkness, as though someone had closed a curtain.

Recoup, plan and re-energise had been my goal but instead I was losing momentum, feeling tired, my confidence dwindling. I had to leave tomorrow and I hoped the road would focus me.

- Sveti Stefan/Ulcinj (48km) -

I had visited Virpazar some years ago with colleagues from the Ministry of Culture in Podgorica, Montenegro's capital. They had had bold and ambitious plans to bring eco-tourism to the area, a model I hoped would flourish with careful planning but for the time being it was a quiet inland area, relatively untouched, lying beside the vast waters of Lake Skadar. Mind you, I had not seen much that day as the area had been shrouded in an ethereal swirl of fog through which I had nervously climbed up the ruins of a castle and peered out over its jagged rocks, enjoying a sense of wild romantic mystery. I was keen to see Virpazar again under a blue sky and to explore the villages along the lake. This would make for a relatively strain-free journey for Tito, and as the lake shared a border with Albania, I hoped to be able to cross from there with ease.

The plan went awry when I missed the inland turning to Virpazar and, before I realised it, Tito and I were hurtling through a long tunnel. We emerged back out into bright sunshine but with nowhere sensible to turn around. I was unexpectedly committed to the coast road. Virpazar was not going to be our destiny after all. Instead it was the coastal port of Bar.

———

Somewhat flustered, I arrived in Bar and parked beside the marina, leaving Tito against a backdrop of rig jangling, bobbing boats while I went in search of a café and a comforting cup of coffee. Bar is a major port, a direct link with Europe and, I mused, an indirect route home. Impetuously, I considered the idea of abandoning Tito here and catching a boat to Venice. The thought of escaping my own journey seemed somewhat spineless but I was becoming increasingly irrational and fed up. The problem was I had lost sight of my journey plan.

I pulled open the road map and reviewed the options. I could take a ferry to Italy, to Bari. From there, a boat could take us to Albania or directly to the Peloponnese in Greece. I walked across to the ferry terminal. There were no crossings to Italy today, and no sailings to Greece – it was not the season. In any case, either journey would be extortionately expensive and therefore a non-starter. Again I unravelled my map across Tito's steering wheel. Stari Bar was a possible option and from there, a road led to Albania. I only had two weeks left before the car's registration documents expired. I could do one of two things; either abandon Tito wherever I was when the documents expired, or do the honourable thing and get him back to Skopje. Albania was the most direct route – it was just a question of where to cross the border.

Chewing determinedly on a mint, I took to the road again. The turning for Stari Bar came and went. Too much mint chewing, and not enough concentration. We were on the coastal road towards Montenegro's most southerly city, Ulcinj. *Should I turn back?* I pulled over, frustrated by my lack of concentration, and tore open the guidebook. *Above all Ulcinj welcomes her visitors. Hospitality to travellers is embedded in the hearts of Montenegrins and nowhere is it more evident than in these eastern corners of the country.* The words had a calming effect. I put Tito into gear and focused ahead. We would go to Ulcinj.

———

The town was alive with hustle and bustle, teenagers coming out of school, young and old mingling or walking arm in arm up the street while others crossed between the slow-moving traffic, giggling to each other at the sight of Tito – this was Bulevar Maršala Tita (Maršal Tito Boulevard). Turbo-folk music blasted from the interiors of cafés heaving with customers. Glass-fronted buildings sat cheek by jowl with old and modern housing and for the first time in weeks minarets adorned the skyline, a sight which took me by surprise but for some reason made me feel at home as I tuned into the language. Ulcinj's population is predominantly Albanian, in an area ceded by the Ottoman Empire, although not without resistance, to become a part of Montenegro in 1880. Understandably, they continued to speak their mother tongue and not the Slavic one, to which I had by now become accustomed to hearing throughout most of my travels.

————

The sign read *'Apartments'* and the building looked meticulously whitewashed, with large balconies extending from each level. I parked opposite. A woman stared curiously at me from her garden as I crossed the road and pushed the doorbell. A plump middle-aged man of medium build opened the door.

"*Dobar dan,*" I said, unsure whether I should be addressing him in Albanian. "Apartment?"

He beckoned me inside with a flicker of annoyance and called to someone in Albanian. A woman came out from the kitchen and eyed me suspiciously as I was invited to remove my shoes (as is the custom in most Balkan homes, whatever their religious beliefs) and followed the man upstairs. I was shown a bright sunny room with one double bed, a single bed and something which resembled a child's cot. I agreed to take the room.

"*Vous parlez* français?" he asked.

"*Mais oui, un peu!*" I said, astonished but delighted that we had a way to communicate. He beamed and led me back downstairs. I brought in my luggage and this time his wife followed me up to the room. She looked at me and pointed meaningfully at the child's cot. *I must sleep in there?* I gulped back a laugh as I realised she was not joking and nodded politely while deciding to appeal to her better-natured French-speaking husband on the subject. He was as pleased to speak French with me as I with him. We sipped Turkish coffees companionably and nibbled on *'kimča'*, a local fruit which looks similar to an olive but has the combined tastes of plum and apple – and is deliciously addictive. And of course I could sleep in the large bed!

- Ulcinj -

Ulcinj looked to be in a great hurry to modernise, with new apartments sprouting up randomly while older buildings were being upgraded. It was hard to believe that I was still in Montenegro; everything felt different here and in many ways familiar. Perhaps it was hearing the Albanian language again and seeing the ferocity of building work which reminded me of Kosovo, although a more relaxed version, by the sea.

Many independent shops lined the street and as I explored I was being acknowledged with friendly smiles. The local takeaway shop served me a spinach-and-cheese burek and a carton of runny yoghurt. The chef watched with amusement as I hungrily devoured the lot – he tried out his few words of English on me but we did not get very far despite his enthusiasm, and an eventual cheery wave symbolised defeat. I left, my stomach contentedly full and my mood considerably improved after the morning's navigational challenges, and I found myself relaxing into the easy rhythm of Ulcinj.

———

The muezzin's soothing chant drifted through the air. I opened my eyes and rolled over in the large comfortable bed to listen. Life felt uncomplicated again, even at five o'clock in the morning. The call to prayer ended and as I stretched out my limbs and drifted back to sleep once more, I decided I would stay another day. Albania could wait until tomorrow.

The owner agreed heartily with my decision and immediately started making coffee for us both, much to the disapproval of his wife. She dragged heavily on her cigarette and scolded him roundly but he shrugged his shoulders amiably and continued to pour out the deliciously rich caffeine-fuelled liquid into two small cups. His wife ran the apartments with an iron fist. I had had to ask her to turn on the electricity for light, and request a bath towel; appeal for loo paper; and (most essential of all), insist the water supply be turned on so I could flush the toilet. The moment I went out, everything was turned off and I was obliged to ask her to turn everything back on again when I returned. She clearly begrudged the expense as it became apparent they lived their life in the kitchen, lit by a single light bulb and limited use of the other services. Yet, parked in their garage sat a top-of-the-range 4-wheel drive Land Cruiser in pristine condition and seemingly untouched. This was one of the many unexpected anomalies of Balkan life which I had come across, could not fathom, and thought better not to question.

During the summer season, tourists flock to Ulcinj from Albania in the south and Kosovo in the east. I remembered my Kosovo colleagues raving about this town, packed to within an inch of its life, with an electric holiday atmosphere, something the more traditional Western traveller could find somewhat overwhelming. On a day like today, in early October, the air was calm, and sunbathers, swimmers and basketball players shared a considerable expanse of sea and sandy beach, a luxury unavailable to them in high season.

Up in the town centre life was less calm. Cars had been parked with abandon along Maršal Tito Boulevard and as I squeezed my way down the street, I was met by a mass of people heading towards me and away from the market, which nestled unobtrusively behind a set of gates. It was late and most people had done their shopping. Both the elderly and middle-aged ladies still manning their stalls beckoned me, but I kept moving until I found a stall selling the olive-shaped kimća fruit I had eaten with my host yesterday. The stall holder was dressed demurely in black from head to toe, her woollen cardigan darned in a number of places and her sleeves carefully rolled back from her wrists. Her blue eyes sparkled as I gestured towards the fruit.

"*Engleski*?" she asked gently.

I nodded politely in response and with ease she broke into English. She gathered handfuls of the fruit into a brown paper bag, her fingers noticeably strong but her hands arthritic from years of manual work.

"Stop!" I said, laughing apologetically, as the bag filled to almost overflowing, "It is only for me."

She looked surprised and then concerned. But my admission seemed to be the catalyst for her to tell me her life story and perhaps, as no one else around us understood English, she was able to captivate my attention completely.

She had been widowed not long ago, earlier in the year. "It is very difficult for me being alone. My sons live in New York. One son, he owns a bus company. He has one hundred buses," she said proudly, and I thought this sounded rather impressive. "The young," she continued sadly, "they are all leaving. There is no life or opportunities for them here."

I picked up a clementine and she chided me gently, "I will find you the ripe ones."

As she selected five rounded, orange-skinned fruit for me,

her voice became upbeat.

"I visit New York often." She smiled a faraway look but as she selected a fifth fruit her expression changed, "But my poor garden, it suffers." She handed me the fruit in another bag and said, "I like to sell what I can at the market when I am here."

And as I offered her some money she shook her head and patted my hands with motherly assurance.

"No, keep your money. You must be careful when you travel."

"Please, let me at least pay you for the *kimća*?"

She accepted and I thanked her once again, touched by her kindness and her story, which was not an uncommon one in the Balkans.

"It has been lovely to meet you." And as I walked away, I realised I had gained an inner strength from meeting this old lady with the sparkling blue eyes, and I felt ready to take on Albania.

———

The old town of Ulcinj sits high on the cliffs overlooking the sea, a view stretching unobstructed to the horizon. Rows of stone houses line either side of narrow alleyways, precariously supporting one another from collapse. Some had been reinforced with concrete and some were under reconstruction or being refurbished, but with a history dating back to Illyrian times, with input from the Romans, Byzantines, buccaneers and pirates, it was no wonder they were showing their age.

I found myself at the door to the ethnographical and archaeological museum and encouraged to enter by the enthusiasm of a young Montenegrin man. The museum was incorporated around an old 14th century church-mosque but it was difficult to find out more than that from the guide, who squeezed my arm with excitement when he learned that I was originally from Scotland. At every opportunity he took great pleasure in drawing parallels between the Montenegrin and the Scottish ways of living and there was no point in my suggesting otherwise. I was whisked from room to room on a wave of Montenegrin/Scottish associations, the array of agricultural exhibits amply illustrating his well-meaning although wildly imagined arguments. I managed to suppress an inappropriate desire to laugh until he insisted conspiratorially that the sheepskin rug wrapped about the poor mannequined exhibit in front of us was from Scotland. I could control myself no longer but, instead of being offended, he laughed too, hugging my shoulders.

The intensive tour of Scottish associations finally ended and reluctantly he released me back into the old town. My footsteps echoed around the empty alleyways as I descended back into the harbour area. Standing some distance away, a young man talked on his mobile phone. He stood between me and the main promenade and observed me with more than just casual interest. A pedestrian walked towards him from the opposite direction and as he neared, I walked towards them both and passed by, striding purposefully towards the promenade to join the many people sitting on the wall eating ice creams and watching the bathers swimming in the ocean. The man was still on his mobile but had moved towards the promenade. He cast me a look from time to time but I stayed within the crowd until I felt the sun begin to burn my face and decided to head up the hill to Maršal Tito Boulevard. The man kept a discreet distance while I window-shopped my way up the street, aware that he continued to wait, watch and then follow. Someone shouted out in English.

"Hello, hello."

Was it him? I was not sure and I decided to ignore the shouts. I passed the burek takeaway and the chef gave me a friendly wave. I reached the boulevard and prepared to cross the busy street between two 4-wheel drive vehicles. Their height hid me and I watched as the man passed, his mobile phone still clamped to his ear. I doubled back around the 4-wheel drive vehicles and retraced my steps. At the corner of the street, I stopped to look in a jewellery shop window. *Had I imagined it, or was this man following me?* At that moment he reappeared and almost collided with me. I continued to scrutinise the window display of traditional earrings, rings and bracelets. He said nothing and walked slowly by. I did not move, secure in the number of pedestrians around me. He hesitated. There were too many people and he moved out of their way and headed back down the hill. I waited. He turned around but saw I was now watching him. He continued to walk away and out of sight. I breathed a sigh of relief, aware that the encounter in Livno had made me forever cautious – or perhaps slightly paranoid.

————

The café, with its huge glass windows, was a magnificent place to watch the world go by. I marvelled at the contrast between modern and conservative dress codes. A woman clothed all in white – white tunic with a white ruffled neckline and three-quarter length puffed sleeves – set off across the road. Her legs were bound in white material and on her feet were black shoes. Her head was adorned with some kind of white hat but she disappeared too quickly for me to take in any more detail and I was left wondering whether she was a nun or perhaps this was the traditional dress of one of the rural communities. My attention was quickly drawn towards an African man walking down the boulevard. He was tall, slim and casually dressed in jeans and a white long-sleeved shirt. Next to him a young girl skipped to keep up with his long stride. It was an unusual sight and I could not help wondering whether they were descendants of the North Africans who had been known to settle within this region in the 16th century. Some had integrated into the way of life, influencing both the dance and music cultures. It was an exciting prospect, although of course the other option was that they were descendants of slave trading, also from the 16th century, or indeed had pirates as ancestors. I had no way of knowing, but they were the first Africans I had seen in the Balkans since leaving Skopje.

It had been an eventful and thought-provoking day, and I returned to my apartment to find the owner sharpening a long bladed knife with clean deliberate strokes. His concentration was such that I did not dare disturb him and I retired to bed wondering what was about to happen.

- Ulcinj/Sukobin-Muriqan Border Control (26km) -

The world appeared to arise two hours earlier the next morning. Unusually, the water was already on and I showered quickly, packed up my bags and ventured downstairs. The kitchen light glowed softly and across the table lay a large dead animal. Was it a cow, or just half a one? I stared aghast at the owner, hunched over it. He deployed the recently sharpened knife across the animal, expertly cutting it into sections. His wife stood at the sink, puffing furiously on a cigarette while washing a large piece of bright red meat under running water. It looked a highly delicate operation and I whispered an Albanian good morning*"Mermengjesi"* into the air. He looked up briefly, raised his knife in acknowledgement and then got back to his butchering, while I shuffled hastily towards the front door and into the street for air.

———

In the event of a human death, it is common practice on the Balkan peninsula to pin an obituary card to a nearby notice board, tree or lamppost for public information. They are frequently seen and always carefully read. This morning, one had been pinned to a tree and was drawing much attention. I watched curiously as people passed by then stopped, or retraced their steps to take a second look. Young and old, all showed interest, but their expressions remained impassive.

———

Butchering duties were complete and the knife was being cleaned. The owner offered me three fresh pomegranates for my journey. I thanked him gratefully, unsure how I was going to eat them, but that could wait. My first challenge was to cross the Albanian border. I filled Tito with petrol and headed along a quiet road that looped then twisted its way through the valley of a steep rocky landscape towards the Sukobin-Muriqan border. We reached a village and traffic tailed back in both directions. At the heart of it two elderly drivers had stopped to talk to one another. No one hurried them; instead we waited patiently while they finished their conversation. This was rural life, where greater levels of tolerance prevail. The landscape was dotted with humble dwellings, gardens filled with vegetables not flowers. Life was simple here, the affluence of Budva a far cry from these locals' reality. We were soon on our way again and the border appeared. With a flickering sense of apprehension, I steered Tito towards the queue of waiting vehicles. This was it. Beyond lay Albania – an unknown quantity. The guidebook's account of abductions and lawlessness had been disquieting, but then the country had been closed to the world. I had friends who had enjoyed working there recently.

"It is a different place from twenty years ago," they had

said reassuringly, but I had no idea what it held for me and for Tito.

ALBANIA

WINTER IS COMING

- Sukobin-Muriqan Border Control/Lezhë (48km) -

We edged painstakingly forward towards the border control behind a queue of eight vehicles. The officer was dealing with both the incoming traffic from Montenegro and the outgoing flow from Albania. He was serious, quick and efficient and, before I knew it, I had a stamp in my passport and with an unexpected flash of a smile he welcomed me to Albania. We had made it into our tenth country!

With confidence levels rising, I headed for Shkodër. The road ran across flat terrain. Piles of rubbish lay discarded by the roadside, and old Mercedes roared passed us every now and then, swerving into the centre of the road with no real thought for vehicles that might be coming from the opposite direction. The air smelt different. We had left the clean, beautifully preened world of tourism behind us and in front lay a world full of new smells, surprises and pollution. A land in transition. It was compelling, fascinating, and so different from anything I had seen on our journey thus far.

Albania had been forcibly isolated from most of the world

for forty years under the leadership of Enver Hoxha and only in 1998, thirteen years after Hoxha's death, did Albania embrace democracy. The result? A desperate bid for modernisation in a country gripped by corruption, pension pyramid scandals, a collapsed economy, frequent leadership changes and entrenched socialist ideals which clashed headlong with capitalism. I was witnessing a moment of this change. It was exciting just to have made it here.

A dilapidated cluster of houses built from a medley of breeze blocks and old bricks housed Roma families, their young children playing perilously close to the road. They were as unaware of the traffic as the drivers were unaware of them, taking no care to slow down. On our right, the silhouette of a castle sat perched on a rocky outcrop, its defending walls etched out against a clear blue sky. With one eye on the castle and one eye on the road, we rounded a corner and onto a single-laned iron bridge across the Bojana River. The traffic moved with great caution as the rickety timber road surface clanked, rattled and moved under the weight of us all. Men sat along the middle sections of the bridge fishing. They looked up as Tito and I went by and their faces registered surprise and curiosity while I marvelled at their complacency, sitting and fishing from a structure which, in my opinion, was likely to collapse at any moment. Safely across, we had the rather nerve-racking task of filtering into a steadily moving double lane of traffic. Whereas others seemed able to barge their way in between the gaps, a Zastava 750 did not have that same powerful capacity. Cars soon piled up behind us, becoming agitated by my hesitancy to pull out. When they could stand it no more, they cut in front of us and disappeared into the two-lane stream.

An opportunity came. It lasted seconds. I accelerated out. The traffic slowed behind us but we had made it. Shkodër loomed, a mass of tall buildings, industrial chimneys and wide boulevards. After our sleepy island travels and inland meanderings, the idea of a city as big as this was intimidating. A wooden sign pointed to Rozafa Castle and spontaneously I indicated right, veered off the two-laned highway and headed up the stony slopes of a dirt track, avoiding the urban challenge ahead. The road narrowed, resembling a farm track, and we climbed until we could go no further.

Rozafa Castle was not the most popular tourist attraction on a Friday afternoon in October. A car park attendant hovered patiently. I proffered him a handful of Lek coins, courtesy of the German couple I had met in Perast. He picked out the parking fee and I walked up to the castle. At the entrance, a sign read *'The enemy throw down to the castle 2,530 wizzbang (some of wich weight 600kg)'*. *Wizzbangs*? I wondered, amusedly. I wished I had had some of those to hand during my encounter with the truck driver on the Pelješac peninsula.

The view from Rozafa Castle would inspire any adventurer: the plains stretched out below the castle in all directions with mountains on the horizon. Lake Skadar lay northwards, a huge expanse of water glistening in a hazy light, beyond which stretched Montenegro. In the immediate foreground was Shkodër. It looked a busy city of colourful tower blocks and a great deal of traffic. From the comforting heights of Rozafa Castle's walls, it seemed too much for Tito and me. To the south, east and west, three rivers snaked their way across the plains and I felt intuitively pulled in one of those directions.

While I mulled over what to do, I ventured into the castle museum. The curator embarked on a tale about Albania's well-known hero Skanderbeg but, with the sudden arrival of a delegation of Albanian officials, I was instantly forgotten. These important guests claimed his full attention and the extent of his knowledge. Meanwhile, I was left to make what I could of the Albanian captions – which did not amount to very much.

Rozafa Castle had charm; it was very much a romantic

ruin to me, from the strange feather-footed birds, looking like sophisticated pigeons peering out from a large enclosed aviary, to the wild flowers and grasses which were growing prolifically across large expanses of the castle's battlements. I sat in the café's courtyard and reviewed the map and guidebook. South appeared to be the best option. Perhaps I would find out more about Skanderbeg in Lezhë, where he had died and was buried in 1468.

It was only 34km. A short journey, yet a shocking introduction to driving in Albania. The fact that Tito was white in colour, slow in speed and compact in size was possibly an unexpected advantage. He could be seen easily and cars could readily overtake him. There was room for another car to fit alongside us in the same lane if need be – which, as it turned out, was necessary on more than one occasion. The Albanian driver is generally male and unpredictable behind the wheel. He is a phenomenon requiring one's absolute attention and concentration on the road if one is to outsmart him and survive. He generally favours the Mercedes, whether old or new, but mainly old. Without exception, he drives at breakneck speed down the single-laned roads with no respect or consideration for anyone else in front, behind or coming in the opposite direction. I certainly had my heart in my mouth on more than one occasion. Staring intently ahead, I hoped to anticipate and avoid what was surely going to be my impending death in Albania, but miraculously Tito and I remained unscathed as we peeled off into the town of Lezhë.

———

L ezhë is a working town, rundown, with only a glimmer of modernisation in the form of glass buildings set amongst a majority of sixty- and seventy-year-old communist socialist apartment blocks. It was 4 o'clock and the town was humming with activity as people went home after work. Many were manual workers, doing what I could not tell, but their clothes were almost black with dirt. Most were walking; some were hoping cars would stop and pick them up, and others crammed into the already packed buses. I drove Tito slowly up the high street like a misplaced tourist. A bearded man in a light blue cap was peering over the balcony of a first floor café. He looked almost bohemian; an artist, maybe, and curiously unusual in this drab environment. I decided to park and investigate.

Tables were crammed onto a narrow balcony. The man in his blue cap was the only other customer. He looked up as I entered.

"*Mirë dita*," I said politely. A waitress appeared and looked enquiringly at me. "Er, macchiato?" I asked, "And, a *mineral pas gaz*?"

The waitress nodded her understanding of my faltering Albanian.

"*Faleminderit*," I said gratefully. It was pitiful that after five years of working in Kosovo this was practically the full extent of my vocabulary. It was true that work commitments had not left me with much available time for anything else. Still, it would have been incredibly useful to know more, particularly at this moment, as the man in his blue cap ventured into friendly dialogue with me. His other language was Italian, which made a surprising and pleasant change to German, but sadly did nothing to aid my ability to understand him.

"*Parlez-vous français*, or English?" I asked hopefully. He had a few words of English and with my somewhat smattering knowledge of individual foreign words we managed to communicate in a stilted mix of languages. Clearly enjoying this challenging form of conversation, he suggested that perhaps we would meet again tomorrow and waved me a cheery goodbye.

I continued to sit watching Lezhë life from my balcony

position. The muezzin's call to prayer pierced the late afternoon air. It seemed to bring out a number of elderly ladies, each dressed in multiple layers of white tunics over loose fitting pantaloons, white socks and black shoes, and with folds of white cloth fastened to their heads. They headed down the street in a group of three, while another woman followed wearing different attire. She had a fitted waistcoat and a voluminous white pleated skirt, which swung over her white pantaloons. She had a black apron tied around her waist, the black ribbon and tassels dangling behind her, while on her head was a black scarf tied tightly around her head and fastened at the nape of her neck in a long tie. These traditionally dressed ladies looked out of place amongst the young Albanians in their western clothes; and they too peered just as curiously at them as I from the local burek takeaway across the way. Above the burek shop rose three floors of apartment blocks divided into many living quarters, each with a balcony from where washing hung, bunches of onions and garlic dried, and flowers and herbs bloomed in terracotta pots. The paint peeled freely off the walls; Lezhë was in need of a facelift.

———

The communist-style "tourism" hotel on the corner of the main street appeared to be my only accommodation option. I parked Tito nearby in what I hoped was a legal space between two cars, removed the key from the ignition and climbed out to the joyful shouts of an old man, who rushed across the road and over to me as fast as his walking stick and legs would carry him. His eyes shone with excitement and his face was alive with emotion as he switched from Albanian to Italian in the vain hope of being able to communicate to me whatever it was about Fiċas that he knew or had experienced. He paused for breath and I asked hopefully, "*Engleski*?" The look of disappointment on his face said it all and I felt instantly wretched for spoiling the moment, denying him the opportunity to chat as he so clearly wanted to do. I watched as he peered nostalgically in through Tito's windows and chuckled to himself. He then walked away with a sigh, his over-sized suit drowning his frail frame, and I was left wondering wistfully what it was he had wanted to tell me.

————

A studious looking young man sat behind the reception desk of the Hotel Liss Uldedaj. As I approached, he slowly lifted his head out of his book and looked at me thoughtfully. Yes, I could have a room on the second floor with a view over the main street and up the slopes to the ruins of Lezhë Castle, he said very decisively. Was it possible to walk up to the castle, I asked. He laughed. He was sure it would be impossible. Apparently, there was no obvious footpath and he seemed to doubt my ability to forge a route – even he had not tried. I bowed to his superior knowledge and instead, taking full advantage of his excellent command of English, launched into conversation with him about life in Albania.

He was your archetypal University student full of ideas, dreams for the future and opinions about the present, although he shook his head despondently at the thought of there being any immediate future in Lezhë.

"Lezhë is still stuck in communist times," he said with regret. "At the coast and in Tirana you have pluralism but here in Lezhë it is still socialism. There is nothing here, no cinema, no theatre and it will be like this for some time, perhaps another generation before it changes." This situation did not seem to affect his mood and I admired his upbeat spirit. He was a man ready for the modern Albania, whenever it arrived in Lezhë, but I wondered if, in reality, he would be able to resist the temptation of Tirana, Albania's capital city which, in his opinion, was moving forward rapidly in a bid to become European and modern.

———

My hotel room was simple. Basic wooden furniture, a huge old-fashioned television set, and an outdated bathroom. A bright blue plastic jug sat in the handwash basin – to be kept filled in case of water cuts. I ate in the only known restaurant in town – the pizzeria in the basement. The chef and waiters were glued to an Italian soap opera on an equally enormous and ancient-looking television set. I was their sole customer. I chose a table where I could see what they were watching and together we followed the Italian drama as it unfolded on screen. They laughed amongst themselves and threw me the odd self-conscious smile to ensure I felt included while I ate in solitary state.

Night had fallen by 7 o'clock. I wandered down Lezhë's high street. Although the shops were open, the products were displayed on shelving from behind full-length serving counters, making it difficult for any form of idle browsing. The main street was lit only by a dim glow from the shops, kiosks and car headlights. Roma children wandered around and men huddled together smoking cigarettes, talking amongst themselves. The receptionist was right; there was nowhere to go and nothing to do on an autumn evening in Lezhë.

- Lezhë/Tirana (70km) -

It was Saturday and washing day. Apartment balconies were festooned in billowing sheets drying in the morning sunshine as I returned to the café balcony for breakfast. My new acquaintance with the blue cap was nowhere to be seen so I headed back down the main street to the town's only tourist attraction, the memorial site of Skanderbeg, the country's 15th century hero. A man forever immortalised in the Albanian psyche for his prowess as a battle warrior, having successfully defended Albania against the Ottomans until his natural death in 1468.

Four fat sheep grazed enthusiastically on the grass either side of the path which led up to the mausoleum. I stepped through a magnificent set of carved wooden-panelled doors set into the walls of Lezhë's former cathedral and into an open space. At one end a walled mosaic of the Kastrioti coat of arms dominated the room, a double-headed black eagle on a bright red background; now the official flag of Albania and formerly Skanderbeg's family crest. In the centre of the room lay Skanderbeg's tomb. A replica of his helmet had been placed on top of the tomb. It was adorned with the head of a long-horned roebuck deer – making it an altogether rather heavy object to be wearing when wielding a sword, a replica of which also lay across his tomb. Disappointingly, I remained none the wiser about this great warrior's past or why there was a deer attached to his helmet. The answers would perhaps lie in the town where I was heading next: Krujë.

———

The highway surface had been dug up for kilometres, its broken surface doing nothing to deter the speed of some Mercedes drivers. They travelled at a death-defying pace, kicking up clouds of dirt and dust in their wake, blinding us all into moments of near collision. I tried to maintain Tito at a slow but constant speed, around which vehicles could pass with relative ease, and minimum danger to us. We turned off into Fushë-Krujë (Krujë on the plain) and onto an even more disastrous road surface. Bumper to bumper, the traffic lurched in and out of potholes, the vehicles cramming together behind us so tightly they were almost shunting Tito up the hill in their haste to reach the top.

The temperature had risen significantly since the morning and I glanced up at Krujë Castle, basking in the light. It had been built by Skanderbeg as part of a defence strategy, linking with Lezhë and Rozafa castles, but unlike these two sites, Krujë was bursting with life, heightened by bus loads of school and college students here on a day's outing. Within the ancient defending walls sat the newly constructed Historical Museum, and the focus of most people's attention. As I passed through the castle gates, I noticed a young man having his palm read by an elderly Roma lady. His hand obediently outstretched, he was listening intently as if his life depended upon what she had to say, while his friends crowded round, whispering quietly to one another. Inside the castle grounds, a market of crafts and less artistic-looking items was strung out across the rough dirt surface, the sellers looking hopefully at everyone who went by. I found myself being pulled along up the steps and into the museum. The guides captivated their young Albanian audiences with tales of Skanderbeg but it was lost on me. Another replica helmet and sword lay across a table and I hoped for more explanation but there was none. A group of four teenage boys lingered behind the rest of their group; they climbed over the ropes and took turns wearing the helmet while photographing one another, sniggering loudly. Before they were detected, they quickly left the scene of their antics and I with them, fearing an alarm would sound any moment and I would be held responsible.

————

E ventually I learned the story of Skanderbeg and believe him to be the buckle that pulls together many individual strands of my Balkan journey into one final twist. Heralded as the great 15th century warrior king of Albania, he was born Gjergi Kastrioti. He was descended from one of the noble families of Albania and with the advance of the Ottoman Army his father's land and wealth came under threat. However, the father struck a deal with the Sultan, trading the young Gjergi for the safe-keeping of his lands. Gjergi was sent to Edirne, where my journey also took me, and here he was trained as a swordsman. He became a great fighter, earning the name of Skanderbeg which, translated, means Alexander the Prince, and was apparently a reference to the much-revered Alexander the Great.

Skanderbeg was expected to convert to the Muslim faith and he fought with the Ottoman armies for many years against the Serbs and other Christian forces. His army lost a battle in Niš in southern Serbia and it was at this moment that he finally took the opportunity to desert the Ottomans and head back to his homeland in Albania. Encouraging the many Albanian clans to bury their differences and fight together as one against the Ottoman army, Skanderbeg earned much respect and success on the battlefield. He married a woman of equal noble standing in the eyes of the Orthodox church and had a son. His allegiance towards Christianity and Europe grew stronger as he successfully led his army against the Ottoman advances. Some say it is because of Skanderbeg's continued success in battle that the Ottoman army was prevented from making a full-scale invasion into Europe through Italy, thus halting the spread of the Ottoman Empire and the Muslim faith – a debate for the historians. What is interesting is how Skanderbeg embraced many religious facets and seems not to be judged or scorned, remaining a hero in Albania and Kosovo, as well as Europe. Puzzling though it may seem, it is his Muslim name Skanderbeg which is more readily expressed, although his roots are Christian. His birth and marriage in the Orthodox church are not questioned, nor his final resting place in a Catholic cathedral. He is a man who appears to have lived, fought and died under the banner of differing religious alliances yet he continues to be revered by all. A tale with which many Balkan families could empathise, and for countries beyond the peninsula, in recognising the complexities of identity.

———

B eyond Krujë Castle lay the Turkish bazaar, filled with individual shops selling handcrafted goods. Floor treadles moved back and forth controlled by the swollen bare feet of women. Their fingers threaded long strands of wool through a maze of taut horizontal threads with amazing speed – another carpet in the making, while piles of their colourful, completed creations were displayed for sale. One shop sold woollen slippers. A teenage boy demonstrated to me the process, enthusiastically finding the correct English words with wool in one hand and timber shoe mould in the other. He grinned appealingly at me in between sentences and I was instantly enamoured. I bought a pair from him, and his mother, who had been shyly sitting in the shadows, glowed with pride.

———

W e were on our way again along the dusty unsurfaced road towards Tirana, and as the kilometres slipped by, the road surface improved immeasurably. My relief was short-lived as the full horrors of driving in Albania were revealed. I learned very quickly to expect the impossible, only made possible by everyone else on the road swerving, braking or, as I did, closing one's eyes and praying for a miracle.

Inside a roadside kiosk not much larger than a telephone

box hung a large skinned animal. A freshly killed cow or sheep? I was not at all sure. Whatever it was, it was attracting quite a lot of attention and a queue of people was forming along the kerb. It was not the only one and I was tempted to pull off the road to take a closer look but it was debatable whether I would be able to communicate with anyone. Having a tendency to feel faint around freshly killed animals, I decided it was best to drive on and was almost immediately brought back to reality by a policeman leaping up and down in the middle of the road waving a handheld lollipop stick, across which the word '*STOP*' was written. Other cars had been halted ahead of us and although this policeman's lollipop-waving action was not done with any real conviction, I pulled over. The policeman sauntered over and stared in through the half-open window.

"*Mirë dita*," I said politely, unwinding the window a little more.

He cast me a watery smile and a "*Mirë dita*" in response. Then, tapping his lollipop stick on the window edge, he said demandingly, "*Pezen*" – or a word to that effect.

What does that mean? I wondered. I took a blind stab at it and handed over my passport. He nodded, looked at it and said "*Pezen*" once again.

So it's not my passport. Maybe he wants the car details, I thought, as I searched for them in my handbag. I handed them over.

He looked at them politely but with more insistence said "*Pezen! Pezen!*"

I searched in my handbag again and handed over my Green Card, hoping this was the "*Pezen*" he was after.

It was not, and, pointing at the steering wheel with his lollipop stick, he shouted, "*Pezen! Pezen!*" at me.

I felt nervous laughter rapidly rising up inside me. I turned off Tito's engine in case that was the offence I was committing, but he started to shout repeatedly, "*PEZEN!*

PEZEN!" waving his lollipop stick in total annoyance. I started handing over document after document until his arms were full, but still none of these items were what he was after. I had exhausted the supply of official papers in my handbag and still had no idea what he wanted.

"Pezen? Pezen?" I mumbled, turning to look at my luggage on the backseat, hoping for inspiration. Suddenly, the penny dropped.

"Ah, Pezen!" I leaned excitedly into the backseat, unzipped the side pocket of my rucksack and pulled out the only other document I had to my name: my international driving licence. "Pezen?" I suggested hopefully.

"Po, po!" he said, looking relieved.

Of course – he was road police! I put it on top of the pile of documents he was already holding and he looked at the front cover with a smile. He did not open it, or show any real interest. I had one and that was enough. Ceremoniously, he handed me back the pile of documents through the window and with a casual flick of his lollipop stick I was dismissed. Desperately stifling a wail of laughter, I started the engine, put Tito into first gear and off we went. The last-minute realisation that I needed an International Driving Licence had involved a panic dash to London; now it all seemed worth it, otherwise who knows what the consequences would have been? I imagine a substantial sum of Albanian Leks would have been a part of the solution.

———

The hectic, jam-packed boulevards of Tirana. I had no real idea where I was going. At each traffic light Roma children would swarm around the mass of cars, furiously washing windscreens while pleading for money. A young girl and boy advanced towards Tito with a bucket of filthy water.

"No, no!" I groaned, but Tito's windscreen wipers were

lifted in a flash and there was nothing to stop their cleaning activities. I had yet to change money and had nothing to give them. As the boy appeared at the window, hand outstretched, I raised my shoulders apologetically to say, *"I'm sorry; I have none."* Undeterred, he started pointing to something on the passenger seat that I could perhaps give him. Was it the bottle of water? He shook his head. Nothing I touched was the object he wanted. On the passenger side a little girl was pulling fiercely at the door. The coat hanger locking device, made by John all those weeks ago in Skopje, flexed but held against her struggles with the door handle. The traffic lights turned green. Whatever the boy had wanted, I had not been able to guess correctly, and he was furious with me. But it was too late; the traffic was moving. My eye caught sight of the multi-coloured cocktail stick I had stuck in the dashboard, a decoration from an ice cream dessert I had had in Bulgaria. That was what he had wanted! But I had realised too late. He had dashed to the side of the road and the queue of traffic pushed Tito and me along the boulevard and out of sight – his wipers still outstretched.

─────

We had reached Tirana; a city of magnificent socialist architecture, and wide boulevards gyrating with the volume of traffic. At its centre, Skanderbeg Square. A statue of the warrior king, sitting triumphantly on his horse, dominated the pedestrianised central section, the Albanian flag fluttering gracefully beside him. Swept along by the sheer number of vehicles, we circled the Square twice before I managed to force my way through it and conveniently landed at the entrance to the Tirana International Hotel. Overwhelmed and considerably stressed by the city experience, I decided we were going upmarket. A faceless hotel atmosphere, but with a spectacular view of the square from my room on the eighth floor and Tito in secure parking more than compensated for the hefty room rate.

- Tirana -

Tirana is a city of culture and contrasts, eager to embrace a new era beyond its closed political past. A vibrant place, though the evidence of communism is everywhere; in the architecture, in the mentality and in the day-to-day functioning of the city, from street cleaner to policeman. It was a chance to experience the remnants of a fast-vanishing system, as the inextricable links with what was, fade rapidly in a time of capitalist awakening.

"*Ku Eshte Vota Ime?*" (Where is my Vote?) the rally boomed. I had somehow to extricate myself from the gathering masses or be engulfed by them.

A Roma man slit the cordoning tape in two and marched towards the crowd, shouting drunkenly, "*ku eshte vota ime?*" A policeman turned and watched in mild annoyance as the man staggered into the melee of chanting protestors, but he made no effort to follow him. I walked away from the parliamentary buildings and took refuge in the entrance to the Dajti Hotel – once a place of luxury where international visitors stayed and where plots and deals were allegedly planned and executed during Enver Hoxha's regime. Now the building looked uncared for, but it had a certain presence and I was curious to view inside. The ground floor housed an exhibition but to enter I had to get through a battery of unfriendly-looking guards. Casually dressed, they sat nonchalantly on old wooden chairs, staring at me suspiciously. If I wished to go inside, I must leave my handbag with them, one of them said aggressively. Perhaps I would come back another day, I said, and retreated hastily.

The National Art Gallery lay close by. It was open yet stood in complete darkness. I pushed the entrance door.

"Yes, yes, it is open," said a man standing at the front desk.

The charge was 300 Lek. I only had two 200 Lek notes. He insisted he had no change. I shrugged and paid 400 Lek. This pleased him greatly and I was escorted to the first gallery room, whereupon he flicked on the lights. I was the sole visitor. A photographic exhibition from Spain took up the whole ground floor. My footsteps echoed around the building.

The gallery attendant diligently followed, turning off one set of lights and flicking on the next as we went. Upstairs was the reason I had come here: a large collection of Socialist Realist art filled the walls. Striking images of men and women resonated from each painting in strong and empowering poses. The paintings portrayed images of inferred happiness, both at work and within family life. A vision fabricated as part of the communist ideal. The artwork was compelling yet threatening. One subject was different. It was night. A clandestine meeting, people around a campfire. Dark colours had been used to paint the scene. It had displeased the museum's Censorship Board, who considered it a negative portrayal of life and immediately all the artist's paintings had been removed from the gallery. The necessity for image control was a reality of communism in Albania at that time. Today it was back on display, a painting expressing a sense of mystery, atmosphere.

———

The staunch architectural style of the communist era is hard to ignore in Tirana. It has a kind of majesty yet at the same time its huge, bold lines can send a shiver down one's spine. Yet Tirana manages to invent new styles from old and incorporate a modern look into as many open spaces as it can. History and time are represented at every corner, although I wondered how long it would be before buildings were knocked down in a bid for complete modernisation. Change is happening fast and respect for architecture seems arbitrarily selective. Old socialist apartment blocks along the banks of the River Lana have been given a modern facelift and are brightly coloured and numbered. Opposite, ultra-modern glass buildings have been erected but they house the shops and boutiques most Albanians cannot afford. The European Trade Centre is one such place. I walked inside, intrigued to see what it had to offer. The shops included well-known top-of-the-range western European brands and an expensive Italian kitchen shop, with designs being sold for 8,500 Euros or more. I wondered who could afford those prices – not many, from the look of things. Like the majority of shops in the complex, it was empty of customers and manned by bored-looking sales assistants. This was a similar scenario to that at the Tzum shopping mall in Sofia, where the greatest activity had come from the floor-cleaning ladies pushing their scissor-shaped mops in synchronised sweeping motions along each floor level. As it had been there, the café was where the soul of the building existed and I squeezed through to the only remaining table. At least here the coffee was affordable and the view over Tirana was free.

———

I took a photograph of a wildly colourful building but a man dressed in black, rather like a minder, came over and signalled to me to stop. Why, I was not sure, but I decided after one more click to move away from the sleek black shiny cars with their smoked windows before I landed myself in trouble.

Nearby, the modern pyramid-shaped Catholic church with its clean well-maintained façade contrasted bleakly with a shabby pyramid-shaped structure crumbling to ruins in the park, defaced by a mass of graffiti. This was to be Enver Hoxha's mausoleum, built by him but in which he was never interred. Instead the building was deteriorating, symbolic of its time but now too closely associated with suppression and a tyrannical leader for many Albanians to bother with its survival.

————

Tirana at night was similar to Lezhë, an odd experience for a capital city. The only light glowed from car headlights or buildings. Away from the wide boulevards, the roads were deeply potholed. I picked my way along in the dark, moving quickly into the pool of light from an open café and then back into the gloom. New buildings sidled up next to old and in amongst these, old earth brick houses stood in fragile groups, filled with sounds of crying children, laughter and the clanking of dishes. Each building style represented the changing face of Tirana; an intriguing mix which included early 20th century single-storey earth brick homes. These remaining houses, clustered together like small communities, were now vastly dilapidated and lived in by Roma families. How long would it be before these structures disappeared, to be replaced by another homogenous style, the poverty-stricken people pushed out of their homes in the name of progress? Today they were there: clinging on to an inner-city life, their future unsure.

————

A dozen people sat around a long table. They stopped and stared at me as I walked in through the door. Clearly, I had made a mistake. This was not a restaurant and to cover my embarrassment I asked hopefully, "Restaurant?"

A young girl of about 12 years was volunteered to speak.

"This is not a restaurant. You must go outside and down the stairs." She blushed while the rest of the table looked at her in admiration and then to me to see if I had understood and would reply.

"Thank you. *Falemenderit.*"

The communication had been successful. They nodded and got back to eating. I retreated quietly and headed for a set of stairs. They wound down into a basement dining room. A table for one was obviously not what the waiter was expecting and he looked suspiciously over my shoulder and then threw me a sympathetic look. I feasted on grilled lamb, vegetables, and potatoes and tried to avoid the many curious stares from the waiters and customers alike. Nervous of the walk back to the hotel, I did not linger over the food and was soon hurriedly threading my way along the dark lanes to the main boulevard and into Skanderbeg Square. The wind was gathering pace and as the first drops of rain began to fall, the sounds of music and singing came in gusty waves through the strong wind. James Belushi was in town. A free concert – but even that did not tempt me. It was a wild night to be outside with too many objects flying about; I did not envy him.

––––––

It was a phenomenal storm which shook Tirana that night. The thunder pounded, the lightning flashed and a gale-force wind whipped up into a fury. No light could be seen across the city. It was 2am as I peered into the eerie darkness from my hotel window on the eighth floor, feeling a million miles away from the world.

- Tirana/Durrës (38km) -

After a fitful night's sleep, morning arrived. The storm had passed and I took one last look at the view over Skanderbeg Square. Skanderbeg and his horse had survived the winds. It was Monday morning and the traffic moved in sudden bursts of momentum around the wide expanse. Chaos ensued, despite two policemen standing strategically at intersection points blowing their whistles, trying to maintain some kind of order. I wondered, from the pandemonium below, how Tirana had not come to a paralysed halt. Cyclists pedalled against the flow, slaloming their way in the opposite direction through the snarled traffic. Men pushing carts entered into the general fray and car horns blared continuously, while drivers blocked one another in an attempt to manoeuvre themselves through the traffic. The mayhem mesmerised me but there was packing to finish and I pulled myself away from the window.

The storm had raged most of the night, followed by torrential rain. Although it had stopped now, dark clouds loomed ominously westwards but today Tito and I would be heading towards the blue skies in the east: to the coast and to the town of Durrës.

We skirted the edges of Skanderbeg Square, passing the old mosque, the Opera House and the majestic ethnographical museum with its impressive mosaic centrepiece. We stayed in the outer peripheral stream of traffic for fear of being sucked in to its centre and I cast a look at the pedestal on which Enver Hoxha's statue used to stand. It was said the great structure had been secreted away before his figure became a public scene of destruction, as has been the fate of many a dictator's statue.

I found myself driving in a bubble of fear, surpassed only by an adrenalin rush for survival against the odds. From behind the wheel of a Fića life on the road was terrifying yet strangely exhilarating. Thankfully, I had not yet witnessed a car crash and certainly hoped not to be in one. Car graveyards were a common sight; towering sculptures of crumpled, written-off vehicles, and I had seen many bouquets of flowers beside the road marking no end of fatal accidents.

———

A headstrong wind pulled and buffeted Tito's light frame but I managed to maintain a steady course following the sunshine eastwards. Tito was not the popular hero he had been elsewhere in the Balkans – perhaps everybody was driving too fast or erratically to have time to notice him. White clouds scudded across the sky as we entered Durrës. A main promenade of hotels and large apartments crowded together. The sea was being lashed up into large waves and the wind whistled around us. The old town sat away from the coastline and the Hotel Lido was tucked up a dead end lane next to a former concrete bunker – now half-submerged in building material.

Another storm was brewing. The wind strengthened in anticipation but for now, at least, there was an opportunity to explore the town. I made for the Roman amphitheatre; although only partially uncovered, it is said to be the largest such structure in the Balkans but as its lengths and breadths were being ferociously guarded by a stray dog, I kept my distance.

Durrës had been dominated by 19th century architecture. Now, however, much had disappeared and what remained was dwindling. It would not be long before it would all be pulled down and replaced. I searched for the old tobacco factory but it was nowhere to be found. A Turkish bath, distinctive by its domed roof, lay unnoticed by its neighbour, a junior school of boisterous young children, its future as a bathing facility questionable. It was sad to see the historic face of the town toppling into obscurity as the race for modernisation and development became a more immediate priority – its popularity as a summer holiday destination paramount to economic development.

Down by the seashore the wind was so strong I could hardly walk in a straight line. Socialist statues struck formidable poses against a backdrop of wild weather and dark storm clouds; they were yet another reminder of the extent of the Partisan resistance movement in operation within the Balkan peninsula during World War II. I took refuge in a café overlooking a turbulent sea with waves pulled by a treacherous undercurrent crashing onto a deserted beach. Trilece was being served: a cake I first tried at the unusually named 'UFO' University café in Tirana and had been hooked on ever since. But this Durrës version surpassed all others. Its mellow mix of vanilla sponge cake, soaked in cold milk and topped with a layer of sweet caramel, looked unassuming but tasted heavenly. It was a welcome sugar boost as I scuttled back to my hotel, avoiding the odd flying object picked up by the wind and which came crashing down to the ground around me, finally reaching safety as the storm hit, bringing with it torrents of rain.

I spent the next few hours dissecting a pomegranate with a penknife and a plastic fork. It was by no means an easy fruit to eat and, with the implements to hand, almost impossible to enjoy. Perhaps there was an easier way to eat a pomegranate but I found its exotic taste more trouble to extract than it was worth.

By evening the storm had cleared and the sun came out in time to produce a colourful sunset display as I went in search of supper. In general it was I, rather than Tito, who had become the object of interest in Albania. I was certainly no Edith Durham or Rebecca West but, as a woman travelling on my own, and out of season, it was taking the locals by surprise and I longed for Tito to take the attention back again because then I could observe without being watched in return.

An area filled with bars and cafés had attracted a large number of customers and I found a restaurant tucked to one side. The menu was incomprehensible to me but the waiter eagerly brought out a board of freshly caught red mullet and I nodded my agreement to a plate of grilled fish and salad. Although it was almost impossible to communicate with anyone, a nod and a few words of French saw me through. In any case, I was more intrigued by the Rastafarian doll sitting on the sideboard opposite holding a rifle, the pose mimicking the socialist realist style of statue. There continued to be much in Albania that I found bewildering and unexpected.

- Durrës/Berat (92km) -

It rained heavily through the night and the temperature had cooled drastically. I put on my jeans, wondering if this was the definitive turning point in the weather for us. At breakfast a retired couple from London listened with some amusement to my quick summary of travels in Tito – although the wife was somewhat distracted by the hotel's resident long-eared rabbit gnawing quietly on a carrot wedged through the bars of its cage.

"You are going to write a book, aren't you?" they said.

I hesitated. "Well, I may try," at which they nodded encouragingly. The man asked for my name, saying he would look out for the book in a year or two. I gave him a non-committal smile, touched by their interest, and said, "It might take me a little longer than that!"

The woman then exclaimed to the waitress, "You must get this rabbit a bigger cage!" and the subject of book writing was swiftly replaced by a more pressing need for animal rights.

———

T he museum gates were open and a red carpet had been extended the full length of the path. I walked up it tentatively and was eyed by a number of museum staff at the front door. The head curator spoke English and enthusiastically welcomed me in. He seemed somewhat nervous and I asked if the red carpet was really for me. He laughed.

"No, I'm sorry. We are expecting a delegation of Canadian government officials at any moment. But please, you are welcome."

I entered a world of Hellenistic artefacts, Roman stonework, Ancient Greek objects, and Byzantine marvels, clay Aphrodite faces and small glass vases, in which the tears of wives and children had been captured and given to their departing loved ones. Although it was small, the museum was beautifully presented. The couple from my hotel appeared. "So many objects to admire," I enthused from across a display case.

The wife rushed off to admire a Hellenic object but he lingered and whispered back, "You know, when you get to my age, you have seen so many marvellous objects, it is very difficult to find the enthusiasm to take in any more, but my wife loves them." He winked and wandered off to find her, with a parting farewell wave.

———

A lbania had got under my skin and although I was tired and eager to get back to Macedonia, I was equally intrigued to see more of this country. I decided to drive a little further south to Berat – considered to be one of the oldest towns in Albania and listed by UNESCO for its wealth of historic buildings. With the expectation of seeing a 13th century castle, an array of old churches, Ottoman houses from the 14th century and a world steeped in the past, I headed out of town, confident that Tito would be fine. My navigation was not so assured and soon we were lurching along a dirt road blighted by potholes submerged in rainwater from the night before and I began to wonder if this was a good idea after all. If this was a sample of what was to come, it was going to be a desperately slow journey. I persevered, following in the wake of other vehicles trying to avoid the red-brown dirty water as it sprayed out from each pothole. Once more Tito was noticed as we passed by. The children waved, while old people smiled quietly to themselves, and again I felt that tenuous connection to the world through which I was travelling.

Although there were no obvious road signs to help me, I found the route south to Rrogozhinë. Roadworks curtailed our speed to a crawl, though some refused to heed the danger signs and flashed past us at every opportunity. Horses and carts, people, bicycles – anything that moved seemed to be on the highway, adding to the challenge of driving without mishap. We regularly got caught behind them, and with not enough acceleration to pass, our progress was limited. The further south we went, the more defence bunkers appeared on the landscape. Domed concrete structures of varying sizes lined the railway route. They popped up at road junctions and in fields. There was no apparent logic behind the placements and I wondered what exactly Enver Hoxha's strategy had been. Did he even have a strategy?

A new stretch of two-laned highway had us racing along at 70 km/h towards the junction with Berat. The road was free of traffic except for a white sports car. It outpaced us in seconds. The young driver pulled into a petrol station ahead as we continued on by. Minutes later, he caught us up and we approached a large roundabout in parallel. The driver wanted a race but, of course, Tito was not up to this kind of a challenge. The white sports car shot in front, taking the Berat exit, but I decided to circle the roundabout again, although I too was making for Berat. I was sure he was just having fun but my Pelješac encounter had made me nervous of drivers who paid me this kind of attention. On the second revolution I came off for Berat, hoping to have put some distance between myself and the sports car, but he had parked further ahead and was looking to see where we had gone. Beyond was a police road patrol and as we went past, the young driver realised there was no way he could race after us. Soon we were comfortably out of sight.

———

A lthough the road to Berat was flat, the condition of the surface was appalling. I navigated cautiously. We were in deeply rural countryside and life appeared quietly removed from the fast-changing Albania I had already witnessed elsewhere. We entered a village. Children pointed excitedly at Tito and once again I found myself laughing at their reactions, as I had done in Romania. Young women nudged their boyfriends, but they looked back at them in horror, unable to see the attraction of a Fića. Bunkers poked up everywhere, like bands of invading Daleks; they appeared in clusters when least expected; others sat alone, and I got a sense of what a "watched" world this must have been, apparently one military bunker having been built for every four inhabitants.

As we approached Berat, the road followed the course of the Osumi River. Two-tiered houses with graceful overhanging roofs of terracotta tiles hugged together, their first floors jettying outwards with large dark timber windows. On our left, grand houses with wide bay windows and arched eyebrow roofs gave an air of superiority. In the town centre concrete-built socialist apartment buildings mingled with their more historic neighbours. We passed the King's Mosque, a stone-built 15th century building considered to be one of Albania's oldest, and turned into a cobbled street which marked the start of the old town. I parked opposite the Mangalemi Hotel. I was in luck. A room was available and I had a view over the many undulating rooftops of old Berat. The muezzin began his call to prayer as the rain fell more persistently. The sound of his voice was muffled by the weather, travelling mysteriously through the empty streets. I sat on the roofed balcony, wrapped in my fleece and rain jacket against the cold, and drank hot soup. Homemade sausages tasted like haggis. I felt strangely homesick. It was followed by the sweetness of baklava – a comfort and a pleasure all Balkan.

———

T he rain fell steadily so I abandoned my expedition into the town and took refuge in a café, much to the delight of the owner and his family. I drank a *Schweppes* while they watched, craning their necks to look at the front cover of my Albania guidebook. I offered it to them and they crowded around, flicking to the central pages and photographs of their country. They admired them, talking in hushed tones. The rain eased, I paid and they came to the door with me.

"*Falemenderit*," the man said gratefully, handing back my guidebook.

It was perhaps the first glimpse they had had of the perceived highlights their country could offer to the curious traveller. I walked down to the river. The rain had stopped by the time I reached its banks. A footbridge spanned its width and I walked to its centre, gazing upstream. Four rainbows pushed through the clouds, each a paler version of the other. Beneath me the river ran fiercely, almost black in colour. I turned and looked downstream. The familiar karst mountain wall, which we had followed along the coast of Croatia, had reappeared and I stared at it in trepidation. Would we still have to conquer its heights to reach Macedonia? I pushed the thought aside and looked up at the castle. The rain started again and in seconds it was engulfed in fog. I was cold and retreated back to the hotel to pull on another pair of socks. I climbed fully clothed into bed, gathering the blanket up to my chin, and fell into an uneasy sleep.

———

I woke with a start. It was 7.30pm and I was starving and still cold. I went downstairs in search of a glass of wine or a *rakija* – anything to get the blood circulating to my feet. The restaurant was full but a retired German couple and a young Dutchman made room for me. They were cyclists and I felt instantly humbled by their energy and enthusiasm. They, in turn, were impressed by my journey and left their plates of steaming food to go out to look at Tito, parked across the road, coming back to say enviously, "You have the 750S, the Sports model!"

I had not realised. Perhaps that was the reason Tito had got me this far.

- Berat/Elbasan (98km) -

The muezzin's call to prayer woke me early. I looked tentatively through the curtains. Blue skies. Sunshine. And… snow! I got dressed quickly and went out onto the balcony. The mountains had a sprinkling of snow. I stared in disbelief. So soon? The sun shone deceptively warm, lulling me into a false sense of security and travel lust. I could journey for another week before the car documents expired. My original plan had been to reach the Greek Peleponnese before looping back to Skopje. *Could I risk it?* I wondered.

The appearance of snow had brought everyone outside to focus on final winter preparations. Logs had been chopped and stacked up the sides of houses to ensure plentiful hearth fires and warmth during the harsh, cold months ahead. The market was in full swing. Fruit and vegetable stands on one side of the street and the meat market on the other, evidenced by blood flowing across the pavement, assuring us all the meat was fresh. A horse had been tethered outside the elegant 15th century King's Mosque, a solid wooden saddle structure strapped to his back. He munched contentedly on a nosebag of delights, ignoring the market buzz around him. I passed a memorial to Margareta Tutulani, *'Heroine e Popullit'* (a heroine of the people), in an adjoining square. She had been hanged by the Nazis for her involvement in the Partisan resistance during World War II, a reminder of the extent to which the Partisan movement had operated in Albania.

———

U p above the town lay the ancient city of Berat. I paid my one Euro entry fee and walked into a world of whitewashed lanes, narrow cobbled alleys, stone churches, mosques, alluring frescoes, painted icons, and fortified walls. The muted sounds of families preparing lunch, talking, laughing and shouting emanated from open windows. A turkey squawked loudly and furiously fanned out her tail as her companion was carried off under a man's arm – today's lunch. Below, lay the industrialised zone of Berat, and rows of socialist-style apartment blocks close to the Osumi River. A man called out to me from the grassed ramparts of the citadel and I walked over to see what he was selling. He spoke English, his weathered face breaking into gentle lines as he smiled. He was dressed in jeans, a checked shirt and a cardigan, the sleeves of which had been carefully rolled up. This was Bujar, who became my unofficial guide; a slim, wiry man with bright eyes and unusually long hair by Albanian standards. His enthusiasm and energy were heartfelt and I found myself compelled to follow him. We plunged down into the depths of an Illyrian water cistern, climbed the heights of the castle walls and squeezed our way up the steps of the remnants of a minaret to admire the view. I was never quite sure whether Bujar was going to rob me and leave me for dead or die protecting me as I embarked on his personalised tour of old Berat.

It was an exhilarating experience, if a little unnerving, as he raced me from one object to the next, shouting excitedly, "Emma, Emma, look, look!" At last, even Bujar ran out of steam and I called a halt outside a café and offered to buy him a coffee. The café was in fact closed but within minutes he had found the owner and it was opened with reassuring smiles. I was then presented with the remnants of an Ottoman smoking pipe, a piece of delicately sculpted pottery which he and Bujar had found in the castle grounds. With discretion, I thanked them but said it would be best to keep artefacts like this here in Berat at the castle and not give them away. Unabashed and nodding sagely, they went off and came back with a large bunch of wild flowering basil. This I could not refuse, and, thanking them graciously, I headed away from the citadel walls, clutching their generous gift of flowering basil sprigs, breathing in their sweet heady scent.

———

The smell of basil filled Tito's interior. My tour with Bujar had greatly delayed my departure and the morning's confidence in embarking further south to the Peleponnese had somewhat dwindled. I looked up at the snow-encrusted mountains. My instinct told me to head for Skopje. This was no time to tempt fate. Resignedly, I put Tito into gear. We would make for the western border with Macedonia.

———

I navigated us northwards back towards Rrogozhinë then dubiously followed a signpost indicating a right turn to Elbasan. I had the feeling we had gone wrong but a passerby assured me Elbasan was this way, so I persevered. The dirt track narrowed significantly and without warning we were on a single-track bridge spanning a wide river. It more resembled a condemned structure than a bridge but there was no going back, short of reversing – an option which seemed even more dangerous than travelling forward. The surface clickety-clacked beneath Tito's wheels as he crossed each concrete section of its fragile construction. I eyed the corroded iron railings with growing misgivings and then, to my horror, I became aware of a modern bridge to our right carrying vehicles in both directions. My hands, clammy with fear, gripped the steering wheel tightly and I counted the seconds until we finally reached the other side, grateful to all the gods for getting us safely over. Tito settled into a 60km/h speed across the plain, following the course of the River Shkumbinit. The mountain range to our left loomed large. That, at least, had been avoided – the route we would have had to take if we had come directly from Tirana. Ahead, snow-covered peaks signalled winter had fluttered across the Macedonian heights. Surely we would reach Skopje before it hit the lowland areas?

——————

Industrial chimneys dominated the outskirts of Elbasan but the vast site on which they sat was silent. Like Vareš in Bosnia and Herzegovina, it was redundant. The economic boom was over, leaving a depressing sight in its wake. I found my way into the historic centre, fortified walls marking the boundary. I parked Tito in a public car park and looked up at the high-rise Skampa Hotel. The guidebook's recommendation lay within the castle walls; I would try there first.

A Muslim lady dressed in a *niqab* walked by. Her dress was the most sophisticated of designs; a rich dark brown material with tan-coloured internal pleats and a black headdress. She crossed the road escorted by a casually dressed man in jeans and I, like everyone else in the street, was momentarily entranced by her striking appearance but as she disappeared into the crowd, my attention reverted to finding accommodation.

Timber steps led down into a walled garden. There was an amphitheatre, an outside terrace, a café, restaurant and hotel with just seven rooms. A young waiter spoke some English and introduced me to someone I took to be the owner. He was a large man with a charismatic character to match. He tried to persuade me to take a room with a balcony shared with two other rooms. I did not like the idea. *Too exposed,* I thought, and plumped for a room with no balcony. He considered that the best suite and we negotiated a price with which we were both happy. The waiter escorted me back to Tito. He took one look at the car and laughed. He had never been in a Zastava before.

"It is so old!"

He watched in astonishment as I unwound the coat hanger from the passenger door.

"Yes, he is old, but he has taken me around the Balkans. Ten countries, in fact," I added for effect.

He jumped in beside me and, much impressed, watched as I went through the procedure of starting the car. He peered curiously at the dashboard as we headed for the hotel. The parking was on a distinct tilt and I planted a brick firmly behind the front and back wheels. I saw him shaking his head in disbelief but he said nothing.

———

Elbasan was a bustling town. The many stares made me conscious of being the only tourist. As the evening light faded, the sunset threw a warm glow against the ancient walls, and I rediscovered the ritual evening stroll I had witnessed throughout the greater part of my Balkan journey. A Roma boy begged for money, a man grilled cobs of corn, and a wide, pedestrianised boulevard filled with people. Young men and women walked in groups of three, a phenomenon I noticed first while working in Kosovo. Why three is the preferred number, I do not know. A group of elderly men, neatly turned out in suits and panama-style felt hats, walked six abreast down the avenue, keeping to the pace of the slowest. Were they in fact two sets of three? They walked with their hands clasped behind their backs in subconsciously synchronised movements, their strides matching each other. They turned this way and that, as one man talked and the others nodded. I watched, fascinated, until my attention was diverted to the park. Here, men of all ages, dressed in layers of warm clothing, thick hats or felt Stetsons, congregated in huddled groups playing chess. I took a photograph but my every move was being observed. They looked up suddenly; some smiled, while others were annoyed that their game was being interrupted. Bicycles were propped against the nearest object, their riders choosing which of the games to follow. Heads leaned together over a chessboard under the watchful gaze of Aqif Pashe Elbasani, his graceful statue giving a certain authority to the setting.

Later that night a television blasted loudly from the next-door bedroom and an eerie feeling crept over me. I put a chair against the door, just in case, and fell into a light sleep. Tomorrow I would be heading back to Macedonia – and home.

- Elbasan/Thanë Border Control (63km) -

It was a slow, steep, but scenic climb on the mountain road through the Jablanica range to the Albanian-Macedonian border. Strings of Enver Hoxha's ubiquitous bunkers lined the hillsides, their numbers increasing intensively as we ascended, reflecting his apparent paranoia of invasion. Finally, we reached the top and I was rewarded with my first view of Lake Ohrid down in the next valley. Macedonia was metres away. I began to smile uncontrollably as we approached the border control. This was a defining moment in my journey, as I realised I was but days away from completing a full circular Balkan voyage with Tito. My passport received an exit stamp. Albania was behind us. One more entry stamp and I would be on Tito's home turf again. *Surely nothing could go wrong now?* I thought.

MACEDONIA

ON THE HOME STRAIGHT

- Kjafasan Border Control/Lake Ohrid (27km) -

"A Fića!" the customs officer exclaimed in surprise. "And where have you come from?"

"Albania," I responded, clearly stating the obvious.

"Your documents please."

I wondered if by some strange twist of fate, I would have trouble getting back into Macedonia. I held back the written Macedonian statement which Liljana (the official owner of Tito) and I had signed at the lawyer's office in Skopje all those weeks ago, permitting me to drive Tito in Macedonia – but he did not ask for it.

"Would you mind getting out of the car?"

A moment of doubt crept in as he began to search through the muddle of discarded objects on the front passenger seat, reminding me of my Bulgarian border crossing, in which a similarly thorough search had been undertaken. He picked up the bunch of now wilting wild basil from Berat and sniffed it. I giggled nervously.

"That's basil."

He withdrew his head from within the car and asked, "Is this all your luggage?"

I nodded.

"What is inside?"

"Oh, mainly dirty clothes," I replied apologetically, "And the red bag is full of books."

"And what is this?" he asked curiously, holding up a slim bottle of liquid.

"Oh, that's a bottle of pear *rakija*." Expecting him to be impressed, I added, "From Vareš."

But his expression did not change. "And how many bottles of wine do you have in the car?"

I pointed vaguely to the couple which lay on the floor under my seat.

"Ok, that is fine. Welcome to Macedonia!"

He patted Tito's roof in farewell and I drove the short distance to the crest of the hill. Stretching out before us, beneath a wide expanse of blue sky, lay Macedonia. Excitement and relief gripped me; we were back in the country from which we had begun our journey.

A spontaneous cry of "Fića!" greeted me from three men who saw Tito approaching. Laughing and clapping, they appeared like a welcoming committee. My adrenalin raced. I felt a large weight lift off my shoulders. I was back in familiar territory. Gliding downhill, I felt carefree.

"Tito, you've done it!" We passed a shepherd herding his sheep alongside the road, free-wheeled into Struga, and through the town to Lake Ohrid. I pulled into a café on the shoreline. We were not quite home; it would still take two days to get back to Skopje, but we had definitely gone full circle. Desperate to share this moment of triumph, I texted friends and the congratulations came flooding back. How I wished they could all be here!

A cool breeze blew across the lake but it was warm in the sunshine and there was no sign of snow. We only needed two more days like this. The water lapped against the shore, long fronded reeds rustled in the breeze and small boats bobbed up and down on the lake. In this peaceful setting I could feel the intensity that travelling alone had required of me totally slipping away.

I took the old shoreline road to the UNESCO-listed town of Ohrid. I could not have believed that arriving back in Macedonia would have such an immediate effect on me and, although I got lost finding the route into the old town, the help of a local obligingly jumping into his car and saying "Follow me!" was a fittingly gracious end to the day's journey. Driving into the square where the resplendent church of *Sveti Nikola Gerakomia* stood, I knew where I was. I parked and walked down to Lucija's home. I had stayed here some years ago and rented the same room as before, overlooking the lake. The view from the balcony was one of my favourites over Lake Ohrid, with nothing but lake in front, sky above, and mountains to each side.

―――――

The old town of Ohrid is a place of narrow meandering lanes, restored Ottoman homes, churches and artisan craft shops. Bars and cafés line the lake; in these one can sit and relax – when the music is not at full volume. Outside the UNESCO-protected area lay a more modern Ohrid filled with the hustle and bustle of everyday life, this mix of old and new adding to Ohrid's heart and soul. It was uplifting and created an unusual harmony. The sun disappeared and the temperature plummeted. I hurried back to Lucija's to pull on some extra clothes. The muezzin's call to prayer resounded around Ohrid while the young continued to drink their coffee and smoke their cigarettes.

―――――

I was freezing. My multiple layers of cotton clothing were not enough. I went out to eat just as the rain began, suddenly and unpredictably. Warmed by a bowl of hearty čorba soup followed by grilled steak and vegetables, I ran back to my apartment by the lake and climbed gratefully into bed with as many clothing layers as I could muster, wrapping a woollen jumper around my head against the icy draft which whistled through the window, and slept.

- Ohrid/Prilep (110km) -

I jumped out of bed, turned on the electric radiator and peered through the curtains. Dark clouds sat low across the lake and the mountains were lost in thick fog. My heart sank. Driving in this was not going to be fun. I wondered if Tito's backlights would be bright enough for drivers to see us in the gloomy light. My initial euphoria at being back in Macedonia had disappeared. Today was going to be challenging.

I decided to travel via Bitola. It would mean Tito having to conquer three mountain passes but the other option was equally mountainous, along the west of the country and back through Gostivar – the route we had taken all those weeks ago from Skopje. In any case, I did not want to retrace my steps and settled for the likely more popular route through the centre of Macedonia and back to the capital.

I was reluctant to set off too early but the fog sat defiantly over the mountains, refusing to budge; I had no option but to pack up and get going.

"Hey guys, look at that car! Isn't it cute?" a woman's shrill American voice exclaimed.

"Oh yeah," answered a male drawling voice, "That's a Zastava. You wouldn't want one of those. It's like a sewing machine on wheels."

"No! Really?" another female voice uttered disappointedly.

I hit the back of my head on the doorframe as I reversed my body out from the backseat to protest but, luckily for them, they had disappeared out of sight.

"Typical American!" I muttered under my breath. "If it's not modern, it's worthless! He has no idea what this car can do. And, more importantly, it is from here, not some import. I bet he doesn't even realise how revered this car is. The Balkan people love their Zastava; something he would never understand with his attitude to life." I fumed some more: "Sewing machine indeed. How dare he?" I checked the oil and water levels and finally jumped into the front seat.

"Let's go, Tito!" I sat patiently, trying to cajole Tito into life but, as the minutes ticked by, my rant of moments ago had turned to laughter. "Well, maybe that American guy had a point. Come on, Tito!"

He hiccupped appealingly then conked out. It took ten minutes until the engine eventually sprang into life. I sat with my right foot firmly on the accelerator pedal until he gained more strength. Now we were off!

The road to the Bukovo Mountain Pass rose steadily. We overtook a cow running down the road towards us and then plunged headlong into thick fog. It swirled around us and I prayed that neither would we come across any more galloping bovines, nor would anyone be travelling too fast behind us. The fog thinned as we reached the pass. The road ahead was so bleak. Not a vehicle had passed us in either direction and as the fog descended once again, I looked nervously at my phone – no signal. A layer of mist covered the windscreen and I flicked the wipers into action. *Squeak, scrape, squeak, scrape.*

An ancient-looking tractor pulling a cart of apples appeared through the mist and preceded us into the town of Resen, a place seemingly lost in its own time warp. The guidebook did not even mention the place but as I drove through, admiring the mansion-sized houses, some of which looked similar in style to those I had seen in Bitola all those weeks ago, I passed a building resembling a French chateau. A sweeping stone staircase led to a *'ceramika'* gallery. I needed to stop and stretch my legs and this looked as good a place as any.

Timber barque boats lined the tiled corridor but every door leading off was locked, an imposing notice sellotaped to the paintwork: *'No guns allowed'*. I was not at all sure where I was or whether indeed I should even be in the building. There was certainly no sign of a ceramics gallery and no one to ask. I could hear voices in one of the rooms but when I knocked all went silent. I retraced my steps, glancing back at this elegant building, mystified as to how a French-style chateau had come to be built here in Resen.

Meanwhile, the sun had reappeared and patches of blue sky filled the horizon. Tito and I set off, ready to take on the next mountain range, pausing momentarily at a humble one-pump garage to top up with petrol.

"Fića! Skopje?" The man seemed delighted to see us so far from the city and waved an enthusiastic farewell as we headed through the countryside towards the Gavato Mountain Pass, unaware of how far we had travelled before reaching his petrol station.

The sunshine was short-lived. As the slow climb began, the fog descended, dense and disorientating. With some considerable effort Tito reached the summit and I sighed with relief – just one more to go! His brakes shuddered, taking the strain for a second time as we slowly descended into the valley, skirting Bitola and a litter-ridden Roma settlement down onto a vast open plain. My feet were warmed by the hole in the gearbox housing and I moved from side to side to ease the pain from my numb rear end caused by the seat's springs, which had failed once more. I was hungry, the route boring, and the weather desperately gloomy. The 37km to Prilep seemed an interminably long way.

Eventually, the town appeared and as we headed into the centre, I could feel a change in Tito. The traffic lights ahead turned red, I put my foot on the brakes and we came to a sliding stop. The lights turned green and we set off across the junction. It was three o'clock but daylight was fading. Would it be too risky to drive on to Veles? There would be another mountain pass to conquer. I mused over the options distractedly as we approached the next set of traffic lights. They turned red. I braked but there was no response. I instinctively moved down into second gear and tried the brakes again – nothing. The brake pedal felt limp under my foot. I lifted the handbrake slowly and we came to a halt. *Now what?* Thoughts of Veles vanished. I had to find a mechanic. I became aware that we were not the only Zastava on the road. In fact, Prilep seemed to be a hub for them – an encouraging, if somewhat surprising circumstance. It was Friday afternoon – never a good time to break down yet, once again, Tito had! The question was *where was I going to find a mechanic?*

———

A woman stood chatting to the petrol attendant, filling her very glamorous-looking Zastava with petrol. Perhaps she could help! The coast was clear. I indicated and turned into the petrol station. We flew down a concrete slope and I hastily pulled up the handbrake as we came within millimetres of hitting the bumper of her gleaming, far superior model. I climbed out into the freezing damp air.

"*Dobar den*. Zastava. Mechanic? I have *problemo*," I said, pointing at her car and then at Tito.

She paid the petrol attendant and came to look at Tito's failed brake pedal. She smiled reassuringly, "*Da, da*. Ok," and picked up her phone. "*Engleski*" and "*Zastava*" were the only two words I recognised as she spoke rapidly to someone. "Follow me!" she said.

"Hvala!"

I travelled in low gear with my hand clutching the handbrake, ready to deploy it at a moment's notice. The last thing I wanted to do was to plough Tito headlong into her shining white Zastava. The road narrowed to a lane and we emerged into a quaint residential square.

A dark-haired man in blue dungarees appeared from behind the doors of a tin shed, more like a lean-to with brown paint flaking off the doors. A lopsided metal chimney puffed out smoke into the cold evening air. She signalled for me to wait.

"Dobar den."

He did not speak any English, but the woman had understood my dilemma and explained the problem to him. He motioned for me to get out and squeezed himself into Tito. Pressing heavily down on the brake, he shook his head.

"Hey!"

Another man appeared from within the shed, opening the doors wide to reveal a small compact garage and just wide enough to accommodate Tito. He was driven inside and the doors firmly shut.

"You stay in Prilep?" the woman enquired.

"Well, yes, I suppose I must. Do you know Pansion Breza?" I asked.

It was the only accommodation mentioned in the guidebook. She did not. We escaped the cold by cramming into the glorious warmth of the garage. In one corner a stove was pumping out volumes of heat and from the walls hung every mechanical tool imaginable. "He is good mechanic," she said confidently. "He knows Zastava very well."

The mechanic was down in the miniscule pit under Tito. While he tinkered away, she gave him strict instructions to take me to a hotel after he had fixed my car. Here I was with a broken-down car, no hotel and no real idea where I was, and the people of Prilep were rallying to my rescue and I was once again humbled by the unhesitating hospitality of the Balkan people. The mechanic smiled politely at me and, having satisfied herself that I was in good hands, the lady wished me a safe journey back to Skopje and departed. All would be well, I was sure of it.

Laughing amongst themselves, the mechanics set about fixing Tito – it reminded me of my first breakdown in Greece. There the garage in Tihero had resounded to similar banter and roars of laughter. As my feet thawed in the cosy atmosphere of the tin shed, I thanked the gods once more. It could well have been a very different story if the brakes had failed as we had been careering down from the summit of either of the last two mountain passes. Luckily, we were both still here and if the brakes could be fixed, we would have only one more mountain pass to conquer before reaching Skopje.

The mechanic emerged triumphantly from the pit. Tito was fixed. He mimed instructions for me to take the car for a couple of circuits around the square. It was just a loose connection between brake pedal and brake pads that had created the failure. It could well have been fatal but all was now well and our journey need not be abandoned on its penultimate day. He guided me to Pansion Breza and bade me farewell. I unpacked my luggage for what I hoped would be the last time and donned as many layers of clothes as possible before venturing out into the freezing cold.

———

I pulled the toggles of my hood tighter around my head. My ears ached from the cold until I could bear it no longer. My breath mushroomed out in front of me like a frozen cloud. How quickly the seasons had changed – winter had arrived.

I walked into the heart of Prilep, to the old pedestrianised Turkish quarter. I was chilled to the bone and sought refuge in a café, indulging in a slice of baklava, oozing with honey and nuts, for solace. This was a truly Macedonian working town, not a tourist attraction. I found myself being observed and as the stares became somewhat unnerving and the cigarette smoke more intense in the café's airless environment, I was driven back out into the cold.

The walls of a ruined mosque looked alarmingly fragile but the minaret stood defiantly tall amongst the crumbling ruins. Shops of tiny proportions bunched together, holding on to each other for support and possibly warmth. I peered through one window: hand-crafted lead pipes leaned higgledy-piggledy against one another. Opposite, a corner shop, with its fast-collapsing timber façade, brimmed with white and yellow candles of every diameter and length. I felt transported back into a world of crafts and skills long forgotten or lost in the homogenous, mass-produced world with which I was familiar.

––––––

The cold gave me a huge hunger and although it was still early, I tucked into baked borlotti beans and meatballs at a traditional restaurant, *Makedonska Kukja*. The waiters eyed me as I demolished the generous servings. The surrounding tables were empty but by nine o'clock this changed. Men piled into the restaurant, staring at me in surprise, and a band of musicians set up their equipment for the evening's entertainment. I was outnumbered and overwhelmed by the massive statures of these Macedonian men who made no effort to hide their interest. Where had I come from and why was I here? I began to wonder that myself, and I decided to beat a hasty retreat. It was perishingly cold outside. The streets were badly lit. I hunched as deeply as I could into my thin jacket. How I wished I had my winter coat and a woolly hat.

The hotel receptionist predicted snow, adding pessimistically that the mountain pass I would cross tomorrow was one of the most treacherous in Macedonia. I asked for newspaper to protect Tito's windows from a possible hard frost. I loved winter but this was a worrying moment. On the penultimate day of our journey I had dealt with a breakdown and now, I was preparing for snow. It was definitely a sign to get back to Skopje as quickly as I could.

- Prilep/Skopje(87km) -

It was bitterly cold outside but there had been no snow or frost. I had breakfast and piled on as many layers of clothing as I could fit under my rain jacket and headed into Prilep town centre. A statue of Phillip of Macedonia stood proudly in the main square. He held a spear double his height and I chuckled to myself. *How could this slight figure of a man, the father of Alexander the Great, possibly have managed to wield a weapon this size with any success?*

The town was filled with activity and I was drawn by the crowds towards the market – definitely the place to be on a Saturday morning. The market teemed with stalls selling jars of honey, cheese, sackloads of peppers, aubergines, tomatoes, apples and every kind of autumnal fruit and vegetables – an organic foodie's heaven.

A surprising number of Zastavas lined the street and for the first time I felt Tito was amongst his own kind. Fićas of all colours and conditions hurtled past and I was propelled back into a time when Zastavas were commonplace, not a novelty, and here in Prilep they were still much used and adored. Of course, there were lots of modern cars too, but Zastavas had a healthy presence and I was delighted to see so many.

I loaded my luggage onto the backseat, removed the newspaper from Tito's windscreen and texted my German friend Anke in Kosovo. She was going to meet me in Skopje to celebrate my return. John had left for an extended work assignment in Bosnia but he had kindly offered me the use of his apartment for as long as I wanted it. I would be finishing my journey directly in front of the place from where I had departed.

Tito was in no hurry to start. He, too, was feeling the cold. I gently raised and lowered the choke, trying my best to remain calm until he kicked into life. I tentatively tested the brakes a few times, just to be sure all was well, and we were off. The road from Prilep ascended with deceptive slowness. At first I was convinced Tito's engine was failing. The temperature dial rose and I hastily went down into second gear. We continued to climb to 994 metres. The Pletvar Pass was conquered. Each kilometre was a kilometre closer to Skopje and my excitement rose at the prospect.

Heading down into the valley, the weather suddenly changed. It was instant, and unexpected. The sun appeared and blue skies stretched in front of us. We passed rows of vineyards into open countryside. I savoured the moment. We were fast approaching the main highway and I had no wish to join the 130km/h EU-funded three-laned racetrack; it appeared there might be another option. Remarkably, the old road still existed, running parallel to the dual carriageway. This would be our final adventure and Tito was in his element. We motored along at 50km/h in blissful isolation; this was our kind of road, all bumps, ruts and potholes.

Eventually, our luck ran out and there was nothing for it but to join the 130km/h speedway. I braced myself as we merged with it. I could feel the change as Tito struggled up the agonisingly slow ascents. He was unable to go at any more than 20km/h and I held my breath every time an articulated lorry appeared behind us. I could hear the frantic crashing down into low gear as the driver took in our speed and prepared to overtake.

Finally, we arrived on the outskirts of Skopje and the traffic speed slowed considerably. The sun seemed to take on a new brightness. I knew my way into town and to John's address and as I saw the sign to the'Centar', I began to grin ridiculously. We rounded the final corner, nipped up the earth bank I had feared on my first ever drive in the car, and we had arrived.

I parked Tito under the same tree from where we had departed on the 6th August 2009 and turned off the engine. It was hard to believe I was actually here, back where we had started. Tito and I had actually made it! We had travelled full circle and here we were back in Skopje.

I wanted to laugh, cry, and jump up and down as the magnitude of what we had achieved began to sink in. It was half-past two on Saturday, 17th October 2009. It had taken just over ten weeks to travel through ten countries: from Macedonia (FYROM) through Greece, Turkey, Bulgaria, Romania, Serbia, Bosnia and Herzegovina, Croatia, Montenegro, Albania and back into Macedonia (FYROM). If the kilometre dial could be believed, my Zastava "Fića" and I had travelled 4,677 kilometres.

I phoned Anke, announcing incredulously, "We're here! We've made it!"

"Well done!" Anke screamed excitedly, "I'm stuck at the Kosovo border! I'll be in Skopje soon. We have to celebrate!"

I continued to sit behind the steering wheel, enjoying the sense of achievement and the sense of relief that I was back in one piece. I began to text family and friends in a state of euphoria.

"Mission accomplished!"

Epilogue

N*ovember, 2009*
     Two weeks later. *'What are your current co-ordinates?'* I smiled at the droll wording. My family had been so tolerant and supportive, and sporadic communication had become the norm, but now I had no excuse and I quickly responded, *'My kitchen. I'm home. '*

The journey was over; Tito was now safely in the hands of a family Liljana knew outside of Skopje, I had flown back to France, and I could now start to think about what was next.

Tito had touched the hearts of so many as we had travelled and through him I had had the opportunity to explore the back roads, meet people and connect with them in a way which would not otherwise have been possible. The respect the Balkan people have for this unassuming car is intangible – unexpected, unpredictable and heart-warming. I had had a unique experience with Tito, through which my knowledge, understanding and appreciation of this beautiful region and the hospitality and kindness of its people had provided me with many fond memories, some hair-raising moments but overall a deep respect for the ordinary people of southeast Europe.

Travelling across the Balkan peninsula in a vintage 31-year-old Zastava had possibly been madness, most probably a miracle, but one thing was certain: I had been travelling with a celebrity and I would miss him dearly.

Acknowledgements

To list all those who have helped, supported, encouraged, berated, counselled, befriended, edited, and who have tirelessly endured me through the whole process of buying the car, travelling, and then writing this tale would indeed take some hundreds of pages. So I am afraid I am taking the all-encompassing group-hug approach by mentioning no names so as not to forget anyone, nor to upset anyone.

I gratefully acknowledge every one of you. You know who you are, and I know who you are, so to you, I would just like to say a big THANK YOU.

About the Author

EMMA CARMICHAEL is a conservation building surveyor by profession and has worked in London and southeast Europe. She has travelled widely and has lived in Sydney, Pristina, Strasbourg and Sarajevo. She is the inspiration behind the bookshop-café Travelling Through… in London. Emma can sometimes be found in London and the rest of the time, she is where she is.

Join Emma's Newsletter and be the first to know about her next writing adventure, and other exclusive news. Sign up via her website travellingthrough.co.uk or follow her on social media.

  facebook.com/Travelling-Through

  twitter.com/@Trvllng_Thrgh

  instagram.com/@Travelling_Through

Lightning Source UK Ltd.
Milton Keynes UK
UKHW011357251119
354202UK00005B/1556/P

9 781916 142305